SOCIAL CONSTRUCTION
OF THE PAST

Representation as power

ONE WORLD ARCHAEOLOGY
Series Editor: P. J. Ucko

Animals into Art
H. Morphy (ed.), vol. 7

Archaeological Approaches to Cultural Identity
S. J. Shennan (ed.), vol. 10

Archaeological Heritage Management in the
Modern World
H. F. Cleere (ed.), vol. 9

Archaeology and the Information Age: a global
perspective
P. Reilly & S. Rahtz (eds), vol. 21

The Archaeology of Africa: food, metals and
towns
T. Shaw, P. Sinclair, B. Andah &
A. Okpoko (eds), vol. 20

Centre and Periphery: comparative studies in
archaeology
T. C. Champion (ed.), vol. 11

Conflict in the Archaeology of Living Traditions
R. Layton (ed.), vol. 8

Domination and Resistance
D. Miller, M. J. Rowlands & C. Tilley
(eds), vol. 3

The Excluded Past: archaeology in education
P. Stone & R. MacKenzie (eds), vol. 17

Foraging and Farming: the evolution of plant
exploitation
D. R. Harris & G. C. Hillman (eds),
vol. 13

From the Baltic to the Black Sea: studies in
medieval archaeology
D. Austin & L. Alcock (eds), vol. 18

Hunters of the Recent Past
L. B. Davis & B. O. K. Reeves (eds),
vol. 15

The Meanings of Things: material culture and
symbolic expression
I. Hodder (ed.), vol. 6

The Origins of Human Behaviour
R. A. Foley (ed.), vol. 19

The Politics of the Past
P. Gathercole & D. Lowenthal (eds),
vol. 12

Sacred Sites, Sacred Places
D. L. Carmichael, J. Hubert, B. Reeves &
A. Schanche (eds), vol. 23

The Presented Past: heritage, museums and
education
P. G. Stone & B. L. Molyneaux (eds),
vol. 25

Signifying Animals: human meaning in the
natural world
R. G. Willis (ed.), vol. 16

State and Society: the emergence and
development of social hierarchy and political
centralization
J. Gledhill, B. Bender & M.T. Larsen (eds),
vol. 4

Tropical Archaeobotany: applications and
developments
J.G. Hather (ed.), vol. 22

The Walking Larder: patterns of domestication,
pastoralism, and predation
J. Clutton-Brock (ed.), vol. 2

What is an Animal?
T. Ingold (ed.), vol. 1

What's New? A closer look at the process of
innovation
S. E. Van der Leeuw & R. Torrence (eds),
vol. 14

Who Needs the Past? Indigenous values and
archaeology
R. Layton (ed.), vol. 5

SOCIAL CONSTRUCTION OF THE PAST

Representation as power

Edited by

George Clement Bond
Institute of African Studies, School of International and Public Affairs, Columbia University, New York

Angela Gilliam
Department of Anthropology, The Evergreen State College, Olympia, Washington

London and New York

First published in 1994 by
Routledge
2 Park Square, Milton Park, Abingdon, Oxon, OX14 4RN

Transferred to Digital Printing 2004

Simultaneously published in the USA and Canada
by Routledge
29 West 35th Street, New York, NY 10001

Typeset in 10 on 12pt Bembo by Florencetype Ltd, Kewstoke, Avon

British Library Cataloguing in Publication Data
A catalogue record for this book is available from the British Library.

Library of Congress Cataloging in Publication Data
  Bond, George Clement
    Social construction of the past: representation as power / George
    Clement Bond and Angela Gilliam
      p.   cm. — (One world archaeology; 24)
    Includes bibliographical references and index.
    1. Social history,   2. Power (Social sciences)   I. Gilliam,
Angela.   II. Title.   III. Series.
HN8.B66   1994
303.3—dc20   93-40053

    ISBN 0-415-09045-8
    ISBN 0-415-15224-0

Contents

List of contributors		*page*	xi
Foreword P. J. Ucko			xiii
Preface George Clement Bond & Angela Gilliam			xvii

Introduction   1
George Clement Bond & Angela Gilliam

Subaltern and 'postcolonial discourse'	2
Relations of inequality	4
Alternative constructions	5
Subjugated knowledge	8
Liberating the past: invention and appropriation	12
Essentialism and the poetics of meaning	16
Insurrections, re-evaluations and the 'western' focus	19
Notes	20
References	21

The representation of ethnicity

1   *Ethnicity and representation*   25
    Leith Mullings

| References | 28 |

2   *Racial representations and power in the dependent development*
    of the United States South   29
    Pem Davidson Buck

Illegitimate anthropology and hegemony	29
The Farmers' Alliance and postreconstruction dependent	
development	31
The Black Patch War and the power of racial representations	35
The social construction of the past	38

Notes   40
Acknowledgements   41
References   41

3   *Sexual politics and the mediation of class, gender and race in
    former slave plantation societies: the case of Haiti*   44
    Carolle Charles

    Women's empowerment in Haiti as counter-power   44
    Haitian sex/gender system and practices of sexual politics   45
    Gender division of labour as legacy of plantation system   49
    Social relations and mediation of sexuality   51
    Conclusion   55
    Glossary   55
    Notes   56
    References   56

4   *Representation and power: blacks in Colombia*   59
    Peter Wade

    Iberian social structures   59
    Discrimination and the ideology of *blanqueamiento*   61
    Race mixture and the ideology of *lo mestizo*   65
    Lo mestizo, blanqueamiento and the black minority   68
    Conclusion   71
    Notes   72
    References   72

5   *From Eden to limbo: the construction of indigenism in Brazil* 74
    Alcida Ramos

    The good, the bad and the dead   74
    The edenic discourse   75
    Innocence found   75
    Nativism and nationalism   76
    From Chateaubriand to Sting   79
    The civilizing discourse   80
    Innocence lost   81
    Olivegreen garb and drab redtape   82
    Out of Eden and back again   84
    Notes   86
    Acknowledgements   87
    References   87

6   *Literacy and power in colonial Latin America*   89
     Joanne Rappaport & Thomas B. F. Cummins

         Alphabetic literacy   90
         Form: orality, literacy, practice   91
         Contents: legal documents and social transformation   92
         Printing and the transformation of visual images   99
         Conclusion   104
         Notes   104
         Acknowledgements   106
         References   107

The social construction of antiquity   .

7   *The construction of antiquity and the egalitarian principle:*
     social constructions of the past in the present   113
     William A. Shack

         Note   117
         References   117

8   *The image of Ancient Greece as a tool for colonialism and*
     European hegemony   119
     Martin Bernal

         Two models for the origins of Ancient Greece   119
         Models of Greek history and anthropology   125
         Note   128
         References   128

9   *The politics of identity in archaeology*   129
     Michael Rowlands

         Identity and categories of the person   131
         Archaeology and nationalism   133
         Archaeologists and development   136
         Archaeology and the postmodern   139
         Conclusion   141
         Acknowledgements   142
         References   142

10   *Gender division of labour in the construction of archaeological*
     knowledge in the United States   144
     Joan M. Gero

        A non-discovery model of knowledge, or knowledge as
        creative construction   144
        The role of gender in the construction of archaeological
        knowledge   146
        Lithic studies   147
        Palaeoethnobotany   149
        Palaeozoology   150
        Interpretation of gender as a social construct in research   150
        Acknowledgements   152
        References   152

11   *Interpreting silences: symbol and history in the case of*
     Ram Janmabhoomi/Babri Masjid   154
     Nandini Rao

        The controversy   156
        Interpreting silences   157
        Symbol and history in the case of Ram Janmabhoomi/Babri Masjid   157
        Symbols at Ram Janmabhoomi/Babri Masjid   158
        Making historical 'facts'   160
        Notes   161
        Acknowledgements   163
        References   164

The scholarship of inequality: the South African case

12   *Lifting the veil of popular history: archaeology and politics*
     in urban Cape Town   167
     Martin Hall

        Textual archaeology   168
        Cape Town in the early nineteenth century   169
        Texts of domination and opposition   172
        Architecture and art   175
        Historical texts in present settings   177
        Conclusion   181
        Notes   182
        References   182

13   *Struggling with tradition in South Africa: the multivocality*
     of images of the past   185
     Andrew D. Spiegel

         Representing Africans as traditional   186
         Traditionality and the land   188
         Traditionality in the tourist industry   191
         Using tradition as a resource in gender struggles   193
         Conclusion: South Africa, anthropologists and tradition   196
         Notes   199
         References   200

14   *Intellectuals in South Africa and the reconstructive agenda*   203
     Mala Singh

         The notion of intellectuals   204
         Intellectuals and the political struggle   207
         The production of knowledge   210
         Intellectuals and the 'powers'   212
         Intellectuals and social transformation   214
         Conclusion   220
         Notes   221
         References   222

     Index   224

List of contributors

Martin Bernal, Department of Government Studies, Cornell University, Ithaca, New York, USA.

George Clement Bond, Institute of African Studies, School of International and Public Affairs, Columbia University, New York City, USA.

Pem Davidson Buck, Social Science Division, Elizabethtown Community College, Elizabethtown, Kentucky, USA.

Carolle Charles, Department of Anthropology, Baruch College and the City University of New York, New York City, USA.

Thomas B.F. Cummins, Department of Art History, University of Chicago, USA.

Joan M. Gero, Department of Anthropology, University of South Carolina, USA.

Angela Gilliam, Department of Anthropology, The Evergreen State College, Olympia, Washington, USA.

Martin Hall, Department of Archaeology, University of Cape Town, South Africa.

Leith Mullings, Anthropology, Graduate Center, City University of New York, New York City, USA.

Alcida Ramos, Department of Anthropology, Universidade de Brasília, Brazil.

Nandini Rao, Tata Institute of Social Science, Bombay, India.

Joanne Rappaport, Department of Anthropology, University of Maryland, Baltimore, USA.

Michael Rowlands, Department of Anthropology, University College London, UK.

William A. Shack, Department of Anthropology, University of California, Berkeley, USA.

Mala Singh, Department of Philosophy, University of Durban-Westville, South Africa.

Andrew D. Spiegel, Department of Anthropology, University of Cape Town, South Africa.

Peter Wade, Department of Geography, University of Liverpool, UK.

Foreword

This book is the fourth in the *One World Archaeology* (OWA) series to derive from the Second World Archaeological Congress (WAC 2), held in Barquisimeto, Venezuela, in September 1990. Despite many organizational problems (Fforde 1991, p. 6), over 600 people attended the Inaugural Session of WAC 2, with more than 450 participants from 35 countries taking part in academic sessions, and additional contributions being read on behalf of many others who were unable to attend in person.

True to the aims and spirit of WAC 1, over three-quarters of the participants came from the so-called Third and Fourth Worlds (see Fforde 1991, p. 7 for details) and the academics came not only from archaeology and anthropology but from a host of related disciplines.

WAC 2 continued the tradition of effectively addressing world archaeology in its widest sense. Central to a world archaeological approach is the investigation not only of how people lived in the past but also how and why those changes took place which resulted in the forms of society and culture existing today. Contrary to popular belief, and the archaeology of some twenty-five years ago, world archaeology is much more than the mere recording of specific historical events, embracing as it does the study of social and cultural change in its entirety.

Like its predecessor, this Congress was organized around major themes. Several of these themes were based on the discussion of full-length papers which had been circulated previously to – or were available to be read at the Congress itself by – all those who had indicated a special interest in them. This book derives from one such Congress thematic session, but it was most unusual in that it was a 'repeat' performance (albeit with several new 'actors') of an earlier WAC-sponsored meeting on the same essential theme (see Preface). In a symbolic way it is fitting that WAC has seen the theme of *Social Construction of the Past: representation as power* as a timeless one (and see *Domination and Resistance*, edited by D. Miller, M. Rowlands & C. Tilley, and *State and Society: the emergence and development of social hierarchy and political centralization*, edited by J. Gledhill, B. Bender & M. T. Larsen). In many ways, *all* the books in the *One World Archaeology* series have been focused around this theme, whatever their particular specializations; in many ways, *all* WAC's ongoing activities since its first World Congress in 1986 have been orientated around this one major concern (e.g. see *World Archaeological Bulletin* 6, 1992) – the deconstruction of power inherent in the very fact of controlling, or even of being able to *claim* to control, another group's or peoples' knowledge about, or of, the past.

The main aim of this WAC 2 theme, and of its resultant *Social Construction of the Past*, was – and is – to focus attention on the nature of such control and, perhaps parenthetically, to cast light on the very nature of what actually constitutes 'historical'/archaeological knowledge. Less obliquely, this book is all about *control* – whether about educational systems concerned with the past (and see *The Excluded Past: archaeology in education*, edited by P. G. Stone & R. MacKenzie and *The Presented Past: heritage, museums and education*, edited by P.G. Stone & B.L. Molyneaux), or about who should be able to define what constitutes ethnic identity at any particular time (and see *Archaeological Approaches to Cultural Identity*, edited by S. J. Shennan, *The Politics of the Past*, edited by P. Gathercole & D. Lowenthal, and *From the Baltic to the Black Sea: studies in medieval archaeology*, edited by D. Austin & L. Alcock), or who it is who should be involved in formulating legislation to 'protect' the evidence of the past (and see *Archaeological Heritage Management in the Modern World*, edited by H. Cleere).

No wonder, therefore, that this is a challenging book, whose enquiries fearlessly expose the racism and sexism, and misuse of politics, literacy and particularized symbolism in the interpretation of the past in the hands of those who wield power at any particular moment in time. This is a book about vested interests; vested interests in 'creating' the legitimacy of past practice. Its analyses happen to range from the modern ascription of white coloured skins to those who in Classical European times may have been black, from the details of ancient Indian temple architecture to those today who wish to create inter-community strife on the basis of such supposed archaeological temple architecture, and to postcolonial intellectual interest in the nature of the development of post-apartheid South Africa. The particular examples and analyses presented here only serve to indicate how many more and diverse the examples could have been.

Not surprisingly, therefore, *Social Construction of the Past* demonstrates that modern archaeological enquiry is essentially a social science, a thoughtful – and rigorous – investigation of socio-cultural attitudes and social constructs. As such, this book not only reflects the way that archaeology has always been a multidisciplinary subject which has drawn its inspirations (and analytical methods) from a host of other disciplinary concerns, but it also exemplifies why it must continue so to be. In the 1990s it is incumbent upon the archaeologist that s/he should also be well versed in sociological (and political?) theory; equally, no legitimate social scientific analysis can any longer afford to ignore (at least) the local historical trajectory of cultural development amongst those communities with whom they choose to study.

This book therefore demands that academic anthropologists, archaeologists, historians, sociologists and other social scientists reexamine the relationships between their respective disciplines. Examples examined in *Social Construction of the Past* demonstrate that the lessons of the use (and abuse?) of female Haitian sexuality, the use of a skin colour base-line, the use of (presumed) ethnographically-legitimated 'tribal' divides, and the use of self-rewarding definitions (and circumscriptions) of ethnic identity, are all essential ingredients, or preconditions, for the understanding (and analysis) of other cultures. And these same areas of enquiry all have important messages for the interdisciplinary investigation of the way that the past is socially constructed, interdisciplinary relationships which have, until now, been singularly lacking from the arena of public debate about the nature of the past.

P. J. Ucko
Southampton

Reference

Fforde, C. 1991. The Second World Archaeological Congress (WAC 2), *World Archaeological Bulletin* 5, 6–10.

Preface

Social Construction of the Past: representation as power began as two sessions at
two different conferences and in two different countries, the co-organizers of
which were the editors of this book. The first one was a joint Invited Session
of the American Ethnological Society and the Association of Black Anthropologists, part of the American Anthropological Association's annual meeting,
15–19 November 1989, and was co-sponsored by the World Archaeological
Congress (WAC). The second session, devoted to the same subject, occurred at
WAC 2 a little over a year later in Venezuela. There it fell within the overall
theme of 'The Social Context of the Practice of Archaeology', and included
papers from a 'Special Forum: South Africa'. The meeting in South America
continued the dialogue about the interlocking relationship between scholarship
and apartheid that had so shaped and defined WAC 1 in Southampton, UK, in
1986 (Ucko 1987). At that time, the strength of the world-wide movement
against apartheid enabled the decision by the WAC Executive to support the
United Nations boycott of South Africa to move forward. Those scholars from
the then socialist countries in Europe and the former Soviet Union had joined
with academics from the Third World to insist that their participation in WAC
depended on the absence of scholars from South Africa.

WAC's First Inter-Congress in Vermillion, South Dakota, USA, in 1989
presaged the transformation in eastern Europe and the resulting complexities
attached to maintaining formal relationships based on resistance to apartheid.
In contrast to the landmark meeting of 1986, few scholars from eastern Europe
attended. There was even speculation that the changing geopolitical relationships and subsequent diplomatic policy adjustments between the government
of South Africa and those socialist countries influenced attendance. Thus, the
issue of apartheid and academic representation revealed the international and
multidisciplinary terrain in which such themes are properly ensconced.

The innovative nature of WAC 1 had been the emphasis on the potential
bonds between the fields of archaeology, prehistory, and definitions of development, including the ways in which they were conceptualized by scholars *and*
indigenous peoples and members of national minorities – irrespective of their

formal professional designation as scholars or not. The strength of the Native American efforts to reclaim and represent their pasts through repatriation of indigenous remains from museums within and outside the United States added an important dimension to the deliberations of WAC 1 in 1986. In engaging the theme, 'Archaeological ethics and the treatment of the dead', the First Inter-Congress in Vermillion continued that focus while broadening it with participation by Tasmanian and Aboriginal Australian activist-scholars.

Social Construction of the Past represents the conjoining of themes from WAC 1 and 2, and confronts the issue of apartheid both as it emerged as part of the Congress debates and as a category of intellectual enquiry. In important ways, the subject of structural inequality and its intellectual correlates is the unifying theme that encompasses this book as a whole.

There are many to whom we wish to express our gratitude for having made this book possible: The Evergreen State College and Teachers College, and Michael Timpane; the Chairs of the various sessions at the conference and Congress mentioned above; the several panel members, and authors of papers discussed, at those meetings, whose contributions are not represented in the published outcome, most particularly Johnnetta Cole, Sylvia Yanagisako, Bernard Magubane, Renagi R. Lohia and the late St Claire Drake. We are very grateful to Pam McClusky and other staff of the Seattle Art Museum, Gretchen Kalonji and Elizabeth Aurich for their suggestions regarding the book's cover design. We also wish to thank Onik'a Gilliam, Alison Bond, Matthew Bond and Lewis Burgess for their assistance. Especial thanks are due to Lambros Comitas for his careful commentary on the Introduction. Finally, we acknowledge the unstinting efforts of Peter Ucko and Jane Hubert in bringing this volume to press.

George Clement Bond   Angela Gilliam
New York City   Olympia, Washington

Reference

Ucko, P. J. 1987. *Academic Freedom and Apartheid: the story of the World Archaeological Congress.* London: Duckworth.

Introduction

GEORGE CLEMENT BOND &
ANGELA GILLIAM

The central unifying theme of this book is that social constructions of the past are crucial elements in the process of domination, subjugation, resistance and collusion. Representing the past and the way of life of populations is an expression and a source of power. These representations may frame relationships of social inequality, and can be intimately related to structures of power and wealth. They contain ideological and hegemonic properties that represent historical and sectional interests. In no way simple, they express a high degree of social and poetic complexity.

As chapters in this volume demonstrate, dominant histories may contain more than one social paradigm and set of principles. Dominant versions of the past are usually vague and general with a capacity to absorb diverging interests and interpretations. Under different social conditions one paradigm and cluster of principles may take sway over others. There are periods, however, during which the dominant renderings of the past cease to have either poetic or social efficacy. Instead, they may become the focus for intellectual debates, political struggles, and popular opposition. Other social constructions emerge as prime contenders for the past with their own interpretations and counter-hegemonic properties. The domains of knowledge, expressed in social constructions of the past, are brought into the arenas of political struggle. The politics of society becomes the politics of knowledge expressed in various fundamental forms of appropriation, interpretation and exclusion. As Lagemann (1987, 1988) makes clear in her history of the Carnegie Corporation, Vincent (1990) in her social history of political anthropology, and Harrison (1991) and Gilliam (1991) in their discussions of decolonizing anthropology, the politics of knowledge is a pivotal aspect of power relations. The meaning and scope of this politics have serious implications for the epistemological underpinnings of anthropology and its claims to an impartial and objective rendering of other cultures and societies. It should be recognized that many anthropologists today do not make this claim and yet, their published works often reveal otherwise.

The chapters in this volume, written by anthropologists and historians, raise a series of fundamental issues related to epistemology, theory, methodology and praxis and to the constraints on historical and anthropological fabrications or constructions. They explore the interrelationship of cultural settings, the politics of knowledge and the ideological components of theory, with theory being simply understood as a body of propositions mapping out a problem area and preparing the ground for its investigation by appropriate methods (Nadel 1957, p. 1), that is, focused in a problematic and establishing criteria of selectivity, or the basis for including data.

These chapters speak to the limits of theories concerning the relation of labour, race and gender to power and class. They reveal that beneath the guise of objectivity and adherence to Weber's imperative of ethical neutrality there lurks a strong partisan rendering of the history and socio-cultural properties of subjugated and oppressed peoples. They make clear that the belief in historical and sociological objectivity has routinely obscured the circumstances of partisan interpretations. The authors demonstrate how power and economic domination establish one rendering of history and culture as objective and ethically neutral and another as subjective and partisan.

These chapters revisit unresolved debates centring on the ability of human thought to apprehend the complexities of social life. They do not assume histories and cultures to be concrete realities and thus, there can be no single correct rendering or version but a multiplicity of interpretations. Thus contemporary political conditions become an essential consideration for analysing scholarly production. Scholars are neither above nor outside societies but integral agents within them, ensuring their perpetuity and at times, attempting to change them. Knowledge is intimately related to power and its representation in its various forms has poetic dimensions that link it to academic canons and the aesthetic standards of public cultures.

Anthropology and history are disciplines that are particularly prominent in constructing the past and contemporary ways of life of 'western' and 'non-western' populations. They do so within the context of historical situations which are not of their own making but whose images they help to shape. The present period of history is one marked by political upheavals and the strong reassertion of the alternative discourses of the intellectuals of subjugated peoples.

Subaltern and 'postcolonial discourse'

The collapse of the Soviet Union and the end of the Cold War have served as global markers for the end of one era and the stirrings of a new one. They have signalled the gradual winding down of the first postcolonial phase with all its accomplishments and failures. The dramatic events in eastern Europe, Africa, the Middle East and other parts of the world during the past few years in areas such as governance, economic reform, civil conflicts such as 'ethnic cleansing' and wars have provided the context for re-examining and reinterpreting the past.

The magnitude of these events should not be allowed to obscure the fundamental accomplishments of 'postcolonial scholars' whose intellectual endeavours have revealed the partisan nature of scholarship itself, exposing the inadequacies of conventional accounts of the past by attempting to include what these accounts tended to leave out (Hall 1978, p. 9). They have disaggregated dominant traditions, reclaimed subjugated knowledge, and included subordinate peoples in the historical record. They have sought to develop theories of consciousness and culture (Spivak 1985, p. 331). In these writings the oppressed have ceased to be the recipients of historical conditions but have become principal actors within them. As a result of these efforts the very foundations of the structure of knowledge are undergoing careful scrutiny.

Colonialism provides the immediate touchstone and background against which many postcolonial scholars and leaders have pursued strategies to reclaim their past and assert their individual and national identities. Rowlands (Ch. 9) suggests that these scholars confronted the problem of breaking with deeply embedded colonial intellectual structures and narratives, and argues that the 'master narratives' of the European nation-states of the nineteenth century were used by the colonized against imperial domination and although they served well in nationalist struggles, they also served in shaping post-colonial narratives. But Shack (Ch. 7) observes that colonial narratives probably had much less of an impact on the colonized than Rowlands and others assert, reminding us that the contributors to *Presence Africain*, for example, rejected European and white American cultural domination, advocating types of black-centred ideologies such as Negritude as well as various forms of socialism. Many recognized their involvement in a struggle broader than nationalism. However, Rowlands and Shack agree that there are profound implications of the past for the present and the present for the past.

Though the postcolonial discourse is intimately linked to the colonial past, in many ways it transcends it in its concern with human conditions and the making of history. It is but one facet of a larger enterprise, the study of subjugated peoples (e.g. oppressed women, minorities, workers, and peasants), the subalterns, a part of that intellectual legacy that focuses on inequality and constructing the activities, consciousnesses, and ways of life of subaltern populations. Generally, the scholars involved in this enterprise align themselves with the subalterns. They employ strategies that reveal them as agents, instigators and actors in producing their own histories and cultures within the conditions of historical circumstances. Their social constructions and the strategies, mechanisms, and reasons for reclaiming, fabricating and inventing them are part of a much broader endeavour, an endeavour that includes studying the relation of knowledge to power, domination to subjugation, and resistance to collusion.

This first postcolonial phase has made apparent the necessity for investigating history from below as well as from above. It has marked the realignment of scholars around theoretical and practical issues and brought the common folk into the controversies of the historical record. The peoples of regions and countries such as eastern Europe, Africa, Latin America, India and the United States are making their own histories. Interpretations of the past are an important feature of their political struggles for individual and collective identities and their claims to power and economic resources. The struggle extends to the use and meanings of dominant icons, images, discourses and written texts (Comaroff 1985, Mitchell 1986, Morrison 1992, Sanjek 1992, Spurr 1993). It centres on the manner in which we understand and represent relations of inequality.

Relations of inequality

Spurr pinpoints an important but controversial feature of domination and subjugation by observing that 'The anxiety of colonial discourse comes from the fact that the colonizer's power depends on the presence, not to say consent, of the colonized. What is power without its object? Authority is in some sense conferred by those who obey it' (Spurr 1993, p. 11).[1] One obvious reaction would be to reject his position and to recite instances of rebellion and acts of resistance, and to refer to James Scott's (1985) work on the weapons of the weak. Unfortunately, the tendency is not to look for ambiguity or for subtle forms of collaboration and collusion that help to create and then maintain the *status quo*.

Charles (Ch. 3) on Haiti and Spiegel (Ch. 13) on South Africa suggest the complexities in distinguishing domination from subjugation and acts of resistance from those of collusion. In her chapter Charles argues that the sexual politics of Haitian women counters male domination and the sexual division of labour, contending that the present politics of sexuality had its genesis in Haitian slavery. During the colonial period, women used 'sexuality to mediate and undermine the race and class hierarchy' (p. 53). Female sexuality subverted the dual class and race systems by creating a free and wealthy mulatto group. Women recognized their sexuality as a resource – capital – a commodity which could be used to establish their autonomy, and which expressed their resistance to the *status quo* and proved an important element in transforming slave society. And yet, because sexuality is treated as a form of capital by many Haitian women today, it may transform them into a commodity, establishing their subjugation in the domain of commerce. The point is that acts of resistance in one domain may lead to one being dominated in another. One might also argue that the creation of a mulatto group positioned between black slaves and white masters might well have preserved the system of slavery rather than transforming it. Spiegel (Ch. 13) points out that supporting 'traditional' precolonial customs and practices may well appear as resistance but in fact they are acts of collusion and subjugation. Traditional and pre-colonial are measured against European notions of progress and development as represented in the 'Aryan Model' of the genesis of western civilization (see Bernal, Ch. 8). Thus, to support the traditional and the precolonial is to justify apartheid in the views of the white South African rulers.

Questions about the consent and obedience of the subjugated and whether an act is one of resistance or collusion are not only a philosophical matter, but may also shape the way in which scholars construct the past. Social constructions of both the past and the present are pliable, flexible and amenable to different interpretations and interests. Anthropologists and historians are master builders and, as a consequence, their roles in the complex fields of domination and subjugation need careful investigation. Their activities are integral parts of the context and substance of contemporary scholarship.

Alternative constructions

Social constructions may reflect the interrelation and interpenetration of structures of thought and human agency interacting within complex economic and political fields. On the one hand, they reflect the ways in which people are defined, apprehended and acted upon by others and, on the other, they define themselves.

A cadre of scholars and their works have become implicated in this process. They become agents and actors within history, actively engaged in fabricating the 'other' and defining their past. Spiegel (Ch. 13) refers to this situation and its consequences, by making the point that some South African anthropologists supported apartheid and actively participated in constructing parochial traditions to legitimize it. Just as important, however (and far more subtle and pervasive), are the seemingly objective works that represent Africans as having only recently emerged from 'traditionalism'. Images presenting Africans in this way, Spiegel argues, are 'the product of a thirty-year exercise of reinventing tradition for the country's Bantustans' (p. 188). Anthropologists are often the ones who define which customs, practices and beliefs are 'traditional'.

The debates by scholars and popular leaders over local history and culture often appear parochial, trivial, and idiosyncratic. In fact, they may be particular instances of more general patterns and processes. In this present period of history, arguments over the past and the validity of established scholarly canons appear to be endemic – witness the heated debates about governance, economic entitlements, and race relations in South Africa, and about multiculturalism and Afrocentricity in the United States (Asante 1987, Schlesinger 1991). Singh (Ch. 14) explores the complex role of intellectuals in conceptualizing the future of South Africa and the great diversity of theoretical opinions even among those who belong to the same social movements. The basic issues in these debates revolve round struggles over nationhood, national identity and national entitlements.

In South Africa the insurrection of subjugated populations has stimulated debates about the fundamental structure of South African society, with scientists and historians experiencing social change as a daily occurrence, and the debates are not only theoretical but also oriented towards practical policies. Singh's chapter (Ch. 14) on intellectuals and the 'reconstructive' agenda clearly brings this home. Her contribution is highly theoretical and yet is constantly tempered by the mundane events of South African politics and the struggle among intellectuals over the reconstruction of South Africa. The context is highly textured and complex. On the one hand, through privatization the white South African government is transforming the white welfare state into a bastion of entrepreneurial activity and, on the other, black political leaders seek to preserve the welfare state and extend it to all segments of the population. Both state and folk histories are in the making, as are the new parameters of class and race. Singh's chapter makes the reader confront the problem of reconciling a class analysis with one that employs the dichotomy of state and civil society, especially during a period of political democratization. What then is the role of the ruling classes and intellectual elites? Singh makes it clear that our notions of class, state, civil society and democracy are of the same order as those of the indigenous intellectuals but with much less power. Their notions may well shape the course of South African history and development. And yet, these indigenous intellectuals are in fact none other than ourselves. The fundamental issue is thus the relation of human agency to the situations, circumstances and conditions of history and the representations of power.

In the United States, the fundamental questions involve: What will be America? Who is an American? and Who is entitled to delineate the universe and establish the criteria of academic discourse? Arguments over these issues have brought into play the full range of political and social actors, revealing the partisan nature of scholarship with the academic as activist and instigator. However, these debates have yet to turn to the more theoretical matter of the individual as agent and instigator in relation to the forces of history and society.[2]

The chapters in this volume indicate not only the pervasiveness of these debates but also the active involvement in them of both activists and scholars. Both Ramos on Brazilian indigenism (Ch. 5) and Wade on Colombia's white/black relations (Ch. 4) point to indigenous ethnic movements whose representatives are actively contesting the established views of their histories and cultures. Having rejected the majority view, indigenous peoples are elaborating their own versions and interpretations. This form of critical appraisal has also emerged within the academy. Gero (Ch. 10) represents this type of alternative academic discourse, one which is both theoretical and self-reflexive. In a systematic manner, she reveals the type of concentration of women in particular activities within archaeology, and from a 'constructivist' perspective she demonstrates the gender component in the construction of archaeological knowledge. Women's contributions in archaeology are relegated to specific domains and their findings subordinated to those of men.

The critique of bodies of accepted knowledge both within the academy and outside it opens channels for reconsidering historical and social fabrications that invent the past and then constrain it. These debates represent the confrontation of alternative discourses. As they begin to reveal the hegemonic and counter-hegemonic properties of historical fabrications and their intimate relation to modes of domination and subjugation and collaboration and resistance, academic guardians of 'high scholarship' may cease to treat them as minor irritants. As Gero (Ch. 10) notes, they often objectify subjective processes.

Said's (1990) observation about 'Third World' intellectuals such as C. L. R. James and Ranajit Guha applies to the contributors to this book. He observed that they 'share a common predilection for alternative versions of a greatly contested history' and that politics 'abuts very closely on the scholarship and research that they represent' (Said 1990, p. 46). Third World intellectuals are part of a submerged intellectual tradition which Said has identified as a 'culture of resistance'. It would be facile to argue that today's culture of resistance becomes tomorrow's culture of domination and that intellectuals move easily from being organic to traditional (Gramsci 1971, p. 5). The acceptance of such an assertion would return us to the mechanical and the parochial, trivializing the force of current social movements. The matter is much more complicated than that.

In characterizing Third World intellectuals, Said points to the issues fostering hegemonic intellectual domination and the persistence of resistance:

> There is an explicit urgency, call it political or human, in the tone and the import of these works that contrasts quite noticeably with what in the modern West has come to represent the norm for scholarship. How that norm, with its supposed detachment, its protestations of objectivity and impartiality, with its code of politesse and ritual calmness, came about is a problem for the sociology of taste and of knowledge.
>
> (Said 1990, p. 46)

As the range of contributors to this volume illustrates, Said's characterization is neither bounded by geography nor applicable solely to Third World intellectuals. The contributions that follow reveal the partisan nature of scholarship by representing conditions of social inequality. From the perspective of mainstream scholarship, they may not always seem detached, objective, or impartial. They may not conform to the code of politesse and ritual calmness. Buck, for example, introduces her contribution (Ch. 2) by situating herself in relation to history and her research materials. Expressing anger, fear and dismay over 'the hegemonic history that was part of [her] white, middle-class heritage' (p. 29) she deals with her theme analytically and self-reflexively. Almost simultaneously, she not only reveals her personal 'bias' but also exposes and rejects the biases of dominant historical versions of white/black relations in Kentucky. Her scholarly thrust goes to the core of mainstream history and anthropology, revealing them for what they are and placing their practitioners within the context of their own history and society. Scholars such as Buck seek not only to represent history in their work but also to transform it. In this sense scholarship is combined with political purpose.

The dominant intellectual elites have claimed authority and objectivity for their cultural productions for a long time. But political and economic tensions, lying very near the surface, have driven other scholars with other interpretations of the past, those who take the subjugated as the point of reference for research and writing. There are periods, however, when the histories and cultures of subjugated peoples are lost or subsumed within dominant or generalized histories. Frequently, the methodological problem is how to reclaim these rusticated bodies of knowledge.

Subjugated knowledge

By identifying two types of subjugated knowledges – the one, buried and disguised, and the other, disqualified and marginalized – Foucault (1980, pp. 78–109) has been central in revitalizing scholarly interests in reclaiming subjugated forms of knowledge and understanding the pervasive nature of domination. Buried knowledge consists of the clusters of knowledge buried and disguised within dominant regimes of formally systematized thought. The formal properties of this form obscure the struggle and conflict that led to the incorporation of other clusters and the domination of one, producing a particular configuration and imposition. What was required was a form of critical assessment that would disaggregate the established regime of thought, liberating the very historical basis of its fabrication.

The chapters by Bernal on European history's images of Greece (Ch. 8), Wade on notions of racial mixtures in Colombian history (Ch. 4), and Ramos on the construction of indigenism in Brazil (Ch. 5) disaggregate the main strands of dominant, totalitarian theories. They reveal the process by which one cluster of ideas gained sway over others and formed the basis for constructing the past differently. In their analyses of dominant bodies of knowledge they identify two contending paradigms: for Greece, Ancient and Aryan, for Colombia, white and black and for Brazil, edenic and indigenism. Each set of ideas and their representations of the past have their own practical consequences. They provide justifications and rationalizations for social and intellectual hierarchies, imperial conquest and the exclusion and subjugation of populations.

Bernal's chapter (Ch. 8) is especially pertinent for unravelling dominant paradigmatic images and analysing the interests that created them. It demonstrates the use of talismanic – or magic – knowledge to distance the colonizer from the colonized, and to 'adjust' scholarship to a ruling class's interest during a particular era. The Aryan Model – developed in the nineteenth century – is just such an adjustment, causing scholars to overlook or dismiss earlier interpretations by Greeks of their own history. The Aryan Model obscured prior models of Greece, and justified the superiority of 'western civilization' and the claims of its ruling classes to conquer, colonize and thereby 'civilize'. It incorporated notions of progress and development against which 'non-Aryans' would be measured, and became the standard for evaluating peoples, their cultures, and their ability to achieve 'modernity'. The Ancient Model was discarded and Greece became the cradle of western civilization and not a gateway for the exchange of ideas. The Aryan Model set the tone for European colonial domination and provided the ideological framework for incorporating and subjugating labour into a capitalist world order. Race, class and geography became merged into a single notion of domination. In the late nineteenth and early twentieth centuries, Africa, the most recent source of slave labour and raw materials, became the lowest rung on the cultural ladder constructed by European scholars and rulers. The Aryan Model and its legacies were most appropriate for the sectional divisions of race, class and ethnicity so characteristic of societies in the Americas.

Wade (Ch. 4) reports the assertion of a Colombian anthropologist that 'the study of blacks was not "anthropology" ' (p. 69). For this statement to make sense one must probe Colombia's dominant rendering of history and its national ideology. At its simplest, it reflected the dominance of whites over blacks and the preference given to whites in Colombian history. Historically, blacks were considered incapable of attaining the standard of progress necessary for development. Their subjugation was thus an expression not only of an historical construction that devalued them but also of the dominant national ideology that claimed Colombia was a nation of mestizos. Given this construction, the history of blacks was in Africa, and that of mestizos in Colombia. National history and ideology combined to justify both exclusion and subjugation of blacks. They were to be an invisible people graced with neither history nor culture.

Ramos (Ch. 5) dissects a more complicated historical rendering in which two dominant notions of Indians run concurrently through Brazilian history, if not the histories of the Americas. Indians are depicted on the one hand as 'noble savages' to be preserved and, on the other, as barbarians to be civilized. Though the two images seem antithetical, they represent the Indian as inferior. Consequently, the white ruling classes may appeal to either image as justification for subjugating Indian peoples and dispossessing them of rights and property. The one voice missing in this historical discourse is that of the Indian. Ramos points out that Brazil's indigenous peoples are organizing themselves and challenging the dominant views of their past. Indians, casting off their role as silent, invisible partners of either the government or anthropologists, are now claiming a voice in the construction of their own history. Their *de novo* constructions are beginning to expose the nature of past struggles and conflicts and the processes of cultural incorporation and subjugation of indigenous knowledges. At this point in time, the alternative discourses and social movements stand in a complementary relationship which does not mean, however, that in the ongoing struggle for political rights one body of knowledge may not become dominant and another be brushed aside and relegated to the margins.[3]

Foucault's second type of subjugated knowledge refers to a whole set of

knowledges that 'have been disqualified as inadequate for their task or insufficiently elaborated'. However, it is through 'the reappearance of this knowledge, of these local popular knowledges . . . that criticism performs its work'
(Foucault 1980, p. 82). Both types of knowledge, the erudite and centralized
and the disqualified and localized, contain and exemplify histories of hostile
encounters that either buried one form of knowledge or pushed it to the
margins. While Foucault was primarily oriented toward reclamation through
genealogical and archaeological pursuits, other scholars have been concerned
with the immediate process of recasting, synthesizing and renewing discarded
interpretations of the past. Their research has focused on reclaiming marginalized knowledge and the history and culture of subjugated and excluded
peoples. This situation applies directly to those chapters in this book that focus
on the history and cultures of formerly enslaved or conquered peoples of the
Americas and Southern Africa.

Cummins & Rappaport (Ch. 6) provide another perspective on the relation
of knowledge to power. They look for those elements which led to the fusion
of Spanish and Andean traditions. Thus, their concern is not so much with
salvaging or reclaiming history but with the consequences of incorporating
literacy into a non-literate society. They view alphabetical literacy as an
innovative and transformative technology that helped to shape Andean history
and culture. With their focus on legal documents, they demonstrate the
fundamental effect that this written material had on economic and power
relations. The ability to use or command this technology conferred power and
affected patterns of inheritance and succession and rights to property and
authority. Here one is concerned with the creation of social inequality based on
the incorporation of an alien technology. The consequences that Cummins &
Rappaport describe for Latin America are also seen in many other parts
of the world as well as in the academy. Literacy is a powerful tool for maintaining one's privileges and appropriating those of others. At times, the
construction of history is closely linked to the level of control of literacy
(Wolf 1982) and at those times the illiterate must look to subaltern scholars to
represent them.

The reclamation of the past has its own complexities and social penalties,
especially for scholars focusing on subjugated populations. These complexities
become abundantly apparent when researchers begin to deal with the problem
of how to retrieve the history and way of life of lower orders such as the
illiterate, partially literate slaves, peasants, or workers, to say nothing of rebel
consciousnesses and insurrections, from documents written by the dominant
elements. Within the United States, these complexities have been particularly
pronounced in issues surrounding slavery and the subjugation of blacks. The
works of scholars such as Aptheker (1943) and Cox (1970 [1948]) are examples
of attempts to analyse fields of subjugation, popular consciousness and resistance. Both paid dearly for challenging accepted wisdom and probing the roots
of the academy's canons. But their work laid a firm foundation for the
generation of scholars that followed. Lamentably, the scholarly legacy of

Aptheker and Cox is not always recognized by subaltern scholars, thereby producing distinctive disjunctions of intellectual continuity.

Genovese (1972), Guha (1983) and Fields (1985) take up this legacy, and engage in an effort to analyse peasant movements, insurgencies and rebel consciousness from colonial documents. Comitas's (1994) study of Greek working-class drug users establishes three sets of discourses, representing distinct versions of history and their commanding voices. There is the rendering of history by historians; the recounting of personal histories and its historical context by the working-class drug users; and finally, the master orchestrating voice of the anthropologist. There is no closure, either empirically or theoretically. Ultimately, the reader becomes the final arbiter, measuring history against history and interpretation against interpretation. The key question raised by all four works is how to prioritize authority among competing voices. Within the arena of public culture, whose interpretations of events should be accorded authority? Most often, scholars attempt to remove themselves from the fray of public combat and should their interpretations or assessments prove false or inappropriate, they usually stand to lose very little indeed. The formulations of scholars are rarely tested within situations of actual social turmoil. Rarely do they have to pay for their misinterpretations. This is certainly not the case for political activists.

In this context, the emic/etic distinction delineated by Harris (1968) seems to obscure fundamental relations of power. This discussion of situation and authority leads to further questions regarding the relation of scholarship to power and praxis, especially in the politically charged racial atmosphere of countries such as South Africa and the United States. Rowlands (Ch. 9) frames the basic issue in relation to academic disciplines and nationhood and nationalism. He observes that 'Nations without pasts are a contradiction in terms and archaeology has been one of the principal suppliers of the raw material for constructing pasts in modern struggles for nationhood' (p. 133). Hall (Ch. 12) points out that in South Africa scholarship has often served the white ruling classes, with one source or type of material being promoted over another to serve the interests and policies of the state. This situation has placed responsibility for the manner in which research is undertaken squarely on the shoulders of the researcher. Thus, Hall attempts to avoid giving preference to written documents over the archaeological record, or artefact assemblage over travellers' accounts, probate records and paintings by viewing the past as a set of complex intertwined texts forming a discourse. Through his careful analysis of three sites, he successfully contests established archaeological wisdom.

Herzfeld (1987) and Bernal (Ch. 8) explore the theoretical and intellectual problems of promoting one stream of historical interpretation over another. Greece's position in western European civilization and western thought provides the terrain for investigation. Herzfeld (1987) discusses the weight that should be given to two types of histories: one produced by nations, states and dominant classes, and the other elaborated by the folk. In the former, timeless, general and pervasive and often incorporating elements of the folk histories, the past appears to be or is presented as enduring and impenetrable. This generalized form of dominant history is 'like myth . . . a "machine suppressing time"' (Lévi-Strauss 1964, p. 24). Its atemporal nature brings it into line with the *status quo* and 'the distinction between myth and history is merely a way of banishing "others" from "history" ' (Herzfeld 1987, p. 44).

On the other hand, folk histories tend to be disjunctive and fragmented with multiple contending versions (Bond 1976, Herzfeld 1987, pp. 42–5). They are often characterized as being incomplete and partisan, representing the interests of a particular parochial constituency (Bond 1976). Since they contest the dominant version of history, they are dismissed by mainstream senior scholars as discordant and political, the emanations of '*bricoleurs*' and not the refined efforts of specialists. But the question is which of these two types is to be privileged or how are they to be used in the construction of models of social history? Herzfeld grounds these problems in anthropological theory and Bernal in central paradigms of western thought. Both explore the centrality and marginality of Greece in notions of western civilization. Comitas (1994) does so from the perspective of the subaltern classes of contemporary Greek society.

Many of the chapters in this volume investigate the processes by which hierarchies of knowledge are established and the political implications of these hierarchies for social relations. Bernal (Ch. 8) on the two legacies of Ancient Greece, Hall (Ch. 12) on South African history and Cummins & Rappaport (Ch. 6) on the power of literacy in Latin America clearly lay out the relation of economic and political conditions to historical interpretations. They delve into both the immediate consequences and the long-term legacies of dominant histories that have subjugated other traditions. Procedurally, their task was one of careful extraction, the unmeshing of multiple pasts from a single encasement. A first step in this enterprise is the recognition of the power of language and those linguistic concepts that draw distinctions between 'us' and 'them'. The underlying methodological problem has become rooted in issues of essentialism, paternalism and distancing. It is a problem that entails invention and appropriation.

Liberating the past: invention and appropriation

The first order is to confront the language of paternalistic domination that resides in the tradition of western liberal thought and manifests itself in the common-sense terms of spatial, temporal and geographical subordinations. The terms are themselves part of the imagery of radical thought that separates a supposed 'western we' from a 'non-western them' or, in the anthropological language of authoritative appropriation, 'the other'. This distinction is given concreteness in terms such as centre and periphery, modern and traditional and north and south. As Fabian points out, this order of spatial and geographical distinction obscures an implicit assumption about temporal progression

(Fabian 1983). It reflects where 'we' have been and where 'they' have yet to reach. In these formulations, our present is their future.

The ideological component of these distinctions is so prevalent and pervasive, so subtle and entrenched, that it frames the thesis of radical thinkers. For example, in his discussion of the Subaltern Studies project, Chakrabarty (1992) situates his argument within the metonymic parameters of centre and periphery but has the wit to break their constraining hold. He explores the manner in which 'the center and the periphery come together in the postcolonial scene of writing history' (Chakrabarty 1992, p. 48). Some scholars may empty the centre, the metropole countries of the imperial past, of its subaltern content, the periphery of its international ruling element, industrialists, commercialists and brokers. These two monolithic categories, centre and periphery, confront each other in a sterile unproductive historical engagement, and history ceases to be about progressive interpenetrations and transformations of relations of power, domination, subjugation, resistance, subversion and collusion. Through an anecdote about attire, an Australian's view of the anachronistic cut of his Indian trousers, Chakrabarty collapses these categories and brings the notion of the periphery squarely into the centre. The postulated past and the present occupy the same temporal space, thereby restoring power to history.

Power within history lies in several domains: one is the relation of text to subject and another is the construction of individual and collective identities (for example, racial, ethnic and national). These social constructions are part of the process of inventing traditions. In the act of creating a written text subjects are transformed into transposable objects. 'We' create 'them' and in so doing, we pretend that we are creating ourselves, if only through contrasts and opposition. But in the process 'we' appropriate 'them', 'we' fix and frame the 'other' through a zealous essentialism, thereby falling prey to the dilemma of dual fabrication.

Most of the chapters in this book explore power relations between peoples framed and phrased in the idiom of race. Inevitably, this thrust leads directly to the fragile, unstable core of 'western social sciences'. It does so with particular pungency in disciplines such as anthropology. Anthropologists are in the unique position of advancing themselves and their discipline through the fabrication of their subjects of study. They make them the 'other' and then situate the 'other' in the timeless void of the ethnographic present (Sanjek 1991). The anthropological 'we' and the native 'other' are intimately tied together, one as active agent, fabricator, or inventor, the 'other' as supposedly passive, the fabricated, or invented. The construction of historical and social configurations gains significance only through a stirring of social and historical imaginations, imaginations usually conditioned by social circumstances and dominant theories. The bind is that anthropologists usually develop paradigms to explain or interpret that which they have themselves created, a scholarly extension of omphaloscepsis. The crisis lies in the limitations of anthropological paradigms to explain historical and ethnographic constructions. As anthropologists, we engage in exploring the internal logic of our paradigms as well as the appropriateness of our data to contemporary theory and political issues. Our scholarly analysis and authority is based upon our own social inventions and fabrications. In our texts we orchestrate the presence of the 'others' as well as their absence. Ironically, in poststructuralist and postmodernist texts the 'others' become no more than an echo. As Mullings (Ch. 1) notes, much of their literature has overlooked the work of Third World scholars who tend to link representation to relations of domination. Instead they focus on texts and textual analysis and not on actual physical circumstances and consequences of subjugation.

In the past our anthropological paradigms have remained aloof from active political realities and the critical analytic assessment of 'subaltern' scholars (Young 1990, p. 160) and indigenous intellectuals and theorists. That day is rapidly passing. Fortunately, the 'others' have the capacity of inventing and interpreting their own pasts and as Singh (Ch. 14) points out, of conceptualizing and constructing their own futures.

Hobsbawm (1992, p. 4) sets out the conditions under which one might expect to find the invention of new traditions. The situation would be one marked by social dislocations – when society is undergoing rapid social 'transformations that weaken or destroy the social patterns for which "old" traditions had been designed, producing new ones to whom they were not applicable, or which such old traditions and their institutional carriers and promulgators no longer prove sufficiently adaptable and flexible, or are otherwise eliminated'. This formulation joins social strain theory (Geertz 1973, p. 205) with a notion of the role of traditional and organic intellectuals in the shaping of history and culture (Gramsci 1971). The invention of tradition is intimately linked to the structure of society and reflects, in one way or another, the potential or real cleavages within it. It is an expression of the history of patterns of differential incorporation of populations (Smith 1991, p. 8) and their sectional interests.

Hobsbawm (1992, p. 9) identifies three overlapping types of invented traditions: 1) those establishing and symbolizing social cohesion and membership of groups; 2) those legitimizing institutions, status or relations of authority; and 3) those whose main purpose was that of socialization. He is concerned with what these traditions do and their connection with social units and processes. Not solely part of the process by which subjects are transformed into objects, these traditions become linked to these objects and secure their continuity. Integral elements of emerging socio-historical configurations, they furnish individuals and collectives with distinct identities and new opportunities. They help fabricate heritage from assorted objects.

Rao (Ch. 11) and Spiegel (Ch. 13) provide examples of the complex factors involved in the invention of tradition. Rao argues that for Indians to assert a postcolonial identity they found it necessary to emphasize tradition. Her analysis of Hindu/Muslim relations in Ayodhya, a city in northern India, points to the continual reinvention of the past to serve contemporary sectional interests. In this context, she explores a dispute between Hindus and Muslims

as to whether Babar, the first Mughal emperor, razed a Hindu temple and
built a mosque on the site. Although there is no archaeological or written
evidence one way or the other, both sides use their own and their antagonists'
contemporary religious norms to claim actions in the past. Both Hindus and
Muslims validated and affirmed their own identities through the supposed past
practices of the other. These invented heritages were brought into the arena of
everyday Indian politics, and became points of debate for political elites and
religious intellectuals.

Spiegel (Ch. 13) describes how the South African government's policy of
inventing African tradition from above has gained support from some
Africans. Following the logic of apartheid, the South African government
created ethnic enclaves or 'tribal homelands' and established indirect rule by
restoring 'traditional' chiefs to oversee renovated 'traditional' administrative
and land-tenure systems. Both the white government and black chiefs claimed
'traditional' authority and powers for chiefs. Great store was placed on restoring the precolonial 'communal' land system which was supposedly highly
productive with no deleterious environmental or societal effects. By renewing
the past, it was argued, consequences of overcrowding and low productivity
could be resolved. Appeals to reinstate a 'traditional' land-tenure system also
came from Africanist opponents of apartheid. However, since there was no
evidence that this precolonial system actually provided equitable allocations
of land and agricultural abundance, the government literally invented new
administrative and land-tenure systems. Cadres of intellectuals came forward
to support this 'restoration' of 'tradition'.

Gramsci's (1971) understanding of the relation of intellectuals to political
and economic formations is relevant to the chapters by Rao (Ch. 11) and
Spiegel (Ch. 13) as well as to those by other contributors to this volume. The
role of intellectuals in inventing and shaping culture and the past is always
complicated. Although they claim dispassion and objectivity it is never quite
clear for whom they speak and whose interests they represent, points clearly
made in Singh's analysis of South African intellectuals (Ch. 14). The latitude of
their autonomy is a matter of constant concern.

The distinction made by Gramsci between organic and traditional intellectuals alerts us to the intimate connection between economic production, basic
social groupings and intellectual activity. He observes that

> Every social group, coming into existence on the original terrain of
> an essential function in the world of economic production, creates
> together with itself, organically, one or more strata of intellectuals
> which give it homogeneity and an awareness of its own function
> not only in the economic but also in the social and political fields.
>
> (Gramsci 1971, p. 5)

An important characteristic of this emergent social group and its intellectual
component is their struggle 'to assimilate and to conquer "ideologically" the
traditional intellectuals' (Gramsci 1971, p. 10) who represent the interests of a

prior epoch. The organic intellectuals act to synthesize and organize a new culture, one which is compatible with the sectional interests of the emerging dominant social group. They are, in fact, engaged in inventing traditions. However, Singh (Ch. 14) and Spiegel (Ch. 13) demonstrate the complex role of intellectuals and the difficulty in assigning them to a simple set of categories.

Gramsci was well aware of the complex relationship between intellectuals and the thick textures of cultural screens that mediate their link to productive modes. But it is not clear whether he fully appreciated the autonomy of contemporary intellectuals and that they were bound by neither situation nor geography. Free to move, the terrain of discourse becomes broad indeed. Obviously, Gramsci did have some appreciation of this situation, as evidenced in his brief discussion of the possible influence of United States 'negro intellectuals' on the 'backward' African masses (Gramsci 1971, p. 21). And yet, he could not have anticipated African intellectual discourse in black American thought and action.

A fierce struggle over the 'history' or 'histories' of Africa is now in full swing. The combat is taking place in the United States and not Africa. While United States black intellectuals of rural and proletarian backgrounds claim an Africa that never was, African intellectuals analyse the historical and philosophical necessities for its invention. Both are engaged in fabrication. They invent a present and, at the same time, elaborate profound intellectual and social critiques of contemporary African and western civilizations and their modes of thought. Mudimbe (1988) provides a francophone perspective on these issues while Appiah (1992) brings to bear the full weight of his elite academic training and social background in Africa and England on the philosophical and practical problems of inventing Africa.

These American and African scholars, while engaging in both the social construction and critique of imagined communities, also provide the basis for interpreting public cultures, as well as ascribing authority to themselves and to their works. Generally, the domain of their discourse is not restricted by economy or locality. Ironically, less reflexive scholars of this mode often succumb to the elegance of their own critique and inventions. By sometimes appropriating the 'other' as an object of thought, they merge unconsciously and unintentionally with the colonial past and its discourse, entwining themselves in their own poetics of meaning.

Essentialism and the poetics of meaning

A world of meaning is constructed through images, or icons, that are the products of particular historical circumstances. Orientalism, Occidentalism and Africanism are examples of such constructions. Manifestations of a particular type of essentialism, they reduce complex and intricate historical and social diversities to a few prominent cultural images. The images become the basis for collusion, cultural screens through which the world is ordered,

interpreted and understood. They have the power to evoke the past, appre-
hending the present, and establishing the basis of 'imagined communities'
(Anderson 1992). These imagined communities, built on clusters of key
symbols that evoke a past that might have been, have a transient and ephemeral present, and a future whose distinctive signature is epiphany. In its own
way, the past is the epitome of the imagined community, since it cannot exist
coterminously with the present. Collingwood notes the complexities of constructing the past when he observes that

> historical knowledge is that special case of memory where the
> object of present thought is past thought, the gap between the
> present and the past being bridged not only by the power of present
> thought to think of the past, but also by the power of past thought
> to reawaken itself in the present.
>
> (Collingwood 1961, p. 294)

Neither the past nor the present enters full blown into our heads.

Whether incorporated into the apparatus of the state or formulated by folk
notions of the past, public history takes on the rhetoric of poetics and the
attributes of property, with claims and counter-claims as to its veracity and its
ownership. Moreover, battles are fought over whose aesthetic principle is
most appropriate for constructing the past in the most convincing fashion, that
is, with the most hegemonic power. No single interpretation of public history
exists, but rather a series of contending fabrications, which pit interest to
power, meaning to experience, and understanding to social consciousness.
Aesthetic and stylistic conventions become points of domination and also of
resistance, and both state and folk histories conform to canons of appropriateness that establish their credibility. As Rao (Ch. 11) and Hall (Ch. 12) clearly
point out, these canons are built upon images, understandings and a shared
constellation of meaningful objects. Though Hindu politicians contest each
other's notions of the past, they rally their followers by employing the same
popular stylistic and poetic forms.

In multiracial societies such as South Africa and the United States, the use
and meaning of key images contained in state and folk histories introduce
further complexity. Hall (Ch. 12) points out that for the South African Cape of
the 1830s and 1840s the image of the lower classes as being homogeneous and
black would be incorrect. There was no clear correlation between race and
class. As he notes 'The Attorney General's full contempt was reserved for the
"lower Irish" ' (p. 170).

Buck (Ch. 2) demonstrates the extent to which social control and power are
embedded in symbols of race, gender and class. The history of the American
south has been rooted on the reality and imagery of the power of whites, with
economic and political power reserved for upper-class white males. 'Whiteness' became the key symbol that elevated and subordinated and channelled
social and class consciousness. For the white population it represented a range
of valued attributes such as justice, goodness and progress, in addition to

power itself. In the traditional historiography of the state of Kentucky whiteness has been part of the apparatus of domination, obscuring long-held social alliances across the lines of colour. Buck's chapter illuminates this use of the ideology of whiteness to subvert shared class interests.

Shack's discussion (Ch. 7) of his mother's use of the Bogey Man is a further illustration of the use of a key image for understanding race relations within the United States. The essential features of whiteness and its concrete manifestation in white males become even more powerful in its reversal and symbolic transmutation as a mechanism of social control and discipline. Instead of white males personifying goodness, purity and justice, Shack's mother (and probably black mothers throughout the South) represented them as evil, veritable Bogey Men. Her rendering, on the one hand, effectively controlled the behaviour of her small son and on the other, exemplified the poetics of resistance in everyday life. Historically, black mothers have been vulnerable socially and yet active politically, highly visible in shaping the counter-hegemonic discourse of black resistance against the social apparatus of cultural domination.

Many of the chapters in this book indicate the power that is attributed to colour in multiracial societies. Mullings (Ch. 1), Shack (Ch. 7) and Wade (Ch. 4) point to the equation of white with progress and development, the Aryan notion of human history. 'Blackness' is framed by a concept of the primitive and non-developed. Progress toward civilization, toward modernity, demands becoming increasingly white. Thus colour itself, an inert substance, is transformed into a political marker that determines the extent of domination. To foster blackness, therefore, may be taken as an act of resistance. And yet, as Buck (Ch. 2) argues, colour is no more than part of the ideological and hegemonic apparatus that enables the subjugation of both black and white workers. As Shack's mother so aptly realized, ideology is itself a powerful factor in daily human behaviour.

Scholarship is not immune to the social environment in which it thrives and the ideology of colour has long been an intricate part of the social context of scholarly activity. That this is rarely acknowledged is in part due to the fact that to mention this relation is to endow it with undue racial sensitivity. To validate scholarship is to give it an 'unraced' identity, and by doing so, the assumption of the universality of implicit 'whiteness' of scholarship is enhanced. Morrison intimates that to omit mention of race in a racialized society is to enhance the power of that society:

> What does positing one's writerly self, in the wholly racialized society that is the United States, as unraced and all others as raced entail? What happens to the writerly imagination of a black author who is at some level always conscious of representing one's own race to . . . a race of readers that understands itself to be 'universal' or race-free?
>
> (Morrison 1992, p. xii)

In this sense, one new strategy of American conservatives is to label racist the person who notes the ethnic composition or lack of ethnic diversity within a given structure, while simultaneously calling for a colour-blind society. Such stratagems have always informed scholarship, and link racism to the twin pillars of 'social reality and scientific truth'. For some scholars 'Racism is thus fundamentally a theory of history' (Saxton 1990, p. 14).

Insurrections, re-evaluations and the 'western' focus

Much of this book is concerned with that which has been banished from the mainstream to the outer reaches. Most of the authors recognize that periodic insurrections of subjugated populations release bodies of knowledge and have led to a proliferation of empirical data and theoretical formulations. These insurrections have been a constant source of new analytic perspectives and aesthetic and stylistic renderings of the past and cultures of populations. One example is the perspective that collapses the distance between the social analyst and the social actor, with the analyst no longer attempting to give the impression of being a detached and dispassionate observer. In fact there are times when the analyst's history, culture and interests appear to merge with those of the actors themselves (Rosaldo 1989), and the scholar's analytic subjective engagement becomes an essential element of the published text (see, for example, Drake & Cayton 1962, Jules-Rosette 1975, Alvarez 1987). It brings into the text Geertz's (1968) two fundamental orientations toward the realities of fieldwork, the 'engaged' and the 'analytic'. The text, in part, retains its context, anchored in reality, yet transcending it. While retaining the personal, it links individuals into the universal attributes of human existence. It derives power and authority from its ability to personalize sociological theory and relate it to particular social situations and human conditions.

However, insurrection has at times led to its own form of negative essentialism in which scholarship and scholars are accorded geographical and 'cultural' designations and preferences. Phrased in terms of the 'non-western vs the western world', this global dichotomy is usually presented as if it captured all the diversity in the world and had intrinsic explanatory power. It is a characterization so deeply rooted in our language of description and analysis that we find it difficult not to use. We may question the essentialists' construction of Orientalism and Occidentalism and yet without second thought preserve the West as the essential point of reference to be used in comparative and dialectical analysis. Even in his perceptive critique of ethnographic essentialism and analysis of Occidentalism, Carrier (1992) uses this dichotomy in much the same way that many scholars bestow centrality to the West. He observes, for example, that 'the way I have cast this privileges the West as the standard against which all Others are defined, which is appropriate in view of both the historical political and economic power of the West and the fact that anthropology is overwhelmingly a western discipline' (Carrier 1992, p. 197). In this

Introduction we too have not avoided making distinctions, but we trust that we have redrawn the contours of the dichotomy without giving explicit or implicit preference to the West. Subjugation is never merely a function of either geography or culture and appearances are often deceiving, obscuring underlying political and economic processes.

The acceptance of the dichotomy and the West as the centre has often led to the belief that the self-proclaimed 'Third World intellectual' has some special hold on knowledge or an intuitive insight into the non-western world. Both the dichotomy and the belief are no more than romantic radicalisms. In this regard, Shack (Ch. 7) notes the absence of the critical voice of the indigenous common folk in academic discourse. The academic spokesman for the common folk may frame the scholarly poetics of subordination and resistance, but fail to represent its substance and the voices of the subjugated. The western and non-western dichotomies often obscure the common ground shared by a body of scholars who explore social inequality, domination and subjugation from a partisan perspective. Certainly scholars may and often do share the same past and conditions as the social actors they study, but it must be stressed that this is by no means essential. The engagement in and critical assessment of explicitly partisan scholarship is the most direct path to an open society and one that oft-times reveals its enemies.

Social constructions are rarely objective and neutral. What is analytically significant is what they do and do not represent or fail to include, and the preference that they give to one body of knowledge over another, and to one set of scholars over others. The politics of knowledge is no more than an element of the politics of society, that is, of domination and subjugation.

Notes

1 Spurr notes that he uses colonial and colonial discourse to designate a series of historical instances and rhetorical functions. Thus, colonial discourse describes aspects of language that survive beyond the classic colonial era and which continue to colour perceptions of the non-western world (Spurr 1993, p. 8). Colonial relations and relations of subjugation may be said to contain the same rhetorical function.
2 Young (1990, pp. 134–40) provides an interesting discussion of Foucault and Said's relation to this issue. The relation of human agency to social and historical determination is a long-standing feature of anthropological theory. Anthropologists have not, however, tended to look at themselves as agents and instigators. They do not usually explore the extent to which their works are the products of cultural and historical circumstances.
3 In less sophisticated hands this type of knowledge excavation could lead to a crude syncretic approach to the social construction of the past. The main concern of these chapters is with relations of power, and not with the genesis of cultural elements.

References

Alvarez, R. 1987. *Familia*. Berkeley: University of California Press.

Anderson, B. 1992. *Imagined Communities*. New York: Verso.

Appiah, K. A. 1992. *In My Father's House*: Africa in the philosophy of culture. New York: Oxford University Press.

Aptheker, H. 1943. *American Negro Slave Revolts*. New York: International Publishers.

Asante, M. 1987. *The Afrocentric Idea*. Philadelphia: Temple University Press.

Bond, G. C. 1976. *The Politics of Change in a Zambian Community*. Chicago: Chicago University Press.

Carrier, J. G. 1992. Occidentalism: the world turned upside-down. *American Ethnologist* 19, 195–213.

Chakrabarty, D. 1992. The death of history? Historical consciousness and the culture of late capitalism. *Public Culture* 4, x.

Collingwood, R. G. 1961. *The Idea of History*. London: Oxford University Press.

Comaroff, J. 1985. *Body of Power, Spirit of Resistance*. Chicago: Chicago University Press.

Comitas, L. 1994. *Opprobrium and Persecution: hashish users in urban Greece*, forthcoming.

Cox, O. [1948] 1970. *Caste, Class and Race*. New York: Monthly Review Press.

Drake, St Clair & H. Cayton 1962. *Black Metropolis*. New York: Harper & Row.

Fabian, J. 1983. *Time and the Other*. New York: Columbia University Press.

Fields, K. 1985. *Revival and Rebellion in Colonial Africa*. Princeton: Princeton University Press.

Foucault, M. 1980. *Power/Knowledge*. New York: Pantheon.

Geertz, C. 1968. Thinking as a moral act: dimensions of anthropological fieldwork in the new states. *Antioch Review* 28, 39–58.

Geertz, C. 1973. *The Interpretation of Cultures*. New York: Basic Books.

Genovese, E. 1972. *Roll Jordan Roll*. New York: Vintage Books.

Gilliam, A. 1991. Militarism and accumulation as cargo cult. In *Decolonizing Anthropology*, Harrison, F. V. (ed.), 168–88. Washington, DC: American Anthropological Association.

Gramsci, A. 1971. *Selections from the Prison Notebooks*. New York: International Publishers.

Guha, R. 1983. *Elementary Aspects of Peasant Insurgency in Colonial India*. Delhi: Oxford University Press.

Hall, S. 1978. Marxism and culture. *Radical History Review* 18, 5–14.

Harris, M. 1968. *The Rise of Anthropological Theory*. New York, Crowell.

Harrison, F. V. (ed.) 1991. *Decolonizing Anthropology*. Washington, DC: American Anthropological Association.

Herzfeld, M. 1987. *Anthropology Through the Looking Glass: critical ethnography in the margins of Europe*. New York: Cambridge University Press.

Hobsbawm, E. 1992. Introduction. In *The Invention of Tradition*, Hobsbawm, E. & T. Ranger (eds), 1–14. Cambridge: Cambridge University Press.

Hobsbawm, E. & T. Ranger (eds) 1992. *The Invention of Tradition*. Cambridge: Cambridge University Press.

Jules-Rosette, B. 1975. *African Apostles*. Ithaca: Cornell University Press.

Lagemann, E. C. 1987. The politics of knowledge: the Carnegie Corporation and the formulation of public policy. *History of Education Quarterly* 27, 206–20.

Lagemann, E. C. 1988. *The Politics of Knowledge: a history of the Carnegie Corporation of New York*. Middletown: Wesleyan University Press.

Lévi-Strauss, C. 1964. *Le cru et le cuit*. Paris: Plon.

Mitchell, W. J. T. 1986. *Iconology*. Chicago: Chicago University Press.

Morrison, A. 1992. *Playing in the Dark: whiteness and the literary imagination.* Cambridge: Harvard University Press.

Mudimbe, V. Y. 1988. *The Invention of Africa.* Bloomington: Indiana University Press.

Nadel, S. F. 1957. *The Theory of Social Structure.* London: Cohen & West.

Rosaldo, R. 1989. *Culture and Truth.* Boston: Beacon Press.

Said, E. W. 1990. Third World intellectuals and metropolitan culture. *Raritan* 9, 27–50.

Sanjek, R. 1991. The ethnographic present. *Man* 26, 609–28.

Sanjek, R. 1992. The organization of festivals and ceremonies among Americans and immigrants in Queens, New York. In *To Make the World Safe for Diversity*, Daun, A., B. Ehn & B. Klein (eds), 123–94. Stockholm: The Ethnology Institute.

Saxton, A. 1990. *The Rise and Fall of the White Republic: class politics and mass culture in nineteenth-century America.* London: Verso.

Schlesinger, A. M. Jr 1991. *The Disuniting of America: reflections on a multicultural society.* New York: W. W. Norton.

Scott, J. C. 1985. *Weapons of the Weak.* New Haven: Yale University Press.

Smith, M. G. 1991. *Pluralism, Politics and Ideology in the Creole Caribbean.* New York: RISM.

Spivak, G. C. 1985. Subaltern studies: deconstructing historiography. In *Subaltern Studies IV*, Guha R. (ed.), 330–64. Delhi: Oxford University Press.

Spurr, D. 1993. *The Rhetoric of Empire.* Durham: Duke University Press.

Vincent, J. 1990. *Anthropology and Politics.* Tucson: University of Arizona Press.

Wolf, E. 1982. *Europe and the People Without History.* Berkeley: University of California Press.

Young, R. 1990. *White Mythologies.* New York: Routledge.

The representation
of ethnicity

1 Ethnicity and representation

LEITH MULLINGS

Representation of inequality has long been contested terrain. Though the emergence of the modern culture concept in the twentieth century permitted a comprehensive critique of race to enter the social science literature, there have always been alternative explanations for inequality. Social reformers, revolutionaries, environmental determinists and Marxist social scientists have challenged biological essentialism. People of colour, often working outside the academy, explored the political economy of race relations, and critiqued the representation of racial and national inequality (see Bond & Gilliam 1994).

Recently, the rise of poststructuralist theory has promoted the emergence of a language which, though generally inaccessible to those outside the academy, supports decentring science, knowledge and the canon, and deconstructing prevailing representations of inequality. But in repudiating the representation of race, much of this literature has retreated from analysis of the relations of race, often overlooking the work of those Third World scholars who definitively link representation to relations of domination and the necessity to challenge them. As notions of indeterminacy of truth easily shade into denial of the reality of slavery, the Holocaust and other forms of oppression, these new studies of race and representation have stepped back from confronting power.

The following chapters, on the other hand, clearly draw the relationship between systems of representation and the social relations in which they are embedded. In placing the study of ethnicity squarely within the context of power relationships, they develop important themes in new approaches to the study of ethnicity. Ethnicity is analysed as: 1) socially constructed, contextually dynamic and historically specific; 2) an arena in which hierarchical relations are presented, reproduced and contested; and 3) interactional, intersecting with other forms of oppositionality.

Contemporary approaches to ethnicity emphasize its historical contingency (Omi & Winant 1986, Balibar & Wallerstein 1991, San Juan 1992). In the formation of nation-states ethnic representation may support an authorized vision of a national past that promotes the conquering group and marginalizes others – usually autochthonous and labouring populations. For example, in

Colombia and Brazil, complementary ideological themes which shift over time denigrate blacks and Indians while camouflaging the existence of domination.

In Colombia, prevailing representations of blacks reflect the changing structural tensions between segregation and discrimination, and the pressures toward ethnic mixing. On the one hand, the notion of *blanqueamiento* (whitening) paints Colombia's history as one of gradual 'whitening': blackness is part of a primitive and backward past that is transcended as 'whitening' moves the nation forward into civilization and modernization. This theme clearly disparages the contribution of blacks and Indians. On the other hand, the more progressive representation of the past as a time of mixedness (*lo mestizo*) affirms the intermingling of population streams. But in celebrating the obliteration of difference, it submerges real differences of race, class and region and denies that racial discrimination exists. Both ideological themes at once subordinate blacks and deny that subordination (see Wade 1994).

Similarly for Indians in Brazil, racial meanings change shape and are played out at specific historical moments. 'Edenic discourse' (of Indianism) portrays the past as an idyllic time of innocence and freedom. As Europeans began to compete with Indians for resources a 'civilizing discourse' (of indigenism) – built on notions of backwardness, savagery, and paganism – emerged (see Ramos 1994). Though these forms of discourse appear conflicting, they are complementary, both constructing a national vision that denies Indians a legitimate voice in their future.

Similarly, in the United States biological explanations for the socio-economic inequality of African Americans gave way to cultural ones. Just as ideologies of assimilation obscure discrimination against blacks in Colombia, in the United States (post?)modern liberal acceptance of the social construction of race often leads to the dismissal of its social consequences and rejection of responsibility for past and present oppression.

Racial representation is important in mediating and presenting struggles and confrontations. In the United States racial representation is crucial to constructing a history that encourages working–class whites to identify with white power holders, facilitating labour control of both blacks and whites (see Roediger 1991). Buck (1994) demonstrates that a racialized version of history – which underplays and distorts the role of African Americans, denies activism to poor black and white farmers, in which race and racism are presented as part of nature rather than a reflection of a specific historical moment – cuts people off from a history that could empower them, presenting protest as pointless.

Ethnicity is also an arena in which representation is contested. As 'reception theory' seeks to document, people are involved in active struggle with images and may challenge, modify or accommodate that which is presented to them (Hall 1973). In Colombia people of African descent have contested ideologies of both assimilationism and 'whitening' through organizations seeking to reclaim their history (see Wade 1994). Indians in Brazil have increasingly turned to mass media to assert their identity and minority rights (see Ramos 1994).

But alternative and oppositional visions are not independent of the categories of the dominant culture (Williams 1977). Charles (1994) raises important questions about how we understand accommodation, resistance and transformation and reminds us that identities are interactional, that representation of ethnicity is linked to nationality, class and gender.

The link between gender and sexuality on the one hand, and ethnicity and nationality on the other, is key to representing community and history. Particularly in situations of colonialism, slavery and other forms of oppression, constructions of gender and sexuality become important instruments for racial othering: men of colour are generally depicted as sexually aggressive while women are portrayed as sexually provocative (see Mullings 1994).

But these representations are not received as whole cloth. Charles (1994) asserts that working-class Haitian women employ sexuality as a type of capital, resisting the norms established by the prevailing sex/gender system through the *contre-pouvoir* (counter-power) of sexual politics. She asserts that sexual politics as practised by enslaved women and free mulatto women modified the basic structure of Caribbean society by creating a mulatto class with access to land. Sexual politics became 'a form of survival, accommodation, resistance and empowerment' (p. 54) which 'mediat[ed] all relations of race, class and culture' (p. 55).

This provocative argument deconstructs historically circumscribed notions of good woman/bad woman, and as such makes a contribution to contemporary explorations into how some women view sexual resources in a commodified society (Alexander 1987). It also provides a supporting case study for the literature rejecting essentialist notions of sexuality, asserting that sexuality is socially constructed and contested (see, for example, Vance 1984, Epstein 1987, Vance 1991).

But society shapes sexuality in intricate ways. It is important to problematize the link between sexuality, reproduction and social reproduction and clearly to draw the constraints within which people make choices about reproduction and sexuality.

Though boundaries between accommodation, resistance and transformation are not always clear, in this case although the norms of the gender/sex system are to some degree contested, they are not transformed. As is evident in Colombia and Brazil, the existence of a mulatto population does not necessarily challenge the denigration of blackness, nor confront the structure of inequality. In fact a mulatto population may function as a buffer, obfuscating the stark realities of a race and class hierarchy.

In examining constructions of the past, in asking how concepts of race, ethnicity and inequality are created and reproduced, these chapters lay the basis for the next phase of work: illuminating the manner in which contemporary global processes give rise to new relations and constructions of identity and ethnicity.

Our analysis of the past shapes our understanding of the present, and sets parameters for how we think about transformative actions to shape the future. These chapters demonstrate that just as mystification of oppression in the past rationalizes its continuation in the present and future (see Wade 1994, Ramos 1994), representation of protest as pointless or ineffective may retard, at least for a time, the development of future challenges (see Buck 1994). As Cabral suggested, the negation of a dominated people's culture is characteristic of the relationship of domination; it is a negation of their history and of their struggle as well (Cabral 1973). The struggle for history is about the present and the future.

Acknowledgements

I would like to thank Juan Flores, with whom I co-taught a seminar on ethnicity, for helping me to think about new approaches to ethnicity.

References

Alexander, P. 1987. Prostitution: a difficult issue for feminists. In *Sex Work: writing in the sex industry*, Delacosta, F. & P. Alexander (eds). Pittsburgh: Clies.
Balibar, E. & I. Wallerstein 1991. *Race, Nation, Class: ambiguous identities*. London: Verso.
Bond, G. C. & A. Gilliam (eds) 1994. *Social Construction of the Past: representation as power*. London: Routledge.
Buck, P. Davidson 1994. Racial representations and power in the dependent development of the United States South. In *Social Construction of the Past: representation as power*, Bond, G. C. & A. Gilliam (eds), 29–43. London: Routledge.
Cabral, A. 1973. *Return to the Source: selected speeches of Amilcar Cabral*. New York: Information Services.
Charles, C. 1994. Sexual politics and the mediation of class, gender, and race in former slave plantation societies: the case of Haiti. In *Social Construction of the Past: representation as power*, Bond, G. C. & A. Gilliam (eds), 44–58. London: Routledge.
Hall, S. 1973. Encoding and decoding in the television discourse. Center for Contemporary Cultural Studies, Stencilled Occasional Paper No. 7, Media Series.
Mullings, L. 1994. Images, ideology and women of color. In *Women of Color in US Society*, Baca-Zinn, M. & B. Dill (eds). Philadelphia: Temple University Press.
Omi, M. & H. Winant 1986. *Racial Formation in the United States*. London: Routledge.
Ramos, A. 1994. From Eden to limbo: the construction of indigenism in Brazil. In *Social Construction of the Past: representation as power*, Bond, G. C. & A. Gilliam (eds), 74–88. London: Routledge.
Roediger, D. 1991. *The Wages of Whiteness: race and the making of the American working class*. London: Verso.
San Juan, E. 1992. *Racial Formations/Critical Transformations*. London: Humanities Press International.
Vance, C. S. 1984. Pleasure and danger: towards a politics of sexuality. In *Pleasure and Danger: exploring female sexuality*, Vance, C. S. (ed.), 1–27. Boston: Routledge & Kegan Paul.
Vance, C. S. 1991. Anthropology rediscovers sexuality: a theoretical comment. *Social Sciences and Medicine* 38, 875–84.
Wade, P. 1994. Representation and power: blacks in Colombia. In *Social Construction of the Past: representation as power*, Bond, G. C. & A. Gilliam (eds), 59–73. London: Routledge.
Williams, R. 1977. *Marxism and Literature*. Oxford: Oxford University Press.

2 Racial representations and power in the dependent development of the United States South

PEM DAVIDSON BUCK

Illegitimate anthropology and hegemony

The analysis of relationships between racial representations and power has been far from a purely abstract process for me. To be fair, I should say that my analysis may well be biased by both anger and fear. To be doubly fair, I might also add that influence by well-placed anger and fear does not necessarily produce an anthropology which is in some sense 'wrong'. These two emotions became gradually stronger in response to the objective conditions I discovered in researching a past whose unfamiliar contours slowly emerged from the mists of the hegemonic history that was part of my white, middle-class heritage. Its contours bore little resemblance even to a more radical version of history that reflected my seventeen years among poor whites in central Kentucky.

There were, in fact, two interrelated sources for these reactions. One was my increased understanding of the past and probable future of racial representations in the ideological justification of hegemony, with the implications that justification carries for the lives of poor whites and blacks. The other was my appreciation of the fact that the anthropology I was producing would be labelled 'non-objective' or 'political' by those who do not accept its premises, with all the implications that might carry for my own life. Collapsing 'the field' (cf. D'Amico-Samuels 1991) and my own community into a single construct, at least for one of my race and class, has meant a process of internal decolonization in response to the continuing battle I had to wage with the elite 'Big Brother' of hegemonic history in my head.

The knowledge embodied in this chapter, like that of any other anthropology, grows from a context – that of continued poverty where I live and teach, among central Kentucky's small white tobacco-growing families. My years here included those touted as the greatest peacetime economic expansion this country had ever known, and have been followed by the increasing hardships of recession, an era characterized by accelerating racism and incarceration rates which have now surpassed even those of South Africa and the former USSR. And, like any other anthropology, it has an agenda – in this case, that of producing a decolonized anthropology and a counter-hegemonic history of poor white tobacco growers, which, returned to those who made it, could empower. Specifically, I wish to address the role of racial representations which promote a spurious identification with white power holders among poor whites, an identification dependent on the belief that race, rather than class, defines self-interest. These representations were carefully fashioned[1] as part of a policy of labour control during reconstruction, when black south-erners, who had won the Civil War in an uneasy alliance with northern armies, attempted to gain control of the fruits of their own labour through farm ownership. These representations were then reproduced to maintain control of poor white labour as well, by keeping farmers divided against each other along racial lines. Such cultural symbols continue to be useful in the containment of class analysis. There is little difference, other than party, between the Willie Horton ad of the first Bush campaign and the many headlines in the early 1900s such as one in a local county newspaper proclaiming 'Negro Murderer Must Hang', placed beside articles referring to the Republican Party's supposed love of blacks or beside articles discussing the importance of a Democratic victory (*LaRue County Herald* 8/9/04, p. 1).

Possessed generally of only a colonized version of their own history, in which there is no rational class conflict and racism is presented as part of nature, most poor white farming families have little basis for reinterpreting their past or challenging the hegemonic interpretation of their future. Thus, poor white identification with white power holders facilitates continued de-pendent development in Kentucky, as millions of tax-payer dollars are spent in 'incentives' and more are lost in tax-breaks (Kingsolver 1989, 1991) to bring in northern and foreign businesses to poor white communities where labour is cheap and schools have been so poor they were declared unconstitutional, while the governor defines public education as vocational training for new industries (e.g. *News Enterprise* 8/10/89).

Among poor white tobacco farmers there is an incipient class analysis, so that Willie Horton and the media construction of crime as a black artefact is actually necessary. Destroying such racial representations by showing their construction by the elite would empower both blacks and poor whites, as class rather than race became the salient feature. This incipient class analysis shows itself in such comments as 'they "control crop prices"', or 'they "want to dump their garbage here because we're just little people"' (cf. Kingsolver 1991 for a discussion of local views of control in a Kentucky community). Such comments are generally dismissed as naive or irrational by members of my class. A colonized anthropology is built on such dismissal and cannot, by definition, grant that the analysis by an oppressed people of the conditions of their oppression has any basic validity.

Poor white tobacco farmers are themselves colonized in this sense, granting only ambivalent validity to their own analysis, so that it remains incomplete and is rarely acted upon. This chapter focuses on two instances where class analysis was given legitimacy by tobacco growers. In the first, the Farmers' Alliance in the late 1800s, race was partially ignored and the structures of dependent development and the class roots of farm poverty were directly addressed. In the second, Kentucky's Black Patch War of 1904–9, tobacco growers had further succumbed to the racial representations of labour control. Consequently they made only a partial class analysis; they saw farmers as a class fighting the owners of the tobacco factories, but they defined the interests of share-croppers out of existence by constructing whites as farm owners and blacks as farm labour. Consequently, despite a temporary win over the American Tobacco company, the Black Patch War, with all its violence, was a much more contained protest than that of the Alliance, and did not threaten the class basis of dependent development.

The Farmers' Alliance and postreconstruction dependent development

The Farmers' Alliance was founded in Texas in 1878 and spread like wildfire, with local chapters being organized in community after community. By 1892 it reached into 43 states and territories, with its strength focused in the South and West. Estimates of membership reach 1,200,000 blacks and 3 million whites (Abramowitz 1953, p. 257), a claim regarded as 'fantastic' by some (e.g. Saloutos 1960, p. 77), despite the affirming evidence of the Alliance's enormous voting power. While the Alliance certainly was not built on black and white equality (cf. Saloutos 1960, Hackney 1969), it did consciously rely on the co-operation of black and white chapters, and many members rejected much of the racial rhetoric on which capitalist power was built (cf. Abramowitz 1953, Goodwyn 1976, pp. 276ff). At the height of its power the Alliance was very successful politically: seven southern state legislatures were dominated by the Alliance; in Kansas 96 of 125 seats in the state legislature in 1890 were held by Alliance candidates. Thirty-eight Congressmen were 'straight-out Alliancemen' (Saloutos 1960, p. 116, Goodwyn 1976, pp. 200, 211).

The Alliance was briefly successful in its two-pronged approach to raising farm income (cf. Rogers 1970, p. 148). First, the Alliance organized co-operative crop marketing, thus controlling enough of the crop to force the monopolistic buyers to meet Alliance price demands. A livestock marketing co-op in Kansas, for instance, had $40,000 in profits to distribute to its members after six months of operation (Goodwyn 1976, p. 145). Second, the Alliance took on the retail system through which farmers had to buy their supplies. Alliance stores provided co-operative buying at much lower prices and experimented, at times successfully, with providing low-cost credit. Its most dramatic success was probably in lowering the cost of jute bagging for cotton bales from 14 cents to 5 cents a yard. The Alliance also advocated a sub-treasury plan by which the US treasury would stand as surety for loans to the

Alliance, using the warehoused crop as collateral. In 1896, however, the People's Party, which acted as the political arm of the Alliance, was beaten in its second bid for the presidency, and the Alliance itself succumbed thereafter to the pressures it had been fighting.

Had the Alliance not been defeated, it could ultimately have destroyed the debt-bondage system which controlled share-croppers and indebted small farm owners (cf. Schwartz 1976, Goodwyn 1976, Weiner 1978). In destroying debt-bondage, it would have restructured the distribution of the fruits of labour to the advantage of the direct producer, for debt-bondage siphoned off most of the value produced by farming families into the hands of their creditors, the landlords and merchants.[2] As it was, however, debt-bondage meant that many Alliance families did not have the economic freedom to determine either where and how they would sell their crop or where they would buy supplies. Many small farmers were therefore handicapped in the Alliance fight against the tobacco and other crop buyers. Even more important, however, they were handicapped in relation to the landlords who also joined the Alliance, fought for and used the Alliance marketing system, and took positions of leadership which they used to further their own interests, rather than those of the poorer rank and file.

The process by which the Alliance was beaten involved clear and conscious political and economic sabotage on the part of both the threatened local elite and a threatened northern elite. Both were in danger of losing their position in the structures of dependent development through Alliance policies designed to end the debt-bondage which, with share-cropping, formed the foundation for capital accumulation for local elites, and through Alliance policies designed to staunch the flow of southern-produced value to the North. Together, these elites exerted control over the media, finances, elections, and over the South's export economy.

The defeat of the Alliance in 1896 was built on three sets of power relationships. First, there was class-based power, operating both within the Alliance and between the Alliance and its opposition. Most large landowners in the Alliance, as opposed to the small-farmer bulk of the Alliance, had no interest in destroying the share-cropping and debt-peonage system from which they benefited as landlords, and resisted the implementation of policies which threatened their privilege, while supporting those which improved their market position. As elected officials many voted for their own class interests rather than those of their constituents (Hackney 1969, pp. 71ff, Schwartz 1976).[3]

The Democratic white power structure outside the Alliance controlled the election process and rigged fraudulent wins for its candidates (Rogers 1970, Goodwyn 1976) after Alliance candidates, either within the Democratic party or as third-party Populists, began winning elections. Fraud appears to have been particularly common in areas with large black majorities, where the white elite was able to buy, steal, or intimidate the black vote (Rogers 1970). When such tactics failed in Alabama, troops were used to instate as governor the Democratic rather than the Populist candidate who had actually won the election (Hackney 1969, p. 69). Local merchants, threatened with the loss of both customers and the power to superexploit through debt-peonage, acted quickly to undercut Alliance stores and buying co-ops (Schwartz 1976, p. 207). In a move which has its counterpart in other areas undergoing dependent development, the editor of a country newspaper in my community, like many others (Hackney 1969), described Alliance policies as 'absurd' and counter-productive (*LaRue County Herald* 4/8/1892, cf. Gaston 1976 [1970], p. 220), just as economic independence movements in Papua New Guinea were described as irrational 'cargo cults' (Buck 1989).

Second, the processes of underdevelopment were built on power relationships which gave the North economic power over the South's export economy. Northern banks controlled the sources of funding for the South, and rapidly began refusing loans to the Alliance, thus helping to break the Alliance's brief stranglehold on agricultural raw materials. Northern manufacturing companies co-operated in refusing to sell to the Alliance. The failure of Alliance buying co-ops, however, was ascribed by much of the media primarily to financial mismanagement (Gaston 1976, p. 1, note, Schwartz 1976, p. 208), as it still is by some social scientists (Saloutos 1960, Rogers 1970, p. 158, Fite 1981, p. 155). Equally important, race and class intersected with dependent development in the defeat of the Alliance, as can be shown by examining accounts of the ideology (Gaston 1976) and history (Weiner 1978) of the New South movement. Dependent development, as is typical worldwide, involved a struggle for power among those being 'developed'. Southerners attempted in varying ways to determine to their own benefit the form to be taken by the northward flow of value and to control the labour force on which that flow depended. Adherents of the New South movement were bitterly opposed to the Alliance, which, if it succeeded in making farming profitable, would absorb a large portion of available labour, raising the price of industrial labour. The New South movement used race and sectionalism to organize support, both from southerners and from northern investors, for their position as an intermediate bourgeoisie benefiting from a flow of value through their hands based on northern industrial capital.

Finally, a third set of power relationships, that between blacks and whites, was critical in the defeat of the Alliance in several ways. First, there was a contradiction within the Alliance itself, in that many black Alliance members worked either as farm labour or as share-croppers, for white Alliance members (Goodwyn 1976, p. 292). Given the greater power of white owners, the often more radical policies advocated by black Alliance leaders aiming at the roots of southern poverty could be thwarted by white leaders. For instance, a cotton-pickers' strike, supported by black Alliances and by many rank and file members of white Alliances, was prevented by the large landowners in the Alliance, who had no interest in paying higher wages to get their crops picked (Goodwyn 1976, p. 292). Schwartz (1976, pp. 282ff) describes the crushing of Populism with Jim Crow legislation, an interpretation which

Gaston (1976 [1970], p. 202) appears to support. Jim Crow established a caste system (cf. Foner 1988), thus dividing poor black and white farmers and augmenting the power of the elite to rule them under a share-cropping system contrary to the interests of all poor farmers, black or white. Equally important, black disenfranchisement directly eliminated between a quarter and a third of the potential Alliance vote. In addition, poll taxes, justified by evoking white supremacy, actually eliminated many poor white voters as well – according to Hackney's (1969, p. 208) estimates, as many as 23 per cent in Alabama. Not only was the Alliance's power at the polls dramatically weakened by black and white disenfranchisement, but Jim Crow legislation also reduced the Alliance's power to protest safely. Further, racism was invoked to gain white support for the power relations thus established between poor whites and the upper classes (Weiner 1978, pp. 222ff). Local county newspaper editors (e.g. *LaRue County Herald* 18/8/1892) predicted the death of white supremacy in the wake of a successful Alliance (cf. Rogers 1970). Sectionalism, with its heavily racist overtones (cf. Gaston 1976, Weiner 1978), played an important part in defeating the Alliance in its political manifestation in the People's Party. Giving a vote to the People's Party, rather than to the Democratic party, was described by newspapers as weakening the party which protected whites against a rising tide of black power (cf. Saloutos 1960, Goodwyn 1976). The issue was thus defined as one of race, diverting attention from economic reform (Goodwyn 1976, pp. 227, 534, Reich 1981, pp. 219, 235).

This attempt to remove white support was one prong of a racially based effort to stop the Alliance. Physical attacks, including those of the elite-directed Klan (Weiner 1978, pp. 61ff, Foner 1988) on black Alliance members and on blacks in general was another (Hackney 1969, pp. 43, 184, Foner 1974, p. 61, Schwartz 1976, p. 286). In addition to intimidating blacks, such attacks involved poor non-Alliance whites in actions which would, by their very participation or silent complicity, force them to define blacks as 'the other' to preserve their own self-respect. The *LaRue County Herald* played its part in this racially divisive process by highlighting black crime and by making the likelihood of lynching for any black who stepped out of line abundantly clear, despite the editor's preference for legal processes of social control.

Racial representations were thus critical in the defeat of the Alliance, both in justifying economic sabotage and in mustering political opposition to policies which were actually in the interest of most of the potential voters, black and white alike. White supremacy was advocated by local newspapers and legitimized by representations of blacks as incompetents who needed white oversight for their own good (*LaRue County Herald* 21/7/04, cf. Gaston 1976). Such representations, and the Jim Crow legislation which accompanied them, have been analysed by a number of authors as a means of ensuring white control of black labour, as a divisive measure splitting the Alliance on racial lines, as a means of reducing the power of the Alliance by keeping poor whites as well as blacks from the polls, and as a means of enforcing share-cropping for both blacks and whites. Waving the bloody shirt and portraying the Alliance as a threat to white supremacy brought many potential third-party poor white voters back into the Democratic fold (cf. *LaRue County Herald* 4/8/1892). These measures were effective partially because Alliance membership was a quarter to a third black and depended for its strength on black–white co-operation, a fact which is played down in most histories of the Alliance (e.g. Goodwyn 1976). Thus, even when a history of farm protest is given legitimacy, it is portrayed as white protest. The decisive factor is ignored and ignorance of the power of class-based rather than racially based action is perpetuated.

The Black Patch War and the power of racial representations

The defeat of the People's Party in 1896 and the subsequent decline of the Alliance was followed in Kentucky, and in much of the rest of the South, by desperation and violence. At least for tobacco growers, on whose history I will now focus, the farm protest which followed reflects the growing potency of the racial representations constructed to contain earlier struggles by poor blacks and whites to gain control of a greater share of the profits from their labour. The effectiveness of these representations can be held at least partially responsible for the success of the American Tobacco Company in holding tobacco growers' revolt to manageable proportions in what is known as the Black Patch War of 1904–9. They can also be held partially responsible for the fact that this was a much more limited protest, addressing only tobacco pricing, rather than questioning the South's class structure based on share-cropping and underpaid farm labour, thus leaving the class basis for dependent development intact.

Starting around 1902 (Shannon 1957, p. 75), the tobacco association affiliates of the American Society of Equity[4] began nearly a decade of struggle for better prices in response to American Tobacco's price reduction as it achieved monopoly status. It advocated co-operative marketing with a grower-determined minimum price and crop reduction to force American Tobacco to pay higher prices for cash crops, and attempted but failed to push relief measures through Congress (Kroll 1965). By 1907 the tobacco association affiliates were advocating grower-owned tobacco factories if American Tobacco refused to buy at higher prices (Saloutos 1960, p. 173).

Some white farmers, many of them from the hillier regions where farms were generally poorer and smaller (Buck & Wenger 1988), refused to join the Society, and were constituted as 'the other' by the use of the term 'hill-billy'. Apparently at least some black families also refused (cf. Waldrep 1984), although according to Cunningham (1983, p. 67) a greater percentage of blacks than whites joined.[5] For both poor white and black farmers, joining would have been difficult without the consent and financial backing of land-owners or other lenders, since joining meant withholding the crop and forgoing the family's only source of income until the Company gave in. In reaction to Equity's success in raising prices, a farmhands' and share-croppers' organization pointed out that they were not sharing in the increased prosperity (Saloutos 1960, p. 171).

American Tobacco exacerbated this economic split between farmers by paying higher prices to hill farmers who refused to join than to lowland farmers (Shannon 1957, p. 77). Farmers responded to this policy with the Black Patch War, directing violence against American Tobacco itself and against hill-billies, whose direct sales to the company amounted to strike-breaking. The war was conducted by perhaps as many as 10,000 Night Riders organized along lines influenced by the Ku Klux Klan and led by an ex-Klansman (cf. Taylor 1963). They may have been Equity members, but in any case acted in the interests of the large lowland growers who were, along with professional men, their leaders (Kroll 1965). They performed Klan-like acts of terror against hill-billies and black labourers and share-croppers (Taylor 1963, Waldrep 1984). The burned crops and barns they left in their wake drove many families to financial ruin, and hundreds of families left the region. Landlords were told not to renew contracts with black tenants and share-croppers (Grantham 1960). It is likely that the exodus of hill-billies and blacks was joined by poorer Equity members as the loans which they had taken from larger farmers to tide them over (Saloutos 1960, p. 178) were called in by richer members. Thus it is probable that large growers enhanced their control of tobacco production during this period, a result of the divisive class and racial policies followed by both American Tobacco and the Night Riders. That some ex-Alliance leaders had turned to the Klan (Goodwyn 1976) now becomes comprehensible: reducing the number of farmers was a way of reducing the supply of tobacco and raising prices for those who remained, a goal which both the Klan and the Night Riders apparently pursued.

Equally important in the struggle to control tobacco prices, the Night Riders attacked Princeton, Russelville, Hopkinsville and several other American Tobacco warehouse towns, causing many millions of dollars worth of damage (Shannon 1957, p. 162) as they burned tons of warehoused tobacco, destroyed communication lines, and fought townspeople and guards who tried to stop them. Additional damage was sometimes caused when the fires spread to the black communities surrounding the warehouses. By 1907 the violence had reached central Kentucky, where it was instrumental in aiding the American Society of Equity's successful effort to restrict the size of the 1908 burley crop (Kroll 1965, p. 224).

The press carried numerous accounts of the violence in Kentucky, some of them sympathetic to the growers, although not to the violence (Shannon 1957, p. 161, *LaRue County Herald* 6/12/06). Such reports acted to the advantage of American Tobacco, fitting with its policy of using the press to further its interests (Saloutos 1960, p. 174). With the state-wide support of non-growers mustered by such reports, Kentucky's new governor, Augustus Willson, who had occasionally worked for American Tobacco as a lawyer (Waldrep 1984), sent in thousands of troops to restore law and order (Kroll 1965, p. 239, Waldrep 1984), saying he would pardon any citizen who killed a Night Rider (Taylor 1963). By 1908 a compromise agreement was reached, but American Tobacco then took measures to prevent a recurrence of this situation by encouraging the cultivation of tobacco outside Kentucky and Tennessee (Saloutos 1960, p. 180). By 1911 the tobacco affiliates of the American Society of Equity had lost most of their power (Saloutos 1960, p. 183).

The use of troops to restore law and order came in response to the enormous success of the combined tobacco-marketing policy of the American Society of Equity and the violence of the Night Riders. By the end of the struggle the New York-based American Tobacco Company (Kroll 1965, p. 132), with its world-wide control of the tobacco market (Saloutos 1960, p. 167), had been forced to agree to co-operative marketing. Prices had risen from approximately $4 per 100 lbs, bringing perhaps $140.00 for a year of tenant family labour, often less than the cost of production, to slightly over $9 (Shannon 1957, p. 166, Taylor 1963, p. 283). Between 70 and 90 per cent of the growers who were left were marketing co-operatively, and American Tobacco had been found in violation of the Sherman Anti-Trust Act (Grantham 1960).

Given what the growers actually accomplished, the immense local middle-class support they commanded, and the effectiveness of their military strategies and intimidation, I think it is fair to assume that without containment prices would have gone much higher, bringing growers out of the poverty in which even the new prices left them, and that tobacco manufacturing might have passed into the hands of the growers, thus destroying much of the tobacco-based structure of dependent development. I think it is also fair to postulate, however, given the organization of the American Society of Equity, that cutting off at least part of the flow of value to the North and to American Tobacco would have benefited large growers and landlords much more than poor black and white share-croppers and debt-peons.

The containment of this revolt is evident not only in the use of force. Ultimately much more important for the preservation of the class structures of dependent development was the incomplete nature of the class analysis on which the revolt was based, an analysis which rested at least partly on the increased acceptance by these protesters of the racial representations of labour control. Unlike the Alliance, the American Society of Equity did not threaten the local elite with the destruction of debt-peonage, a policy facilitated by the manipulation of the symbols of racial representations. The *LaRue County Herald*, for instance, portrayed blacks as lazy labour and whites as industrious farm owners. The paper published 'jokes' such as one about a lazy black cook who preferred jail to the offer of bail and a job (14/3/07). Editorials referred to the nine out of ten blacks who refused to work hard enough to earn the decent wages offered in the South and preferred to move to the North (8/12/04). It regularly published obituaries of blacks who had been good servants, and continued to emphasize black crime.

The inaccurate construction of whites as members of the same class, in opposition to blacks, and consequent lack of attention to the interests of the poorer members of the Association, both black and white, meant that the American Society of Equity could ignore the class relationships which drained the value produced by poor farming families into the hands of the local elite. Nevertheless, Equity policies did threaten northern profits. Consequently, they received tremendous support (cf. Hackney 1969, pp. 325ff, Weiner 1978, pp. 222ff) from local merchants, from 'prominent farmers', and from the editor of the local paper. Slowing the flow of value to the North would enhance the position of the local elite as an intermediate bourgeoisie in their competition with northern elites for increased shares of the value produced by farming families, a competition structured by dependent development. This relationship is made clear in the *LaRue County Herald* by the merchant campaign for roads into the county seat, by 'buy local' admonitions, and by editorials extolling the virtues of a farming community which could afford to buy more, a set of relationships which would hold good only in areas with a large percentage of small-holders.

Such struggles continued until 'economic development' had successfully organized the North's direct control of the southern economy and had produced a cheap, racially segmented labour force. At that point, the New Deal government handed farmers a few of the measures for which generations of tobacco farmers had fought. For tobacco farmers alone this included the right to control marketing and bargain from a position of power in setting prices (Lobb 1989), and burley tobacco remains one of the few profitable crops left to family farmers.

But the transformations of underdevelopment, and the power relationships it organized, meant that those concessions could no longer help the small farmer. Burley farmers are poverty-stricken despite burley's profitability, since the allotment system allows each farm to market a very limited amount of tobacco in order to restrict supply and keep prices up (cf. Wenger & Buck 1988, Kingsolver 1991). Small farmers, disproportionately black, were driven from the land by New Deal policies which gave big farmers incentives to remove tenants and share-croppers and to consolidate and enlarge their holdings (Badger 1980, Daniel 1985, Kirby 1987). The dispossessed became wage labour in cities, where their descendants, particularly those who are black, are now being disproportionately incarcerated (cf. Buck forthcoming).

The social construction of the past

Past and present intersect in central Kentucky in a social construction of the past based in racial representations and classism which deny an active part in history to poor black and white farmers. Such a social construction of the past currently empowers a white elite at the expense of those on whom they depend for capital accumulation, people whose history has involved an active, but defeated, process of resistance and accommodation.

Students from this area are subjected to history books which teach them that the activities of their grandparents and great-grandparents were defeated, not by a massive exercise of power, but by their own irrationality, naiveté, or inability to organize. Their textbooks refer to Alliance leaders as 'whiskered prophets' and 'mannish' women who had 'peculiarities', and omit reference to black–white Alliance co-operation (Bailey & Kennedy 1983, p. 539). This is a social construction of the past which is demeaning. It defines farmers as powerless, and then blames them for their 'apathy'.[6]

Symbols of racial representations continue to define parameters for historical analysis of the Alliance, even for those who deny the validity of the image of the apathetic, unorganizable farmer. Photographs of Alliance meetings and discussions of the Alliance generally focus on white chapters, with only lipservice paid to the importance of black chapters and leadership (cf. Abramowitz 1953 for an important exception), a position easy to take since, due to prevailing racism, the Farmers' Alliance and the Colored Alliance were unable to merge, despite their co-operation. Goodwyn, for instance, mentions blacks peripherally many times, but does not integrate their role into his basic analysis. Instead, he has a chapter on the Alliance's 'approach' to black America. The Alliance, in other words, was 'really' a white organization which could choose to approach blacks, rather than an organization whose strength *depended* on the solidarity of black and white farmers alike in confronting both the agricultural buying and selling monopolies and the local elites dependent on draining value out of farming families. While admitting the importance of farm protest, this construction of the past nevertheless maintains the myth that only whites are active in shaping history.

Thus the hegemonic construction of the past contains no active blacks or poor whites, is without *class* conflict (Genovese 1971 [1968], pp. 300ff) or dependent development, and presents racial antagonisms as part of nature. Third-party political efforts in this past are doomed to failure and can be categorized as irrational (cf. Schwartz 1976, pp. ix, 135ff). Such a construction of the past makes serious challenges to the present distribution of power unlikely, since they appear to be pointless (cf. Goodwyn 1976, pp. viiff), and by omission, cuts people off from knowledge of their own history. A black student who says his father was *given* the vote, or a tobacco grower[7] who says the allotment system, which raises prices through production control and until 1983 (Lobb 1989) gave farmers significant control of the marketing process, was the best thing that ever *happened* to farmers, has been cut off from a history which could empower by defining protest as both possible and sometimes effective. Farmers *wrung* the allotment system from reluctant power-holders through violent and non-violent protest, just as blacks *fought* for the vote.

Further, white farmers who now define lazy labour as black labour and blame farm problems on labour problems, have bought into a newer version of the racial representations of labour control which stopped the Alliance and contained the Black Patch War. These representations rear their heads in my white students' perceptions of blacks and Hispanics as too lazy to work, turning instead to drug trafficking and welfare. Such racism, to which the white rural survivors of a century of dependent development often continue to subscribe, is seen by whites as natural only because of a careful manipulation of both past and present. The power of the Alliance, with its interracial co-operation, is obscured; films such as *Mississippi Burning* obscure black–white co-operation by presenting the Civil Rights Movement as one in which whites acted for the benefit of passive blacks. And the drug issue is presented as one in which blacks and Hispanics benefit financially from their destruction of themselves and their communities, while the role of white addict demand and of white elites in organizing the trade is generally down-played.

These representations reflect the importance of the labour of poor blacks and whites in the American version of the superexploitation on which capital accumulation is based for certain geographical and demographic segments of the population, as it is for Third World populations organized around the needs of dependent development (cf. Frank 1967, Meillasoux 1981, Wenger & Buck 1988). Because their role is critical, it is particularly important that their past appears to contain no effective counter-action, and that their labour appears unimportant. Hence, many social scientists continue to dismiss the importance of the crop production of poor black and white farmers (e.g. Fite 1981, pp. 20, 79); hence, black history, as presented in white history, is 'lost, strayed, or stolen' and poor white farm history has, until very recently, followed it into oblivion.

Such constructions deny the power of class-based activity by constructing a racial lens through which to view the world. In its divisiveness, such a lens facilitates the exercise of power needed to emplace and maintain the Third World conditions on which dependent development is based. The reproduction of this racial lens has become particularly important again in the 1980s because, as this examination of the history of farm protest demonstrates, poor blacks and poor whites have shown themselves perfectly capable of uniting, and may do it again. Class-based support among so-called rednecks for the policies of Jesse Jackson, for instance, would at least have threatened the power of capital to determine in its own interest the distribution of the fruits of poor white and black labour, blocking the spread of Third World conditions to a growing segment of the American population.

Notes

1 DuBois (1963 [1935]), Schwartz (1976, p. 30), Cox (1976, p. 50), Weiner (1978, pp. 35ff, 159), Greenburg (1980, p. 388), Reich (1981), Foner (1988) and Roediger (1991) all discuss the construction of racial images, and their divisive effectiveness. That farmers have in fact supported policies contrary to the interests of the small farmer is amply documented by Badger (1980), Daniel (1985) and Kirby (1987) among others.
2 Note, however, that Alliance policies never threatened capitalism itself, but asked only for a better place for farmers within the capitalist system, as both Saloutos (1960, p. 69) and Rogers (1970, p. 148) point out.

3 See Weiner (1978) for a general discussion of the conflicting interests of small farmers and planters and of planters and merchants.
4 My accounts of the Black Patch War and of the American Society of Equity are based on reports in the *LaRue County Herald*, a local county weekly newspaper, as well as on secondary sources such as Shannon (1957), Saloutos (1960), Taylor (1963), Kroll (1965) and Waldrep (1984).
5 It is not clear from published reports whether black farmers were referred to as hill-billies. The origin of this term is unclear; if in fact it refers to the geographical location of refuters in hilly terrain, then it is also likely that most of those referred to as hill-billies were white. More blacks lived in flatter, former plantation areas, and a larger percentage of blacks than whites were share-croppers who could be either forced or backed by their landlords in joining the boycott.
6 Gaventa (1980) discusses the ideological use of the term 'apathy' and the conditions of powerlessness which produce quiescence. Paige (1975) considers the conditions under which agrarian revolutions are possible, complementing Gaventa's discussion of the creation of apathy or quiescence.
7 My discussion of local white farmers' attitudes is based partly on seventeen years of living and ten years of teaching in a poor white tobacco-growing area, and partly on comments made by participants in 'Tales of Ourselves', a project I directed, funded by the Kentucky Humanities Council, to produce stories based in local culture for newly literate adults. Additional historical information comes from the archives of the *LaRue County Herald News*, resulting from the merger of the *LaRue County Herald* with another local newspaper.

Acknowledgements

My thanks to Angela Gilliam and Faye V. Harrison for continuing stimulation and criticism of this work, and to George Bond for an enlightening comment he made after its presentation.

References

Abramowitz, J. 1953. The Negro in the Populist movement. *The Journal of Negro History* 38, 257–89.
Badger, A. 1980. *Prosperity Road: the new deal, tobacco and North Carolina*. Chapel Hill: University of North Carolina Press.
Bailey, T. & D. Kennedy 1983. *The American Pageant*. 7th ed. Lexington, Mass.: D. C. Heath & Co.
Buck, P. Davidson 1989. Cargo-cult discourse: myth and the rationalization of labour relations in Papua New Guinea. *Dialectical Anthropology* 13, 157–71.
Buck, P. Davidson Forthcoming. With our heads in the sand: the racist right, concentration camps, and the incarceration of people of color. *Transforming Anthropology*.
Buck, P. Davidson & M. Wenger 1988. The domestic dynamics of development: articulation, rearticulation, and the rural family. Paper presented at American Anthropological Association Annual Meeting, Phoenix, Arizona.
Cox, O. 1976. *Race Relations: elements and social dynamics*. Detroit: Wayne State University Press.
Cunningham, W. 1983. *On Bended Knees: the Night Rider story*. Nashville: McClanahan House.
D'Amico-Samuels, D. 1991. Undoing fieldwork: personal, political, theoretical, and

methodological implications. In *Decolonizing Anthropology*, Harrison, F. (ed.), 68–87. Washington, DC: American Anthropological Association.

Daniel, P. 1985. *Breaking the Land: the transformation of cotton, tobacco, and rice cultures since 1880*. Urbana: University of Illinois Press.

DuBois, W. E. B. [1935] 1963. *Black Reconstruction in America*. New York: Russell & Russell.

Fite, G. 1981. *American Farmers: the new minority*. Bloomington: Indiana University Press.

Foner, E. 1988. *Reconstruction: America's unfinished revolution*. New York: Harper & Row.

Foner, P. 1974. *Organized Labour and the Black Worker – 1619–1973*. New York: Praeger.

Frank, A. G. 1967. *Underdevelopment in Latin America*. New York: Monthly Review.

Gaston, P. [1970] 1976. *The New South Creed: a study in southern mythmaking*. Baton Rouge: Louisiana State University Press.

Gaventa, J. 1980. *Power and Powerlessness: quiescence and rebellion in an Appalachian valley*. Urbana: University of Illinois Press.

Genovese, E. [1968] 1971. *In Red and Black: Marxian explorations in southern and Afro-American history*. New York: Pantheon Books.

Goodwyn, L. 1976. *Democratic Promise: the Populist moment in America*. New York: Oxford University Press.

Grantham, D. 1960. The Black Patch War: the story of the Kentucky and Tennessee Night Riders, 1905–1909. *South Atlantic Quarterly* 59, 215–25.

Greenburg, S. 1980. *Race and State in Capitalist Development*. New Haven: Yale University Press.

Hackney, S. 1969. *Populism to Progressivism in Alabama*. Princeton: Princeton University Press.

Kingsolver, A. 1989. Toyota, tobacco, and talk: who has 'the say' in rural Kentucky. Paper presented at the American Anthropological Association Annual Meeting, Washington, DC.

Kingsolver, A. 1991. Tobacco, Toyota, and subaltern development discourse: constructing livelihoods and community in rural Kentucky. Unpublished Ph.D. thesis, Department of Anthropology, University of Massachusetts at Amherst.

Kirby, J. 1987. *Rural Worlds Lost*. Baton Rouge: Louisiana State University Press.

Kroll, H. 1965. *Riders in the Night*. Philadelphia: University of Pennsylvania Press.

LaRue County Herald and *LaRue County Herald News*. Hodgenville, Ky. Microfilms stored at LaRue County Library.

Lobb, R. 1989. Interview with retired LaRue County agriculture teacher.

Meillasoux, C. 1981. *Maidens, Meal and Money: capitalism and the domestic community*. Cambridge: Cambridge University Press.

News Enterprise. Elizabethtown, Ky.

Paige, J. 1975. *Agrarian Revolution: social movements and export agriculture in the under-developed world*. New York: The Free Press.

Reich, M. 1981. *Racial Inequality: a political-economic analysis*. Princeton: Princeton University Press.

Roediger, D. 1991. *The Wages of Whiteness: race and the making of the American working class*. London: Verso.

Rogers, W. 1970. *The One-Gallused Rebellion: agrarianism in Alabama, 1865–1896*. Baton Rouge: Louisiana State University Press.

Saloutos, T. 1960. *Farmer Movements in the South, 1865–1933*. Lincoln: University of Nebraska Press.

Schwartz, M. 1976. *Radical Protest and Social Structure: the southern Farmers' Alliance and cotton tenancy, 1880–1890*. New York: Academic Press.

Shannon, F. 1957. *American Farmers' Movements*. Princeton: Van Nostrand.

Taylor, M. 1963, 1964. Night Riders in the Black Patch. *Register of the Kentucky Historical Society* 61 (4), 279–99; 62 (1), 24–40.

Waldrep, C. 1984. Augustus E. Willson and the Night Riders. *Filson Club History Quarterly* 58, 237–52.

Weiner, J. 1978. *Social Origins of the New South: Alabama, 1860–1885.* Baton Rouge: Louisiana State University Press.

Wenger, M. & P. Davidson Buck 1988. Farms, families, and superexploitation: an integrative reappraisal. *Rural Sociology* 53, 460–72.

3 Sexual politics and the mediation of class, gender and race in former slave plantation societies: the case of Haiti

CAROLLE CHARLES

Women's empowerment in Haiti as counter-power

Power is a very difficult concept to define. Mintz (1985, p. 166) observes that 'few concepts in the social sciences have caused as many disagreements'. The concept refers to or suggests a relationship of domination/subordination. More importantly, it helps clarify under what conditions groups of people in a particular society are maintained in a hierarchical and unequal relationship without the compulsion of open force and violence. The concept has always been used as the central axis of the political field where politics is defined as the interplay of power relationships. The concern with power in turn has always had a masculine attribute, for politics tends to be construed as inherently male. Political participation and political activities are male concerns; they belong to public life. In contrast, problems that concern the private domain are those generally associated with women. Power conceptualized in this manner is western and patriarchal and always has the meaning of control, of domination. It means 'power *over*', and it has the quality of property owned by certain people. Those who have acquired power work toward maintaining it by attempting to be invulnerable and closed. Following this view, reality becomes compartmentalized in order to support the separation of the self/ personal from the public/institutional, and the continued view of these individuated domains of power. Yet, power relationships also define the boundaries of rights and obligations and the conditioned process of inclusion/exclusion of distinct social groups, in particular women within the whole society. Thus, the concept of power must be examined in both the private and public domains.

Contemporary feminist perspectives on power differ. Power is not viewed as property possessed by those who dominate. Rather it is seen as a process where people transform themselves personally and collectively. Feminists speak of 'power *with*' rather than 'power *over*'. Power derives from energy and strength in people (Albrecht & Brewer 1990, p. 8). Women's empowerment may take different forms (Tilly 1986, Staffa 1987, Jelin 1990, Albrecht &

Brewer 1990, Charles 1991). It may take the form of a counter-power. For example, when in the context of foreign dependency and extreme poverty as in Haiti, women's struggles evolve around issues of global changes as they affect the global society, rather than focusing on their specific subordination. This focus is not, however, a unique Haitian phenomenon. Feminists of colour have made similar observations regarding the perception of gender issues among black women in both the Americas and in Africa (Bastide & Mintz 1974, Comhaire-Sylvain 1974, Sudarkasa 1981, Pala 1981, Steady 1981, Davis 1981, Mullings 1984).

Indeed, Haitian women, in particular of working-class and peasant backgrounds, tend to be reluctant to attack directly the issue of male dominance and gender hierarchy. This points to the complexity of the forms of expression of that dominance in Haitian society. Indeed, to speak of male dominance without looking at the socio-historical context, and without looking at how women can resist that dominance and even undermine it by redefining its terms, does not help to explain strategies and mechanisms of empowerment that women have created outside the political arena.

Many Haitian feminists have observed that Haitian women have subtly created mechanisms of *contre-pouvoir* (i.e. counter-power) against the existing sex/gender hierarchy.[1] This is manifested in the meanings given to sexuality by Haitian women, particularly in the rural areas and among women of poor urban strata. As will be argued further below, sexual politics goes against the conventions and norms established by the prevailing sex/gender system and against the prevailing gender division of labour. Although women of all strata and classes in both urban and rural areas have developed strategies of resistance, it is particularly among women of working-class backgrounds that sexuality takes a completely new social meaning and becomes a type of capital, a resource.

This chapter attempts to analyse the roots and dynamics of this sexual politics and argues that such a counter-power is part of the strategy of resistance/survival, yet it also embodies empowerment. This counter-power implies a particular definition of sexuality. The body becomes a resource that can be used to gain economic independence and access to resources or to negotiate a better position in gender and class hierarchies. This use of the body cannot be understood without looking at the historical roots of the sex/gender system and the gender division of labour. Although these two systems originated with the creation of the independent Haitian nation-state, their presuppositions are rooted in Africa and the slave-based colonial plantation society.

Haitian sex/gender system and practices of sexual politics

The material basis of male dominance and of the gender hierarchy (the sex/gender system) generally resides in men's control over women's labour.

This control is exercised by excluding women from access to essential productive resources and by restricting their sexuality. While the sex/gender hierarchy informs the sexual division of labour in the economic sphere, it is particularly in its relationship to the kinship system that ways are socially created to satisfy sexual needs, to reproduce people, and to construct gender roles and identities. These two dimensions of the sex/gender system permeate all social structures of a given society (Rubin 1975, Ortner & Whitehead [1981] 1989).

In Haiti, however, patriarchy as a specific form of the sex/gender system is very complex. The legacy of slavery, the maintenance and transformation of certain African cultural practices, the resistance of poor and working people against the oppressive and predatory practices of the Haitian state, and the need to survive in a situation of poverty and underdevelopment have all had different effects on patriarchal relationships.

As Rubin (1975) argues, the kinship system is the most empirical form of a sex/gender system. Kinship is more than a list of biological relatives: it is a system of categories and statuses that often contradicts genetic relationships. It determines obligations, genealogical status, lineage, names, rights of inheritance, forms and patterns of conjugality and mating, norms and conventions governing sexuality, as well as people in concrete social relationships.

Although in Haiti there are few studies of kinship and the sex/gender system, some of the most important features and content of kinship relationships are evident. The extended patriarchal family structure and bimodal forms of conjugal relations – legal marriage and *plasaj*, or common-law conjugal relations – tend to be dominant (Simpson 1947, Comhaire-Sylvain 1961, Bastien 1961, Comhaire-Sylvain 1974, Allman 1980, Laguerre 1984), although about 46 per cent of Haitian households are female-headed and many women are not engaged in a long-lasting conjugal relationship (1971 Census, Allman 1980, p. 20).[2] There are three other forms of union, however, that do not entail cohabitation. They are *rinmin*, (to date), *fiyanse* (to be engaged) and *viv avek* (living with). Although all of these involve sexual relations and some form of economic support, they differ in residence, legal and social standing, and in economic and social obligations. Nonetheless, *rinmin* and *fiyanse* tend to precede the dominant forms of conjugal relationships (Allman 1980), Lowenthal 1984). Forms of conjugal relationships are also informed by class. Even though in the rural areas legal marriage is less prevalent than common-law and visiting unions, it increases with elevations in class and status. Likewise, in the urban area, the nuclear families based on legal marriage tend to predominate among the middle class and the bourgeoisie.

Most historical accounts on the social organization of family life and household structure in Haiti have focused on the existence in the rural areas of the *lakou*, a large household compound where a male patriarch, the head of the extended family, lives with his wife, concubines and offspring. Although the *lakou* has tended to disappear, some of the social relations embedded in it continue to exist. Many peasant households are still polygynous. A male peasant, in addition to his wife and children from a legal or consensual marriage, may have one or two mistresses with children who live on other plots of land that he owns (Moral 1961, Laguerre 1984).

In the rural areas, as well as in poor urban areas, there is a tendency for women to enter a union (a consensual mating) or to marry legally when they get older. Age at the first union is relatively late, averaging 20 years old (Allman 1980). There is no pressure for females to marry as they reach puberty. Yet there is social acceptance of sexuality, as long as the woman observes a strict code of behaviour aimed at protecting her reputation, in order to ensure a legal (decent) marriage or a formal common-law conjugality.

> Women follow a developmental cycle of conjugal unions. Children
> are born to young women in their twenties while still living in the
> family of orientation. Then the mother leaves that household to
> form a conjugal household with the father of her children.
>
> (Allman 1980, p. 22)

Norms and conventions about sexual behaviour differ for men, however. On reaching puberty, men are granted certain freedoms. Yet, the comportment of men *vis-à-vis* their partners is conditioned by the forms of conjugal and mating relationships. Responsibilities may vary in terms of economic assistance, time spent, type of residency established, and support and obligations to children.

The Haitian constitution does not differentiate between legitimate and illegitimate children. Since 1805, any discrimination against children born out of wedlock has been outlawed. Nevertheless, the status of the children depends on the recognition of the parents. A bilateral pattern guides inheritance patterns: all children – male and female – have equal right to the property of both parents. However, there is a tendency for male children to become privileged in gaining access to the resources inherited from their parents.

In most poor households, rural and urban, there is a sexual division of labour. In addition to paid work, Haitian women perform most of the household chores. They may delegate chores to children according to age and sex. Most responsibilities fall to the girls. Moreover, many women are heads of household, or are responsible for single female family–centred households. Men will only perform 'female' tasks under extraordinary conditions, like childbirth, illness, prolonged absence of the woman from home, or when other kinswomen are not available. Child-rearing, however, is an exception (Comhaire-Sylvain 1974, Lowenthal 1984). In fact, parenting is independent of the relationship between spouses. Men often point out that they have the duty and the right to care for their children. They are proud to claim that they participate fully in child-care, although this is less the case in urban areas because of the availability of domestic workers even among poor working-class households.

Until the 1980s, relatively few Haitian women participated in formal politics. They gained the vote only in 1957, and until the 1970s married women had the legal status of minors. In the case of divorce, there is no provision for child-care or alimony. Even within progressive circles – let alone among traditional male-oriented political parties or groups – women's place is still in the kitchen.

In Haiti, the sex/gender ideology praises the male's sexual prowess. In urban areas, poverty and corruption have had some important effects on sexual practices. Particularly among the middle class, men compete with each other and acquire status by having a great number of mistresses. Since there is a large supply of women as a special kind of commodity, competition among women is fierce. During the last thirty years under the dictatorship of the Duvalier family, many influential and affluent black males have tended to have many mistresses, in particular mulatto women of the middle class.

In spite of the fact that more than 40 per cent of conjugal relations are not legally sanctioned, the ideology of marriage is still strong. Indeed, a considerable proportion of female expenditure is on cosmetics, luxury goods, and jewellery, all of which can enhance women's sexual attractiveness and thus increase their value as commodities.

Whereas in the urban centres the dynamics of sexual and conjugal relations have tended to take the symbolic form and meaning of a commodity relationship, in the rural areas and among urban women of popular strata, sexual and conjugal relations are more complex. Interestingly, women participate actively in the making of these sexual meanings, infusing a new dynamic to these relationships.

Sexual encounters that lead to the formation of households are from the beginning social. Both males and females manage their sexuality in these terms. For women, their sexuality is an important resource. It is a form of capital. As they clearly express it '*kom se karo te'm; se lajam'm*' ('my body is a piece of land; it is my money') (Lowenthal 1984). The dominant ideology is that sex is not fun but *work*. For men, the aim is to increase their potential access to a wide range of partners – '*Gason se chen*' ('men are dogs') (Lowenthal 1984). Therefore, men may simultaneously marry, maintain a consensual wife in a second household, and conduct one or more relatively stable extraresidential affairs with varying degrees of responsibility. Women must formally dedicate themselves to a monogamous relationship even though they may enter serially and consecutively into several kinds of unions. Unionforming is always an arrangement, a deal. This is expressed in the way a relationship is described. All other forms of sexual encounters which do not lead to a formal union like '*fe afe – fe kondision – fe desod and byin avek*' ('to have an affair or to have pleasure') (Lowenthal 1984) are informal ties where sexuality in its physical aspect takes precedence over the social aspect.

The impact of the sex/gender system and of the ideology of sexuality differs in town and country. Nonetheless, with the potential of economic independence and the high proportion of female-headed households, working women tend to end unsatisfactory conjugal or mating relationships more easily. A significant number of women in their thirties and forties deliberately opt out of the conjugal system, either temporarily or permanently. They depend on the labour of their sons or on hired labour, and they devote their time to commercial marketing activities. The same pattern holds true for working women in the urban areas. They are quite satisfied to escape the disadvantages of conjugality and, when successful, they are praised by other women for their achievement.

Gender division of labour as legacy of plantation system

Haiti is distinctive in many ways. During the eighteenth century, it was the richest colony in the New World, deriving its wealth from the production of sugar, coffee and cotton. Through the exploitation of slave labour, St Domingue was France's *premier* colony. Yet 200 years after the most successful slave revolution in human history (in 1804), the first black republic and the second independent state in the western hemisphere is in shambles. Haiti is now the poorest country in the hemisphere. With an estimated population of around 6 million, the average annual per capita income was only $270 in 1980 (Walker 1984); the World Bank estimated that during the same period more than 80 per cent of the population had an average income of under $150 (Foster & Valdman 1984, DeWind & Kinley 1988). Other indices of poverty provide an even more graphic sense of current conditions: malnutrition is widespread; infant mortality is 115 per 1000 live births; only 20–27 per cent of children go to school in the rural areas. Moreover, Haiti is extremely dependent on foreign assistance. From 1972 to 1981 foreign assistance financed approximately 70 per cent of the total of Haitian development expenditures (DeWind & Kinley 1988; for a more detailed analysis of the contemporary economic situation, see Foster & Valdman 1984, p. 28, Walker 1984, pp. 205, 226–30, Valdman 1984).

A counterpart to the poverty is the extraordinary concentration of wealth and privilege. Income distribution is highly skewed and income inequality dramatic. In 1981, 0.4 per cent of the population received more than 46 per cent of the national income. This concentration of wealth and power in the hands of a small elite residing in the capital has led to a centralized structure of decision-making in all spheres of life (Hooper 1984). The Haitian bourgeoisie, which controls the most important economic sectors and yet includes only 2 per cent of the population, derives its wealth from the exploitation of the peasants and the urban working classes (Valdman 1984, Dupuy 1989).

The rural nature of Haiti means that over 60 per cent of the population lives off agriculture. Beyond the large landowners – 2 per cent of the rural population – who own large estates and employ wage labour or share-croppers, and various groups of middlemen who buy from the peasants and sell to the export houses, the bulk of the rural population is composed of peasants (Girault 1981, 1984, Nicholls 1985).

Among the peasantry, there is a rapidly growing class of landless wage earners, who form approximately 10 per cent of the rural population. In addition, there is a rural sub-proletariat, totalling perhaps 35 per cent of the population, that works as unpaid labour on small estates owned by relatives. And finally, there is the largest group of peasants, comprising over 50 per cent of the rural population, who own their own property. This independent peasantry uses mainly family labour and occasional wage or in-kind labour. The size of their plots varies, but they usually average around 3 acres. Many independent peasants also farm land through the system of metayage.[3]

The peasants' economic dependence on the middleman is reinforced by paternalistic social bonds. Indeed, the category of middleman is somewhat misleading, for many are also prominent landowners, merchants, or politicians, purchasing coffee from the peasants and selling it to the merchant houses (Girault 1981). Often as merchants, they advance credits and goods from their stores to the peasants in return for future coffee harvests.

Haitian women's participation in economic activities has always been significant. They make up 48 per cent of the workforce; of this number, 70 per cent are peasants who farm and raise animals (1982 Census). This percentage does not include women working in the informal sector. In the agricultural sector there is no strict division of labour by gender. Women participate in all activities related to production. Usually, the woman is responsible for production on a piece of land and shares some of the revenues with her mate (Moral 1961). Peasants produce both coffee for export and subsistence crops or provisions. In other words, the majority of Haitian women of all social and economic backgrounds work. Women are responsible for almost all food distribution, controlling 80 per cent of that trade. They are the link between the rural areas and the towns and cities. Though the distribution of food is entirely controlled by women, the distribution of the export crop is a male domain (Girault 1982).

Women are generally charged with meeting the bulk of domestic needs from the cash generated from the sale of their produce. Thus men are clearly dependent on the labour of women. The potential of transforming provision marketing into a profit business is real. This possibility for economic independence significantly enhances a woman's bargaining power within the household and family and at the same time shapes the meaning of womanhood and its relations to sexuality in the rural area. These forms of gender relations have emerged from the contradictory and complex nature of the Haitian state.

Indeed, although the Haitian state was the result of an alliance between free black and mulatto leaders and the masses of slaves against the colonial power, its creation was characterized by conflicts. There were huge differences between the rebel slaves and the emerging political and economic elite over the meaning of freedom and economic independence. For an important fraction of the emerging elite, freedom during slavery had meant full political rights and recognition of their economic status as planters. With the creation of the state, these two goals could be realized. Control of the state became the most important means to accomplish these goals.

Such accumulation of land became possible with the creation of the Haitian nation, when most of the vacant estates passed into the hands of the state, which became the biggest landowner and the sole purveyor of land. Thus access to state power meant access to wealth by acquiring land through concessions, privileged prices for buying and leasing, and inheritance.

For many slaves, the experience of freedom began during slavery. Freedom and independence were gained through marronage.[4] Likewise, the practice of selling surplus food and the freedom to dispose of these gains further re-inforced the slaves' understanding of the meaning of freedom. The former slaves – now peasants – used every possible means to retain their freedom and independence. It was only when all possibilities were closed that they became share-croppers or tenants. With the creation of such a peasantry, the ways in which capital could directly penetrate the agricultural sphere were reduced. Only a formal subsumption of labour, in contrast to a real subsumption with the creation of wage labour, could be achieved.[5]

This contradiction became the centre of the ongoing struggle between large – and small – holders, between labour and the new representatives of capital. After independence the Haitian state, controlled by the ruling elite of planters and landowners, began a continuous offensive to keep the freed labour force on the plantation. By the mid-nineteenth century the agrarian question was still a burning issue. The code of 1826, which had replaced the *Reglement des Cultures* of 1800, still prevailed. The law stipulated that workers on plantations were obliged to stay on the estates for three- to six-year contracts. They could not travel without a pass, send their children to school in the towns, or engage in trade. Any violation of these rules meant punishment for vagabondage (Charles 1990).

In spite of this law, the rural areas were changing. In addition to large private holdings, there was a large state domain which was occupied in many areas by lessees and squatters, and a free independent peasantry in the hills or scattered on the plains. In order to maintain their way of life, a new gender division of labour emerged to pool fully family labour, especially the labour of women. This gender division of labour relied not only on women's labour for the bulk of peasant production which was channelled to the market, but also on the reproductive role of women, and thus on the norms and conventions of the sex/gender system. It is thus in that context that practices of sexual politics and sexuality may take the meaning of capital or of commodity. This process of empowerment using sexuality also has its roots in experiences of sexual relations during slavery.

Social relations and mediation of sexuality

Many scholars have sought to understand the roots of the prevailing sexual division of labour in Haiti, in particular the specialization of women in trade. For scholars like Bastien (1961), Leyburn ([1942] 1966), and more recently Neptune-Anglade (1986), this pattern of division of labour and trade originated with the military draft of the nineteenth century. For others, like Herskovits (1937) and Simpson (1947), they are a retention of African culture, because women dominate in trade in some areas of contemporary West Africa. Both arguments, however, are simplistic. The first tends to isolate the Haitian case, since in many other parts of the Caribbean women also predominate in trade (Mintz 1974a). The second downplays the role of slavery in mediating these cultural practices.

While one cannot claim that slavery completely wiped out the culture of enslaved Africans, it is nevertheless sound to argue that African culture was both transplanted and transformed by slavery.

> Neither the masters nor the slaves were able to transfer to the Caribbean setting any adequate version of their ancestral culture, and since the slaves in most situations had insufficient opportunity to use the master's cultural tradition as a model, the cultural forms typifying plantation life were usually contrived out of what the slaves themselves could transfer from Africa and were permitted to retain, combined with those features of European culture that they could learn.
>
> (Mintz 1974a, p. 27)

There is no historical documentation that such a gender division of labour with women controlling trade existed during slavery. But it is possible that the creation of Caribbean peasantries after the abolition of slavery, their confinement to less favourable land, and their poverty and sheer resistance to state control meant that these peasantries tended to perpetuate and reproduce cultural practices from the past. In fact, one could argue that these conditions provide the context for the emergence of the gender division of labour and the distinct sex/gender system: the need to create and reproduce an extended family as a primary source of labour supply and the need to maintain the cohesion of the household against state control. It might well be that these conditions forced Haitian males to concede control over certain economic activities to women. Moreover, the women were able to seize this opportunity and reinforce their relative autonomy because of their experience of sexuality as a way to mediate race and class relations during slavery and their understanding of their important role in the reproduction process (Reddock 1985, Bush 1987, Smith 1987, Morissey 1989).

Most discussions of the sexual politics of master–slave relations during slavery tend to emphasize the practice of rape by white planters and the resistance of slave women to that oppression (Hine 1981). Although during slavery time sex and abuses were always intertwined as forms of expression of white power, the dynamics of sex and power were significant for the development of Creole societies and in particular, for the development of race and class relationships (Smith 1987, Bush 1987, Morissey 1989). Moreover, if we also conceive of resistance as the capacity to create something different, something that challenges the existing system of domination, then sexual politics from the perspective of slave and free coloured could have different consequences. In that vein, sexual politics, in addition to infanticides and abortions, were part of the mechanisms of resistance/survival by slave women. It was not that sex benefited women but rather that slave women could use sexuality to mediate and undermine race and class hierarchy.

> Slave women learned the value of sexual ties with European men and sometimes aggressively sought them. Economic motives and dealings might be rewarded then by a slave woman's freedom, or by food, clothing and petty luxuries for herself and her kin.
>
> (Morissey 1989, p. 147)

One of the most important elements that can be used to support this argument is indeed the presence of that large number of freed persons in many Caribbean and Latin American slave-based societies. Given the relatively large number of free blacks and mulattos, some very wealthy (as in Haiti), it is difficult to explain their existence only as a result of rape. It is clear, however, that any form of sexual relations between a slave woman and a white master was conditioned by the coercive nature of the slave system.

The most fundamental relation in slave-based plantation societies was the bipolar racial and class division between white master and black slave. Yet the evolution of Caribbean slave-based societies resulted in the creation of a social context where class/race (or class/ethnicity) tended to be confounded. For example, slave-based societies are generally conceived of as polarized, dichotomized societies. At one pole is the black/slave labourer and at the other the white/master–planter class. Yet the multiple realities of slave societies never corresponded to that polarization. During slavery, though the most fundamental relationships were the overlapping class and racial relationships between masters/slaves and whites/blacks, the same dynamics also created other types of class and race relations. A case in point is the process of formation and consolidation of a free and wealthy mulatto group, as in Haiti. The emergence of this particular group had its basis in both race and class relations in the colonial social formation (Charles 1990).

Although there is no clear relationship between miscegenation and manumission, there is, however, a correlation between miscegenation and the process of development of a free coloured or mulatto stratum in the slave colonial society. Indeed, sexual contact between black female slaves and white masters was widespread and persistent. As a result, manumission of a female black or mulatto slave attached to a white master in an informal union could follow. Concomitantly, many offspring of these informal unions were usually given freedom. In most French Caribbean slave-based plantation societies, sexual and mating relations, in the form of concubinage between whites and blacks and whites and mulattos, were allowed in spite of the restrictions imposed by the *Code Noir*. Restrictions on mixed unions were in fact inefficient given the illegitimate birth statistics. In Martinique, for example, from 1727 to 1749, the number of illegitimate births was slightly less than that of legitimate ones, a ratio of 166:173. Between 1749 and 1759 the figures were inverted to 100:91. Then between 1800 and 1823, the old restrictions clearly broke down. During that time, there were 425 legitimate births for 1000 illegitimate ones (Elizabeth 1972, pp. 156–7).

The extent of informal unions had important consequences for race and class relations in Haiti. Often the best lands passed to the mulatto offspring of white planters – so much so that it inspired bitter comment. Hilliard d'Auberteuil, a French statesman, wrote that the *Code Noir* was subject to great abuse on the part of black women:

> How many negresses have profited from it and appropriated the entire fortune of their masters, brutalized by libertinage and incapable of resisting their power over feeble and seduced souls . . . The wealth of families has been sacrificed to passion, has become the price of debauchery, and respectable names have fallen, along with the best lands, to legitimized mulattoes.
>
> (Elizabeth 1972, p. 158)

Such sexual politics also existed in other Caribbean and Latin American plantation societies. For example, Mexico in 1810 had a freed mulatto population of 624,000 and around 10,000 slaves. The mulatto group represented more than a tenth of the total population. The same pattern could also be found in Ecuador and Uruguay. A 1781 census of Quito and Guayaquil in Ecuador shows a total of 27,528 free coloured to 4,684 slaves (Bowser 1972, pp. 19–58).[6]

In Jamaica and St Domingue a few free mulattoes came to share the same economic position as some rich white planters. In St Domingue on the eve of the Revolution, mulattoes owned a third of the land, a quarter of the slaves, a quarter of the properties, and had good positions as merchant traders and artisans (Debien 1950, Hall 1972).

Through the mediation of sexual relations, social structures and relationships took different features and different meanings. The development, for example, of the non-white freed group, their accumulation of wealth in some areas, and their assimilation and acculturation to European values had a significant economic and social impact.[7] Thereby, the legal and racial differences created by the dominant white group *vis-à-vis* blacks and mulattoes redefined the character of many Caribbean colonial societies. The result was a three-tiered social structure despite the politically fragile status of the free population. In that process, black slave women and free mulatto women used sexual politics as a form of survival, accommodation, resistance and empowerment. These past practices are clearly part of the collective reconstruction of the dynamics of sexual politics in contemporary Haiti.

Conclusion

This chapter has attempted to explain in part the dynamics and the specificity of the sex/gender system in Haiti. It argues that these relationships are complex and must be analysed taking into account the role of slavery, its mediation in the transfer and retention of certain African cultural practices, and the impact of the new social relations that emerged with the formation of the Haitian nation-state on gender hierarchy. It is thus clear that in a situation where gender inequality is compounded, on the one hand, by class and racial inequality, and, on the other hand, by national dependency and underdevelopment, sexual politics and reliance on informal networks and reciprocity are means that women use to cope with all these sources of oppression and inequality. These strategies of sexual politics are part of the capacity and creativity of women to give meanings to their sexuality in negotiating their space in the gender/sex system and the gender division of labour. Thus, sexual politics tends to mediate all relations of race, class and culture, and we should take these distinct experiences into account in any project aiming to eliminate gender inequality. It is obvious that it is through a redefinition of femininity, family, marriage and motherhood based on these various and complex historical experiences, that these relationships and processes of the sex/gender system mediate race, class and gender hierarchies, and that issues of empowerment of women, and of Haitian women in particular, can be fully defined.

Glossary

Plasaj: common low or consensual union. The literature also refers to this form of union as concubinage, a practice of mating prevailing during slavery time encompassing all members of the slave societies across race and class.

Fè désod and byin avèk: a casual encounter.

Rinmin: literally a date or an affair which might include sexual relations.

Fiyansé: a more formal date, an engagement.

Viv avèk: could be equated to *plasaj* yet it is more casual and less engaging.

Lakou: the form of spatial organization of household and residency. Some argue that it is rooted in the compound of West African households while others claim that its origin is clearly linked to the organization of the big slave house.

Karo t'èm: a *karo* is a measure unit of land from the French *carreau*. It is equivalent to about 3 acres of land.

Code Noir: black code.

Notes

1 For a definition of the gender/sex system and its multiple and complex forms, see Rubin (1975), Hartman (1981), Ortner & Whitehead [1981] 1989, Collier & Yanagisako (1987).
2 In 1980, for example, 48 per cent of women were not engaged in a conjugal relationship (Allman 1980).
3 Metayage is a form of economic arrangement similar to the share-cropping system. A peasant works on a piece of land that he does not own. In counterpart, he pays rent, which can take the form of cash and/or products. There is a contract between the owner of the land and the direct producer. The terms of the contract, as well as the nature and proportion of the rent, vary.
4 Marronage consisted of a movement away from the plantation through rebellion, escape and desertion. It was a common practice in all slave-based societies. Marronage could be individual or collective. Substantively, it was also the attempt by runaway slaves to create an alternative way of life. In colonial societies like Jamaica, Cuba, Brazil and Haiti, the movement was so widespread and powerful that in some areas maroons completely controlled their territory (see Price 1979 for a fuller account).
5 See Marx's (1971, Section G) argument in 'Results of the Immediate Process of Production' where he develops the category of formal and real subsumption of labour (and see Marx 1976).
6 In 1800–2 the free black and mulatto population of Puerto Rico was 48 per cent of the total free population. In Brazil, it was around 60 per cent, in Cuba and Jamaica 25 per cent, in Martinique 40 per cent and in Curacao 62 per cent. The freed colour group in St Domingue was 40 per cent of the population in 1784. In the United States, however, in 1800 the freed population was only 5 per cent. Moreover, in most Caribbean societies mulattoes were the most important segment of the freed population (Cohen & Greene 1972, p. 10). Generally, it was difficult for a free person to enter into 'white' professions. However, it was possible for mulattoes to enter trades. In many British Caribbean colonies, free mulattoes unwilling to work on the sugar estates migrated to towns and came to dominate important sectors of trade (Hoetink 1967, Hall 1972, Bowser 1972, Labelle 1976).
7 Cohen & Greene (1972) suggest that with the accumulation of wealth by many mulattoes the previous unions of whites with slaves were supplanted by those of whites with free coloured or mulattoes, particularly in areas where the latter were numerous and prosperous. For Cohen & Greene, the complex colour coding which prevailed in most Caribbean and Latin American slave societies may have been operative in terms of marriage preference and social status.

References

Albrecht, L. & R. M. Brewer (eds) 1990. *Bridges of Power*. Santa Cruz: New Society Publishers.
Allman, J. 1980. Sexual unions in rural Haiti. *International Journal of Sociology of Family* 10, 15–39.
Bastide, R. & S. Mintz (eds) 1974. *La Femme de couleur en Amerique Latine*. Paris: Anthropos.
Bastien, R. 1961. Haitian rural family organization. *Social and Economic Studies* 10, 478–510.
Bowser, F. 1972. Colonial Spanish America. In *Neither Slave nor Free*, Cohen, D. & J. Greene (eds), 19–58. Baltimore: Johns Hopkins University Press.

Bush, B. 1987. White 'ladies', coloured 'favourites' and black 'wenches'; some considerations on sex, race and class factors in social relations in white Creole society in the British Caribbean. *Slavery and Abolition*, 245–50.

Charles, C. 1990. A transnational dialectic of race, class, and ethnicity: patterns of identities and forms of consciousness among Haitian migrants in New York City. Unpublished Ph.D. thesis, Suny-Binghamton.

Charles, C. 1991. Feminism and power: the struggles of Haitian women in Haiti and the diaspora, 1930–1990. Paper presented at the HSA, Boston, Tuft University.

Cohen, D. & J. Greene (eds) 1972. *Neither Slave nor Free: freedmen of African descent in the slave societies of the New World*. Baltimore: Johns Hopkins University Press.

Collier, J. F. & S. J. Yanagisako (eds) 1987. *Gender and Kinship: essays toward a unified analysis*. Stanford: Stanford University Press.

Comhaire-Sylvain, S. 1961. The household in Kenscoff Haiti. *Social and Economic Studies* 10, 192–222.

Comhaire-Sylvain, S. 1974. La Paysanne de la region de Kenscoff. In *La Femme de couleur en Amerique Latine*, Bastide, R. & S. Mintz (eds), 149–170. Paris: Anthropos.

Davis, A. 1981. *Women Race and Class*. New York: Vintage Books.

Debien, G. 1950. Gens de couleurs libres et colous de St Dominique devant la constituante. *Revue d'Histoire de l'Amerique Française* (Montreal) 4, 211–32.

DeWind, J. & M. Kinley 1988. *Aiding Migration*. Boulder: Westview Press.

Dupuy, A. 1989. *Haiti in the World Economy: class, race and underdevelopment since 1700*. Boulder: Westview Press.

Elizabeth, L. 1972. The French Antilles. In *Neither Slave nor Free*, Cohen, D. & J. Greene (eds), 134–41. Baltimore: Johns Hopkins University Press.

Foster, C. R. & A. Valdman (eds) 1984. *Haiti – Today and Tomorrow*. New York: University Press of America.

Girault, C. 1981. *Le Commerce du cafe en Haiti: habitants, speculateurs et exportateurs*. Paris: Centre National de la Recherche Scientifique.

Girault, C. 1982. *Le Commerce du cafe en Haiti*. Paris: Centre National de Recherche Scientifique.

Girault, C. 1984. Commerce in the Haitian economy. In *Haiti – Today and Tomorrow*, Foster, C. R. & A. Valdman (eds), 181–204. New York: University Press of America.

Hall, G. M. 1972. Saint-Domingue. In *Neither Slave nor Free*, Cohen, D. & J. Greene (eds), 172–93. Baltimore: Johns Hopkins University Press.

Hartman, H. 1981. The unhappy marriage of marxism and feminism: towards a more progressive union. In *Women and Revolution*, Sargent, L. (ed.), 1–42. Boston: South End Press.

Herkovits, M. J. 1937. *Life in a Haitian Valley*. New York: A. A. Knopf.

Hine, D. 1981. Female slave resistance: the economics of sex. In *The Black Woman Cross-Culturally*, Steady, F. C. (ed.), 289–300. Cambridge, Mass.: Schenkman.

Hoetink, H. 1967. *The Two Variants in Caribbean Race Relations: a contribution to the sociology of segmented societies*. London: Oxford University Press.

Hooper, I. 1984. The monkey's tail still strong. *Nacla* Nov./Dec., 24–32.

Jelin, E. (ed.) 1990. *Women and Social Change in Latin America*. London & New Jersey: Zed Book.

Labelle, M. 1976. *Ideologies de couleur et classes sociales en Haiti*. Montreal: Presses Universitaires de Montreal.

Laguerre, M. 1984. *Urban Life in the Caribbean: a study of a Haitian urban community*. Cambridge, Mass.: Schenkman.

Leyburn, J. [1942] 1966. *The Haitian People*. New Haven: Yale University Press.

Lowenthal, I. 1984. Labor, sexuality and the conjugal contract in rural Haiti. In *Haiti – Today and Tomorrow*, Foster, C. R. & A. Valdman (eds), 15–34. New York: University Press of America.

Marx, K. 1971. *Un chapitre inedit du Capital*. Edited and translated by R. Dangeville. Paris: Union Generale d'Editions.

Marx, K. 1976. *Value Studies*. Edited and translated by A. Dragstedt. New York & London: New Park Publication.

Mintz, S. 1974a. *Caribbean Transformation*. Baltimore: Johns Hopkins University Press.

Mintz, S. 1974b. Les Rôles economiques et les traditions culturelles. In *La Femme de Couleur en Amerique Latine*, Bastide, R. & S. Mintz (eds), 15–147. Paris: Anthropos.

Mintz, S. 1985. *Sweetness and Power*. Baltimore: Johns Hopkins University Press.

Moral, P. 1961. *Le Paysan Haitien*. Paris: Larose et Maisonneuve.

Morissey, M. 1989. *Slave Women in the New World*. Boulder: Westview Press.

Mullings, L. 1984. Uneven development: class, race, and gender in the United States before 1900. In *Women's Work: development and the division of labor by gender*, Leacock, E. & H. I. Safa (eds), 41–54. South Hadley: Bergen & Garvey.

Neptune-Anglade, M. 1986. *L'autre moitié du developpement*. Montreal/Haiti: Arce.

Nicholls, D. 1985. *Haiti in Caribbean Context: ethnicity, economy and revolt*. London: Macmillan.

Ortner, S. B. & H. Whitehead (eds) [1981] 1989. *Sexual Meanings: the cultural construction of gender and sexuality*. Cambridge: Cambridge University Press.

Pala, A. 1981. Definition of women and development. In *The Black Woman Cross-Culturally*, Steady, F. C. (ed.), 209–15. Cambridge, Mass.: Schenkman.

Price, R. 1979. *Maroon Societies*. 2nd edn. Baltimore: Johns Hopkins University Press.

Reddock, R. 1985. Women and slavery in the Caribbean. *Latin American Perspective* 44, 63–80.

Rubin, G. 1975. The traffic in women: notes on the political economy of sex. In *Toward an Anthropology of Women*, Reiter, R. R. (ed.), 157–210. New York: Monthly Review Press.

Simpson, G. E. 1947. Sexual and familial institution in Haiti. *American Anthropology* 44, 655–74.

Smith, R. T. 1987. Hierarchy and the dual marriage system in West Indian society. In *Gender and Kinship: essays toward a unified analysis*, Collier, J. F. & S. J. Yanagisako (eds), 163–98. Stanford: Stanford University Press.

Staffa, S. 1987. Dimension of women's power in historic Cairo. In *Islamic and Middle Eastern Societies*, Olson, R. & S. Al-An (eds), 62–99. Brattleboro: Amana Books.

Steady, F. C. (ed.) 1981. *The Black Woman Cross-Culturally*. Cambridge, Mass.: Schenkman.

Sudarkasa, N. 1981. Female employment and family organization in West Africa. In *The Black Woman Cross-Culturally*, Steady, F. C. (ed.), 49–65. Cambridge, Mass.: Schenkman.

Tilly, L. A. 1986. Paths of proletarianization. In *Women's Work*, Leacock, E. & H. I. Safa (eds), 25–41. South Hadley: Bergen & Garvey.

Valdman, A. 1984. The linguistic situation in Haiti. In *Haiti – Today and Tomorrow*, Foster, C. R. & A. Valdman (eds), 77–100. New York: University Press of America.

Walker, J. 1984. Foreign assistance and Haiti's economic development. In *Haiti – Today and Tomorrow*, Foster, C. R. & A. Valdman (eds), 205–30. New York: University Press of America.

4 Representation and power: blacks in Colombia

PETER WADE

This chapter is concerned with the notions of race mixture that exist in Colombia, their relationship to the system of power that produced and sustains them, and their construction of the past (and present and future), with specific reference to the black population of the country.

Racial discrimination against blacks is legitimated by an elite ideology which constructs blackness as belonging to a backward past in the process of being transcended by modernization and integration into a whitened mixed-race population. At the same time, the ideology of mixedness is flexible enough to encompass claims that the past is a history of mixture which has undone any racial or ethnic purity. Hence blacks are the same as everyone else and have no grounds for complaint since they suffer no discrimination as blacks. Challenges to inequality are thus defused, while discrimination is legitimated: different variants of the same basic ideology underwrite both effects.

I start by outlining a basic tension in Iberian social structures, then showing how two variants on the basic theme of race mixture emphasize the different sides of this tension. In the co-existence of these two variants, and the possibility of slipping from one discourse to the other, lies the cultural politics of racial inequality for blacks in Colombia.

Iberian social structures

The Iberian colonial enterprise was marked, in ethnic terms, by a contradiction of power. On the one hand, there were factors reinforcing the segregation of indians, black slaves and white settlers. The Spanish Crown wanted to keep indians separate from whites and enacted much legislation towards this end. Many colonists would have preferred to keep all blacks as slaves. On the other hand, there were factors encouraging the breakdown of simple ethnic and social barriers and differences. In essence, neither Crown nor colonists had the power or the resources to police a system which tried to force blacks and indians into strictly defined subordinate roles. In addition, Crown and colonists themselves undermined these roles. Manumission of slaves was practised by individual owners and, as the result of self-purchase by a slave, was a right upheld in courts against the objections of disgruntled slave-owners (Bowser 1972). Colonists, often faced with a shortage of white women, frequently took black and indian women as informal partners and, much more rarely, as wives. Blacks and indians, despite decrees against marriage and sexual relations between them, also mixed widely in certain areas. The mixed-blood offspring of these unions inevitably undermined simple classification into a triadic ethnic system.[1]

Two sets of forces, direct results of the system of power of the Iberian colonial enterprise, thus co-existed and interacted: 1) discrimination which kept blacks and indians in subordinate positions as free, semi-free or bonded labour, and as cultural inferiors; 2) the breakdown of discriminations both through the inability of the colonial presence to police them, and through the actions of whites, blacks and indians which undermined them. A major medium for the latter process was 'race mixture', a complex of physical and cultural transformations in which 'blacks' and 'indians' became various types of 'mixed' people.

These two processes did not simply co-exist in parallel, they interpenetrated. Discrimination entered into the very heart of mixture, both physical and cultural, creating a finely graded hierarchy of socio-racial types and cultural *mores*. Although the middle strata were, and are, full of ambiguous and contestable identities, they are structured by the three polar nodes of white, black and indian, with white firmly at the top of the triangle. Thus mixture, rather than a horizontal combination of elements, involved movement up and down a hierarchy of value.

At the same time, mixture could, according to historical circumstances, penetrate discrimination so entirely as to undo it. For example, in some Latin American countries, mixture has proceeded to a point at which black minorities and discrimination against them barely exist – Paraguay, for instance (Rout 1976).

Systems of power produce systems of knowledge (Foucault 1980, pp. 109–33), and as the power structures of the Iberian colonial enterprise were characterized by the tension noted above, so the system of knowledge that emerged from it displays the same tension, giving rise to different, although related, representations of the past, the present and the future. These representations share some common ground, but lead off it in rather different directions. They are contestable, and contesting them means challenging the relations of power that underlie them, but they are not simply illusions or false ideologies foisted on to 'the people' by an elite. They constitute the parameters for comprehension of society and criteria for assessing truth and falsehood. As Foucault (1980, p. 133) says, 'The political question . . . is not error, illusion, alienated consciousness or ideology; it is truth itself'. Clearly truth in this sense does not lack a certain positionality. As I will show below, ideas about the association between progress and whiteness in Colombia are strongly linked to the literate ideology of a political and intellectual elite which was perhaps most public from independence to about 1940 (Graham 1990, Wright 1990). But this ideology is rooted in the social structures of the country and, although different people have different relationships to such ideas, in some respects they appear self-evident: whiter people *do* on average have more power, wealth and education; blacker and more indian people are on average poorer and more peripheral to the main currents of development. These structures are experienced reiteratively and indeed reproduced by many people during their lives, even while some may contest them and belie them with their actions and beliefs.

In the next sections, I will look at notions allied with discrimination and race mixture in Colombia, drawing out the representations of the past involved and the location of the black minority. Despite Foucault's strictures on the use of the notion of ideology, I retain it as a useful term without, however, implying an opposition between ideology and 'truth'. Instead I use ideology to mean a system of knowledge.

Discrimination and the ideology of *blanqueamiento*

Discrimination against blacks has been a continued feature of Colombian society. In colonial New Granada,[2] the so-called *sociedad de castas* existed, *casta* being the general term for the various people of different categories who made up the middle and lower strata of society. There was a tremendous concern with descent and status, as the higher strata tried to protect their 'racial purity' and social status, and the lower and middle strata tried to encroach on their privileged terrain.

Jaramillo Uribe (1968, pp. 181–6) gives accounts of long litigations in late eighteenth-century New Granadian society about alleged acts of defamation of honour by casting slurs on a person's racial heritage or by attributing to them a racial status below that which they claimed as their right. Juan & Ulloa ([1758] 1772 I, p. 30) observed in eighteenth-century Cartagena that 'every person is so jealous of their tribe or caste, that if, through inadvertence, you call them by a lower degree than what they actually are, they are highly offended, never suffering themselves to be deprived of so valuable a gift of fortune'. When Gaspar Mollien travelled through Colombia in 1822, he passed along the Cauca valley and noted that 'the muleteers, proud of being white, are ashamed to go on foot, so it is difficult to distinguish the rich from the poor'. He also observed that 'the pride inspired by colour is no less great in the valley of Cauca than in the colonies of the Antilles' (Mollien 1824, pp. 282, 285).

In the obsessive concern with colour and status that characterized this *sociedad de castas*, only one thing was certain: to be black or indian was bad, to be white was good. To be rich alone was useful, but inadequate: to enter universities, the Church or the administration required proof of *limpieza de sangre*, clean blood, and any doubtful heritage was a major obstacle. True, after

1783 the Crown could by decree dispense a *cédula de gracias al sacar*, a royal cleansing, a certificate of whiteness, and as from 1795 this license could be bought for about twice the price of a prime slave. But universities or the Church often found it hard to swallow this side-stepping tactic and long litigations sometimes dogged the attempts of royally cleansed individuals to act on their new status (Mörner 1967, p. 45, Rout 1976, p. 157). Interestingly, black blood seems to have been harder to get rid of, socially speaking, than indian. In the rather artificial and academic *casta* nomenclatures of eighteenth-century New Spain and Peru which pedantically describe and classify types of racial mixture, a Spaniard–indian cross could return to Spaniard within three generations in New Spain or four in Peru, if each offspring again united with a Spaniard. For a Spaniard–black cross, it took five steps in Peru, while in New Spain no such possibility was envisaged (Mörner 1967, p. 58).

The *sociedad de castas* ultimately crumbled as a result of the continuing race mixture that had brought it into being. But its polar categories – black, indian and white – remained and the cult of whiteness which paid tribute to the high value of a light-coloured skin and European features remained also, as did the 'damned link' between black (or indian) and low status (Friedemann & Arocha 1986, p. 40). After independence, the political elites all over Latin America faced an intellectual dilemma as they tried to define their nationhood on a world stage dominated by countries who either had few 'mixed' people (e.g. Europe) or had kept them firmly behind a barrier intended to protect white racial purity (e.g. the USA). As a compromise, these elites often, although not always, eschewed the simple condemnation of blacks and indians, since admission of some kind of 'mestizo' identity was largely unavoidable, and to damn blacks and indians risked admitting an unremediable basis for national progress. The solution instead lay in 'whitening', in diluting the bad with the good (Graham 1990, Skidmore 1974, 1993, Wright 1990). In 1824, the British consul reported that

> the preponderance of African blood along this very extensive line of coast [the Atlantic littoral], in agitated times like the present, cannot fail to excite serious reflections in this country. Those in power . . . feel the full importance of the expediency of inviting Europeans to find homes in Colombia . . . where their descendants must improve the moral and physical properties of the Colombians.
>
> (Humphreys 1940, p. 267)

Blacks were not seen as good material for the developing nation and Agustín Codazzi, the Colombian geographer, who helped map the new republic in the 1850s, commented tersely on the blacks of the Chocó department of the Pacific coastal region that 'A race almost all of which passes its days in such indolence is not that which is called to make the country progress' (Comisión Corográfica 1958, p. 324). Bushnell (1954, p. 144) also observes that new liberal immigration laws promulgated in 1823 were designed to encourage white immigration in order to outnumber coloured people and defuse the threat of 'race warfare'. Race warfare was only a concern during the 'agitated times' of the newly formed republic of Gran Colombia (1819–30), but the underlying idea of the inferiority of blackness ran much deeper and was by no means confined to Colombia. For Venezuela, Rout reproduces a 1924 bulletin of the Chamber of Commerce which states that 'whitening the population as much as . . . possible' should be the objective of a 'fair . . . well thought-out policy' since 'all Venezuelans . . . have in this goal the same supreme interest' (Rout 1976, p. 258).

This kind of attitude is evident in still more recent publications. In a 1953 book on the geography of the Cauca region, Arroyo writes that

> the black has not been able to free himself of the moral deficiency of improvidence and since the indian is introverted and indifferent, it is vital to engineer a better direction for the mixtures, starting centrally from white towards red and from white towards black . . . so that the descendants remain influenced by the dominant characteristics of the European stock.
>
> (Arroyo 1953, pp. 104, 110)

Arroyo states that eugenic policies should aim for a morphological type similar to that of 'the ancient Mediterranean civilizations', while indian–black unions should be avoided since they produce 'tenacious or insoluble sub-types which retard racial uniformity and are refractory to the dominant capacity of the white race' (Arroyo 1953, pp. 110–12). Camacho Perea, writing on the department of Valle del Cauca, a little further north, also envisages the eventual creation of a 'cosmic race': he notes that the black is well adapted to tropical climates and arduous labour, but 'without stimulus he gives himself over to laziness'. The black who lives in the river valley itself is described as being of a melancholy type with

> a disposition to music and indolence. He submitted to the apathetic nature of his spirit and was constantly lazy, almost vegetative. He contents himself with the easy sustenance of fish and plantains along the banks of the Cauca and its affluents.
>
> (Camacho Perea 1962, pp. 82, 88)

González Ochoa remarks more dramatically that the importation of blacks was 'one of the greatest errors committed by any statesman or sociologist of all time', since they are 'an inferior race' which, luckily, was controlled and punished to a degree which 'prevented the black race, prolific like no other, from taking over the continent' (González Ochoa [1942] 1960, p. 129).

Underlying the comments of these intellectual elites is a common ideology: that of *blanqueamiento*, or whitening. This is based on race mixture, but it construes it in a discriminatory fashion: blacks and indians mix into a mestizo population, but in doing so are erased from the national panorama and absorbed into the white race. The latter is changed, but its dominant essence remains. Increasing racial homogeneity reinforces national integration as everyone is becoming mestizo, and the mestizo in question is of light skin and Caucasian features, rather than heavily mulatto or indian in appearance.

As historical processes, both *blanqueamiento* and the emergence of national identity are based on a certain construction of the past, and the future. The past is seen as traditional, backward; it is also seen as heavily black and indian, a time when blacks were slaves (an antique, backward form of labour relation) and both blacks and indians were numerous. Progress is modernization; it is also the increasing integration of blacks and indians into modern society where they will mix in and eventually disappear, taking their 'primitive' culture with them. In the temporalization of this ideology lies part of its apparent self-evidence and hence power. Those in charge of leading the nation *forward* have always been 'white' people, guiding the country away from a past which began in indianness and slavery and which has become increasingly mixed.

In Colombia, this temporal scheme is powerfully reinforced by a spatial schema, which again has been formed and changes over time (Wade 1993). Simplifying greatly, the central Andean regions have historically been the locus of power and wealth. They were also home to the majority of white settlers. The Pacific and Atlantic coastal regions were both settled by smaller numbers of whites and had significant numbers of slaves. They also remained comparatively underdeveloped economically. Equally the eastern lowlands give on to the Amazon and Orinoco basins, very underdeveloped and home to mostly indian populations. Thus black and indian regions are also poor, rural and uneducated regions. Indian culture appears very distinct to mainstream national culture and is seen as primitive, while the black culture of the Pacific region, although actually heavily Hispanicised, is also seen as backward and rustic by non-blacks.

As migrants from the interior colonize peripheral indian and black regions, and as blacks and indians from these regions migrate to the interior in search of work and education, they all experience directly the racial hierarchies of Colombia as they self-evidently exist. And they partially recreate them. Colonists bring economic 'progress' (of sorts) to peripheral areas just as they 'whiten' them with their presence. Black migrants to central cities move up the hierarchy of place and often end up with the whiter partner (Wade 1993).

In short, then, from this point of view, a certain trajectory of history is constructed in which the country is envisaged as an entity which is historically transcending its past, associated with blacks, indians, and backwardness, by means of a process of spatial and racial integration, an integration which is inherently progressive. Backwardness, blacks, indians and their 'primitive' cultures will be eliminated.

This ideology, or system of knowledge, is not of course uncontested, but neither is it simply a false consciousness propounded by the elite. It derives from real social relations and processes underlain by power differences. Power and wealth are connected with whiteness and whiter regions of the country. For blacks, in the past and today, vertical social mobility has tended to go hand in glove with more contact with white regions and people, with assimilation to non-black culture and with unions to lighter-skinned partners. Thus progress, whiteness and whitening are strongly linked in social practice. This is not to argue that *blanqueamiento* is actually 'true'; it is not in itself true or false, since it is a value system that provides criteria for judging truth and falsity but it is embedded in historical and contemporary social experience and practice. Although different people have different relationships to *blanqueamiento*, it informs everyone's understanding in some way (Wade 1993).

Blanqueamiento holds up an image of nationhood based on a specific representation of the past. In doing so, it projects a future homogeneity and the obliteration of difference. But it also puts difference into relief. By valuing whiteness and envisaging the elimination of indianness and blackness, it points up racial and regional difference. Furthermore, since the valuation of whiteness clearly translates in practice into discriminating against blacks and indians (the utopian vision of a whitened racial homogeneity notwithstanding), difference is inevitably reiterated by the ideology of *blanqueamiento*. In this it contrasts somewhat with the allied ideology of *lo mestizo*.

Race mixture and the ideology of *lo mestizo*

Lo mestizo is an abstract concept of 'mixedness'. It celebrates the obliteration of difference in a democratic, non-hierarchical form. Rather than envisaging a gradual whitening, it holds up a generalized image of the mestizo in which racial, regional and even class differences are submerged into a common identification with mixedness. *Blanqueamiento* implies this as a future goal, while undermining it with its reiteration of difference; the ideology of *lo mestizo* takes up the same theme, but glorifies it as a current as well as a future focus of identification. Like *blanqueamiento*, the ideology of *lo mestizo* links emerging nationhood with the predominance of the mestizo, this time not construed necessarily as a whitened mestizo. These two visions are thus variations on the same theme and share a common middle ground.

Again we can look to the literary productions of an intellectual elite for this ideology. Its clearest expression is perhaps in the cult of the mestizo which characterized much Mexican writing about race and nation in the nineteenth and early twentieth centuries (Knight 1990). José Vasconcelos, for example, coined the term *raza cósmica* for the mestizo 'race', and argued for the superiority of the hybrid. Knight comments:

> It was with the Revolution that the mestizo cult blossomed. 'In the great forge of America', wrote Manuel Gamio, 'on the giant anvil of the Andes, virile races of bronze and iron have struggled for centuries.' From this struggle emerged the mestizo, the 'national race' of Mexico, the carrier of 'the national culture of the future'.
> (Knight 1990, p. 85)

Knight argues that in Mexico this mestizo cult became allied to *indigenismo*, the glorification of the indian, since the indian was to be integrated and 'mestizo-ised' in the process of becoming Mexico's national symbol. Either way, says Knight, these ideologies remained in the 'conceptual prison' of racism even while they rattled its bars: they still made reference to ingrained, even genetic, human differences (Knight 1990, p. 87). The point is, however, that they explicitly denied the assumed superiority of the European, racially and cultur-ally, while still projecting an image of mestizo homogeneity.[3]

For Colombia, this indigenista variant on the ideology of *lo mestizo* is much less pronounced, due mainly to the sparseness of the indian population, currently reckoned at about 1 per cent of the total.[4] Instead statements tend to emphasize a tri-ethnic mix, glossing over differences of race and region. Luis López de Mesa, psychologist, philosopher and intellectual, writing in 1934 on the formation of the Colombian nation, admits that white immigration would tend to 'enrich the qualities of our racial fusion', but the emphasis is as much on the social input of skills and habits as on the 'enrichment of [Colombia's] good stock' (Lopez 1970, pp. 122–3). In his view, while blacks and indians are not seen as an ideal heritage, transmitting certain traits of laziness (Lopez 1970, pp. 19, 97), neither are they roundly castigated for contaminating the Colombian nation: 'creole laziness is conditioned by elements which can be dominated', such as ill-health and undisciplined habits (Lopez 1970, pp. 20–1). Instead, there is a powerful emphasis on mixedness and lack of social distinc-tion. 'We are Africa, America, Asia and Europe all at once, without grave spritual perturbation', and this results in 'an integral [democracy] without distinctions of class or breed' (Lopez 1970, pp. 14, 15). This affirmation of democratic mixedness, while it also marginalizes blacks and indians, diverges from the outspoken condemnation of them characteristic of *blanqueamiento*. Rather the emphasis is on mixed populations, and blacks and indians as such tend to vanish into peripherality, appearing occasionally, like the blacks of the Cauca valley who are 'constantly lazy, almost vegetative' (Lopez 1970, p. 108). There is a compromise in defining national identity: blackness and indianness become marginal and inferior, but too great an emphasis on 'contamination' is avoided since this would lead to an overly negative view of Colombian nationality and its future.

In a more recent book which tries to delineate features of a Colombia social psychology, Rubén Ardila considers the concept of 'race' and rejects it as having no basis in biology. He then slips almost unawares into rejecting its social significance on the same grounds, reinforcing this with the idea that Latin America is a mestizo continent 'for which race has practically lost all meaning'. Colombia is 'definitively a mestizo country', although in some regions 'certain homogeneous groups can be distinguished' (Ardila 1986, pp. 59–62).

Morales Benítez, the Colombian writer and politician asks

When did the mestizo emerge? I have no doubt that this historical
moment is the same as the instant at which people born here after
the Discovery became conscious that these lands belonged to them.
(Morales Benítez 1984, pp. 32–3)

He continues, characterizing 'our artisans and modest carvers' under the
domination of the Spanish rulers.

There they were, with their rough faces, of irregular shape, sometimes with slanting eyes, some with black layers in their skin, and
with some white colouring, listening to orders. And no one was
to challenge [those orders]. . . . This insolence would not be
tolerated.
(Morales Benítez 1984, p. 34)

Here racial differences are only hinted at by references to phenotypical appearance and are in any case submerged in a common destiny of liberation from
'foreign' domination. The issue of usurpation of indian land by non-indians of
all kinds is casually transformed into the issue of Creole[5] subjugation to
Spanish rule. The trajectory of race mixture is thus intimately linked to the
project of national independence. The 'mestizos' face up against the (foreign)
'whites'.

This ideology clearly has a specific view of the past and of the trajectory of
history. Like that of *blanqueamiento*, it sees mixture and the emergence of
nationhood as intimately linked to the transcendence of a traditional and
backward past, and the progression towards modernization. But with the
glorification of the mestizo as a mixture of black, indian and white, rather than
a whitening of black and indian, the inferiority of the traditional past tends not
to be so strongly associated with blacks and indians. To do so would clearly be
to undermine the basis of the mestizo and the superiority of the hybrid.
Instead, positive qualities of the blacks and indians are proposed: the blacks'
'resilience' and 'vigour', the artistic achievements of past indian cultures and so
on. Also, history tends to be cast as a progressive emancipation from domination (especially foreign domination), whereas *blanqueamiento* maintains a
dominant position for whiteness (and hence by implication for Europe and
North America). Nevertheless, in either case, blackness and indianness are
construed as ultimately belonging to the past and as ultimately to be super-
seded by a generalized mestizo type. The difference lies in the extent to which
blacks and indians are simply 'submerged and hence ignored as particular
ongoing ethnic categories and populations with specific claims and cultures,
and the extent to which they are actively disparaged as inferior.

The ideology of *lo mestizo* can take on the appearance of a falsity or pure
rhetoric. Frequently, it is part of a nationalist platform propagated by political
elites seeking to create a unified basis of support. Glossing over difference is a
fairly transparent strategy in this respect. Yet, as with *blanqueamiento*, ideology
is not an illusion, but is a system of knowledge in dynamic relation to the

power structures of the society, past and present. Race mixture has been and
continues to be a vital and everyday part of Colombian society. A widely
agreed-upon trope in Colombia, and in other Latin American societies, is
'*Todos somos mestizos*' ('We are all mestizos'). Although different people have
different relationships to this statement, it is enunciated by people of all classes
and colours (except perhaps those classifying themselves as indians). Pacific
coast blacks might say this, for example, attributing purity of blackness to
Africans. Their claim to be 'mestizos' could be contested by lighter mestizos
who would classify them as 'blacks', or quite possibly as *negros negros* (black
blacks, i.e. 'real' blacks). Upper-class whites might, on the other hand, claim
to be *blancos* and have that claim contested by others who would affirm, as did
one mulatto informant, that 'to speak of whites in this country is an irony,
because we're all mestizos'. The point remains, however, that race mixture is a
fact and a notion that forms part of everyone's ideas about society and, in
certain circumstances, about themselves. The possibility of surpassing racial
difference by a claim to *lo mestizo* is a real one, even if it is surrounded by
contestation and negotiation.

Thus far, I have outlined two versions of race mixture and their ideologies
of history and progress. They derive from the two sets of interrelated processes – mixture and discrimination – that have characterized the social structures of Iberian society. The argument can be schematized as follows.

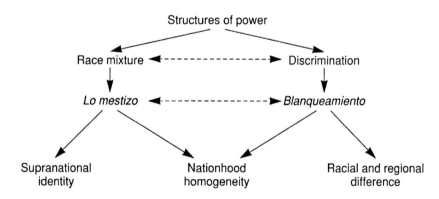

Just as miscegenation is not opposed to discrimination but interweaves with it,
so *lo mestizo* is not simply the opposite of *blanqueamiento*. Not only do they
share a common ground, but the discourse of *lo mestizo* can easily slip into that
of *blanqueamiento* and vice versa. There is no hard and fast line between them.
More importantly, the neutral democratic discourse of *lo mestizo* tends to be
subverted by the hierarchical discourse of *blanqueamiento*. Both harmonize
with people's lives and experiences, but the latter expresses real inequalities
and power differences which the former attempts to transcend. In addition, the
latter also privileges certain categories of people – the lighter-skinned, those
who live in central regions – who are the most powerful and who stand to gain
from the dominance in social practice of this version of the ideologies about

race mixture. In this sense, the ideology of *lo mestizo* is a weaker and more transient discourse.

Lo mestizo, blanqueamiento and the black minority

The black population of Colombia is by no means a homogeneous or easily defined category. Blacks concentrate in various different regions which have been affected differently by both processes of mixture and discrimination. Thus, for example, blacks in the Pacific coast region constitute 80–90 per cent of the population, have experienced relatively little race mixture and have been and still are subjected to powerful discriminations. Blacks on the Atlantic coast are a minority and are much more mixed. Patterns of discrimination are also less clear cut. Thus the definition of 'black' is ambiguous – although less so in areas like the Pacific coast – and there may easily be discrepancies between claimed and ascribed identities of 'black'. Bearing in mind these complexities – which are of importance for how racial inequality may be challenged – blackness with respect to ideologies of *lo mestizo* and *blanqueamiento* has a specific position. Blacks may be actively disparaged as primitive, inferior, irresponsible, lazy and so on; or they may be praised as the stalwart labourers of colonial and postcolonial society, whose valuable inputs into the emerging mestizo stock may be seen as toughness and resilience or perhaps as 'expressive warmth' or a certain magical religiosity (Morales Benitez 1984, p. 61). In either case, as noted above, *blanqueamiento* as the more powerful ideology tends to cast blackness in an explicitly inferior light. In short, blacks are constructed as a forgotten, inferior and residual element in the national panorama. In Friedemann's (1984) words, they become 'invisible'. As Friedemann has shown at some length (1984; see also Friedemann & Arocha 1986), this invisibility is sustained institutionally. Despite the large black population that exists in Colombia, in the field of the humanities, studies of blacks are a minority interest. The vast majority of anthropological and archaeological studies concentrate on indians: according to Friedemann (1984, p. 538), between 1936 and 1978, 271 individuals became professional anthropologists – only 5 have worked on blacks. The reason for this discrepancy lies, I think, in the ideology of *lo mestizo*. In terms of archaeological study, indian culture can be seen as an artistically rich and complex input into Colombian culture: it is part of the glorious heritage of *lo mestizo*. Indians also form an attractive target for contemporary investigation because of their apparent separateness from the national social system.[7] Culturally (though not of course politically) they appear to stand outside it – the more 'authentic' they are, the more they are apart. In this sense, they can be seen as outside the entire ideology of race mixture. For the academic community, they can constitute the exotic, foreign, anthropological 'other'.

Blacks, on the other hand, fulfil this role less easily. Their culture does not have the exotic 'Africanness' of some aspects of Cuban or Brazilian black culture; they simply appear to have a variant of 'Colombian' culture. Put another way, blacks are seen culturally as just one part of a mestizo nation (ideology of *lo mestizo*). Hence the remark reported by Friedemann from an anthropological colleague to the effect that the study of blacks was not 'anthropology' (Friedemann 1984, p. 509). To the extent that more evaluative ideologies of *blanqueamiento* penetrate the academic community, black culture can also be subject to denigration as an 'inferior' variant of Colombian culture.

In terms of archaeology, blackness is not considered to have a history in the same way as indianness. Its archaeological history is seen as entirely located in Africa, history 'lost' or at least severely fragmented when Africans came to the New World. Of course, specialists in black studies make a point of rediscovering this history (e.g. Escalante 1964, Friedemann & Arocha 1986), but its relevance to Colombian nationhood and its historical roots are generally construed as less significant than indian history.

Institutional support given to the interpretation of indian culture, past and present, can have various effects. Representation of the glories of the indian past can legitimate a sense of identity and claims to ethnic continuity. It can also draw attention away from current problems and evoke disparaging comparisons between then and now. Contemporary studies may avoid these problems and focus on current claims and inequalities. Even these, however, can have the effect, albeit unintended, of encouraging the 'museumification' of indian cultures. Thus representations of the past and present can feed into the politics of domination.

For blacks, the situation is rather different, since this institutional support is largely lacking. For them, the cultural politics of domination occur, on the one hand, by condemning blacks and black culture as inferior (ideology of *blanqueamiento*) and, on the other, by denying that these people have any specific problems – such as racial discrimination – or that their culture has any real specificity (ideology of *lo mestizo*).

Contesting these ideologies is a difficult process, one which several black organizations (Gutiérrez Azopardo 1980, p. 87) and black and non-black individuals nevertheless attempt. Strategies include the *reivindicación* (reclaiming) of black history and black culture through investigation and publication, and the documentation of racial discrimination in the economic, political and cultural realms. However, these strategies encounter numerous obstacles.

The classic charge against someone, black or white, who attempts to bring up the issue of blacks and racial discrimination is, ironically enough, that of racism or more usually 'racism in reverse'. This appeals precisely to the notion, implied in claims of a Latin American 'racial democracy', that Colombia is basically a homogeneous nation racially speaking, that black Colombians are like any other Colombians, that although mere differences of skin colour exist people are blind to them, because after all *'todos somos mestizos'*. If poverty is a problem, it is a problem for blacks, whites and mestizos, and to concentrate specifically on blacks is to favour them unfairly over other equally deserving candidates. Thus by appealing to the ideology of *lo mestizo*, an attempt is made to declare as false this challenge to the ideology of *blanqueamiento*.

A second problem, although some would not construe it as such, also stems from the ideology of *lo mestizo*. I emphasized above that 'ideology' did not simply mean false rhetoric or illusion. Race mixture does exist and one of the characteristics of Iberoamerican societies is that racism against blacks is not thoroughgoing. Channels exist for upward mobility which, as long as it is individualistic and entails conformity to the cultural *mores* of the non-black world, is accepted by non-blacks:[8] channels exist for blacks to form unions with non-blacks, giving birth to lighter-coloured offspring. The implications of this are threefold. First, the differential impact of this process over time and space has created the diversity of blackness and black identity in Colombia, undermining simple solidarities. Second, appeals to the ideology of *lo mestizo* are strengthened: blacks are the same as other Colombians, they can be successful, they can intermarry. The question of how many and under what circumstances is ignored. Third, blacks themselves may take this path. Rather than challenging the devaluation of blacks and black culture, they may take advantage of the opportunities open to them which inhere in the ideology of *lo mestizo*. In doing so, not only do they leave uncontested the ideology of *blanqueamiento*, but also they actually appear to endorse it (whether or not their own motives are shaped in this way) by apparently distancing themselves from blackness.[9]

The third problem underlies the second. The ideologies of both *lo mestizo* and *blanqueamiento* are hegemonic. Many blacks basically endorse images of the inferiority of blackness. This is more than 'false consciousness', it is embedded in the structure of society. Many blacks are in the lowest-ranking strata and regions of the society: therefore blackness and black culture are strongly associated with poverty, ruralness, peripherality and all that these imply. Stereotypes constructed around blackness which emphasize laziness, lack of ambition, a fun-loving and irresponsible nature – images often projected on to subordinates by a dominant population – are partially accepted by some blacks (Wade 1984, 1993). Challenging ideas about the inferiority of blackness is thus hampered by the self-evident nature of the social position of many blacks and their partial concurrence in the morally evaluative stereotypes that are constructed around this. Alongside this, the ideology of *lo mestizo* penetrates as well. Thus many blacks say that racial discrimination is a negligible or minor factor in their lives, that colour differences are unimportant, that opportunities are open to them on an individual basis, that marriage partners are decided by 'personal' factors alone (rather than 'social attributes').

Conclusion

The double construction of the past as both 1) an era of blackness and indianness leading towards a whiter present and future, and 2) a time of general democratic mixing, setting the stage for a contemporary state of mixedness, at once subordinates blacks and denies that subordination.

These representations are articulated through the twin ideologies of *lo mestizo* and *blanqueamiento* which, deriving from the historical structures of the society, constitute systems of knowledge with which people apprehend their reality and against which they struggle in order to change it.

Notes

1 These processes are documented in a wide variety of sources (e.g. Mörner 1967, Lockhart & Schwartz 1983).
2 This territory included roughly what is today Colombia, Panama and Ecuador.
3 Knight (1990) notes that some positions in the indigenista camp veered away from the glorification of the mestizo towards the cult of Indianism proper.
4 Censuses of 1912 and 1918, the last to include racial categories, put the indigenous population at about 8 per cent of the total. The 1985 census did enumerate the indigenous population, arriving at a total of about a quarter of a million individuals, out of a total of some 28 million people.
5 Creole refers to a person born in Latin America, as opposed to an immigrant from Europe. It was often used to refer to locally born Spanish people, but could also designate anyone born locally.
6 Zambo refers to an indian–black cross. *Tente-en-el-aire*, literally 'keep yourself in the air', is a name drawn from the eighteenth-century *casta* nomenclatures: it designated someone who was going neither up nor down the hierarchy, but was 'in mid-air'.
7 This can be seen as partly a result of past patterns, since in the colonial period indians had a different legal status from blacks. They were officially decreed to belong to a different 'republic' and they could not legally be enslaved. The efficacy of these decrees was, of course, dubious to say the least, but it cannot be denied that indians had the basis for a legal separation from the non-indian world.
8 Fernandes (1969) terms this a system of 'accommodation'.
9 Banton (1967) recognized this many years ago.

References

Ardila, R. 1986. *Psicología del hombre colombiano: cultura y comportamiento social*. Bogotá: Planeta.
Arroyo, M. A. 1953. *El Cauca es así*. Popayán: Editorial Universidad.
Banton, M. 1967. *Race Relations*. London: Tavistock.
Bowser, F. 1972. Colonial Spanish America. In *Neither Slave nor Free: freedmen of African descent in the slave societies of the New World*. Cohen, D. & J. Greene (eds), 19–58. Baltimore: Johns Hopkins University Press.
Bushnell, D. 1954. *The Santander Regime in Gran Colombia*. Newark, DE: University of Delaware Press.
Camacho Perea, M. 1962. *El Valle del Cauca: constante socio-economico de Colombia*. Cali: Imprenta Departamental.
Comisión Corográfica 1958. *Jeografía física i política de la Nueva Granada*. Bogotá: Banco de la República.
Diez, J. A. 1944. *Itinerarios del tropico*. Quito: Editorial Industria.
Escalante, A. 1964. *El negro en Colombia*. Bogotá: Facultad de Sociología, Universidad Nacional.

Fals Borda, O. 1979. *Historia doble de la costa*, Vol. 1. *Mompox y Loba*. Bogotá: Carlos Valencia Editores.

Fernandes, F. 1969. *The Negro in Brazilian Society*. Translated from the Portuguese by J. D. Skiles, A. Brunel & A. Rothwell and edited by P. Eveleth. New York: Columbia University Press.

Foucault, M. 1980. *Power/Knowledge: selected interviews and other writings, 1972–1977*. Brighton: Harvester Press.

Friedemann, N. de 1984. Estudios de negros en la antropología colombiana. In *Un Siglo de Investigación Social: antropología en Colombia*, Arocha, J. & N. de Friedemann (eds), 507–72. Bogotá: Etno.

Friedemann, N. de & J. Arocha 1986. *De Sol a sol: génesis, transformación y presencia de los negros en Colombia*. Bogotá: Planeta.

Gómez, L. 1970. *Interrogantes sobre el progreso de Colombia*. Bogotá: Colección Populibro.

González Ochoa, G. [1942] 1960. La raza antioqueña. In *El pueblo antioqueño*. Medellín: Universidad de Antioquia.

Graham, R. (ed.) 1990. *The Idea of Race in Latin America, 1870–1940*. Austin: University of Texas Press.

Gutiérrez Azopardo, I. 1980. *La historia del negro en Colombia*. Bogotá: Editorial Nueva América.

Helg, A. 1990. Race in Argentina and Cuba, 1880–1930. In *The Idea of Race in Latin America, 1870–1940*, Graham, R. (ed.), 37–69. Austin: University of Texas Press.

Humphreys, R. A. (ed.) 1940. *British Consular Reports on the Trade and Politics of Latin America*. London: The Royal Historical Society.

Jaramillo Uribe, J. 1968. *Ensayos sobre historia social Colombiana*. Bogotá: Universidad Nacional.

Juan, J. & A. de Ulloa [1758] 1772. *A Voyage to South America*. Translated from the Spanish by J. Adams. 3rd edn. New York: Alfred A. Knopf.

Knight, A. 1990. Racism, revolution and *indigenismo*: Mexico, 1910–1940. In *The Idea of Race in Latin America, 1870–1940*, Graham, R. (ed.), 70–113. Austin: University of Texas Press.

Lockhart, J. & S. Schwartz 1983. *Early Latin America*. Cambridge: Cambridge University Press.

López de Mesa, L. 1970. *De cómo se ha formado la nación colombiana*. Medellín: Ed. Bedout.

Mollien, G. 1824. *Travels in the Republic of Colombia, 1822–1823*. London: C. Knight.

Morales Benítez, O. 1984. *Memorias del mestizaje*. Bogotá: Plaza y Janes.

Mörner, M. 1967. *Race Mixture in the History of Latin America*. Boston: Little Brown.

Rout, L. 1976. *The African Experience in Spanish America: 1502 to the present day*. Cambridge: Cambridge University Press.

Skidmore, T. 1974. *Black into White: race and nationality in Brazilian thought*. New York: Oxford University Press.

Skidmore, T. 1990. Racial ideas and social policy in Brazil, 1870–1940. In *The Idea of Race in Latin America, 1870–1940*, Graham, R. (ed.), 7–36. Austin: University of Texas Press.

Wade, P. 1984. Blacks in Colombia: identity and racial discrimination. Unpublished Ph.D. thesis, Department of Social Anthropology, Cambridge University.

Wade, P. 1993. *Blackness and Race Mixture: the dynamics of racial identity in Colombia*. Baltimore: Johns Hopkins University Press.

5   From Eden to limbo: the construction of indigenism in Brazil

ALCIDA RAMOS

> The Indian became important for the English mind, not for what he was in and of himself, but rather for what he showed civilized men they were not and must not be.
>
> (Pearce 1988, p. 5)

The good, the bad and the dead

The history of Indian–white relations in Brazil has run along two parallel lines: one, manifested in the rhetoric of the 'noble savage' living in a placid Eden of innocence and freedom; the other, revealed in the attitude of the superior white whose moral responsibility it is to rescue the Indian from barbarism.[1] We may call the former the 'edenic' discourse of indianism, and the latter the 'civilizing' discourse of indigenism. This is simply a classificatory device to help put across some ideas on the subject, for the two positions are opposed only in appearance. We cannot forget that while the edenic discourse proclaimed the imaginary Indian the enviable representative of Paradise on Earth, flesh and blood Indians were being killed, plundered, goaded into Christianity and denied their ethnic identity. At the same time, while a whole host of civilizing agents, from missionaries to royalty, writers and administrators, proposed the transformation of the Indians into 'civilized whites', these same Indians were being physically exterminated or shoved into the lowest ranks of the social hierarchy. Indeed, both discourses are part and parcel of the edifice of inequality that has characterized the relationships between Europeans and indigenous populations since 1492. I shall focus on these two seemingly conflicting, but in fact complementary, visions of the Indian, calling attention to the purposes each one has served in the effort to construct a nation out of Brazil.

The edenic discourse

From Caminha, Pedro Alvares Cabral's scribe during the voyage that led to the discovery of Brazil in 1500, to Sting, the rock star who in 1989 campaigned for the preservation of Amazon jungle and Indians, the edenic discourse, with its many versions of the 'vision of Paradise' (Buarque de Holanda 1977), has been a constant ingredient in the construction of the complex imagery surrounding the figure of the Indian. From the Renaissance to postmodern times western imagination has been prodigal in fantasies exploring the ever-present theme of the Indian as a natural phenomenon.

In crossing the centuries, the rhetoric of Paradise on Earth has changed emphases, styles and tropes, but has maintained the tone of contemplative fascination for the exotic. It is, essentially, the discourse of the distant white who does not live at close quarters with the Indians and does not compete with them for resources, natural or otherwise. I shall refer briefly to four moments of the edenic discourse: the first moment of bewilderment at discovery, the nativistic moment in the eighteenth century, the indianist moment in the nineteenth century, and the ecological moment in the twentieth century.

Innocence found

The first response of the Portuguese who arrived on the coast of Brazil in 1500 was to praise the benign climate, the fertility of the soil and the innocence of the Indians. In this new world of neither cold nor hot weather, 'anything you plant will grow', in Caminha's colourful expression: no winters, no scarcity, no plagues, no persecutions. This perfect landscape was prodigally supplemented by natives who seemed to be the brown-skinned sweet version of Adam and Eve before the fall, displaying unselfconscious nudity and everything else that goes with Paradise. Sixteenth-century Europeans gorged themselves on this paradisical scene just long enough to establish their definitive presence. The idyllic interlude lasted but a few decades. It was an ephemeral reaction that did not restrain the western impulse to conquer both nature and people. Soon the initial edenic rhetoric gave way to the civilizing discourse that was built on the precise opposite of Paradise – savagery, backwardness, paganism, brutality. The following century witnessed the most aggressive moves against indigenous populations. Among these were the attacks on coastal villages by settlers, the catechist campaigns by Jesuits and other missionaries, and the westward expeditions under the leadership of the so-called 'Bandeirantes' (Morse 1965). These were adventurers from the coastal settlements who, under the banner of protecting and widening the colony's borders, were in fact promoting the first massive gold rush in Brazil, devastating Indian villages as they found them, and thus sealing the fate of whole populations for centuries to come. In that period entire indigenous peoples were exterminated either by arms or by bacteria. By the beginning of the eighteenth century, the coastal Tupinambá, the first Indians to meet the Portuguese, were extinct. The same happened to the Tapajós of the Amazon. The 1600s were not especially strong in producing edenic discourses. This was a time for conquest, not 'poetry'.

Nativism and nationalism

The nativistic moment in the eighteenth century and the romantic moment in the nineteenth century are best depicted in paintings, music and especially in literature. The difference between them is subtle and may even be somewhat artificial, but it is useful in the attempt to identify the similarities and differences in the political and ethical modes of those two centuries regarding the Indian issue.

In a sense, the nativistic era reflects the shock waves of the Enlightenment as they reached Brazil: the fascination with the unspoiled native, the aesthetic value of nobility of character,[2] the spiritual potential of the pristine purity of the New World. Perhaps the most outstanding example, with its religious overtones, is the poem entitled *Caramuru*, first published in Lisbon in 1781 by José de Santa Rita Durão. An Augustinian friar, he is identified with the eighteenth-century group of baroque poets from the Province of Minas Gerais. The poem is an epic about a Portuguese man, Diogo Alvares Correia, who went native and married Paraguassu, an Indian woman who went white. These characters are allowed to cross the cultural boundaries only because the Indian is portrayed as a dignified, courageous, monogamous, impeccably honest figure, unspoiled by greed or any other sin. In the poem Diogo Alvares, already a noble white, becomes even nobler with his metamorphosis into *Caramuru*. Never mind that Durão, in the process of glorifying his hero, did a thorough cleaning job of his character, removing embarrassing stains such as accepting the sexual favours of young Tupinambá girls, or passing on to the Portuguese Crown large plots of land he acquired through his marriage to Paraguassu (Candido 1967, pp. 201–2). Diogo Alvares, the Portuguese colonizer who, shipwrecked, landed on the coast of Bahia in the first half of the sixteenth century, becomes *Caramuru*, the hero in Paradise (Barros 1968).

The real Diogo Alvares seems to have been anything but a nobleman. In his stern demystification of Caramuru, Mendes de Almeida (1876, p. 21) points out his obscure origin, writing 'it is not certain whether he was the survivor of a shipwreck, a convict, or a deserter from Crown or private ships'. Furthermore, Mendes de Almeida attributes what he calls 'this legend or pious fraud' (Mendes de Almeida 1876, p. 18) to the efforts of Alvares' apparently numerous illegitimate offspring (he also had three legitimate daughters all married to non-Indian men) to erase the 'irregularity of their origin' (Mendes de Almeida 1876, p. 21). Caramuru, he says, 'had no greater importance than that which resulted from his knowledge of the Indians' language; but like him there were others on the shores of Brazil' (Mendes de Almeida 1876, p. 21).[3]

Paraguassu, in turn, when taken to the Court in Paris, brings along the innocence and purity of the Indian and adds to these virtues the indispensable qualities of wifely dedication and fidelity, all enhanced by a christianized persona. 'Like the most authentic heroine of European tradition', she is depicted in white and rosy skin, rejecting the nudity of her companions, and displaying a pious concern for the spiritual fate of her fellow Indians.[4] In changing her name to Catarina and thus becoming a homonym of both the Queens of France and Portugal, she completes her civilizing process 'in an opposite and symmetrical movement' to that of her husband. They are together in 'the same ideal situation of ambiguity' (Candido 1967, p. 208), ideal, that is, for the rhetorical style of Durão's century and for the reinterpretations of the romantic times that followed.

The couple represent the best of two worlds. But the fusion of these worlds is only possible because the whites – represented here by Friar Durão – projected their own ideal virtues on to the Indians. The proclaimed nobility of the whiteman was thus enhanced by his social and sexual intercourse with the noble savage, so long as that savage was domesticated by his own religion. Only thus was it possible to create *Caramuru*, the European with the strength of character and psychological malleability that was required to colonize the new land. This image of the easily adaptable Portuguese who populated the colonies in Africa and America, thanks to his lack of prejudice toward black and Indian women, was to remain in the ideological apparatus of Portuguese colonization for centuries to come.

Caramuru is the quintessence of the edenic discourse at the service of exalting the feats of the colonizing whites to the benefit and appreciation of the colonized Indians. Whites and Indians are thus inextricably intertwined in the same historic destiny, the destiny of an emerging nation. It is not a mere coincidence that 'the Portuguese dominion in Brazil was showing the first signs of declining, and the colonial system itself was beginning to run into contradictions with local realities' (Candido 1967, p. 202). In such a context, the literary elite of the colony was encouraged to promote a 'Brazilian historical tradition, in order to justify the political individuality of the country' (Candido 1967, p. 203). On the other hand, it may also be of some relevance that the author, Durão, lived for many years in Italy and in Portugal, where he died. Proximity to the epic traditions of those countries and distance from the interethnic realities of Brazil may well have influenced his choice of rhetorical mode – the heroic epic – and vision of cultural harmony – Indians and Europeans jointly building a common world.

In the following century, we find the romantic moment also glorifying the Indian from a distance. Two major writers, José de Alencar and Gonçalves Dias, have become the main representatives of indianism, a literary movement whose thrust was the building of the Brazilian nation, now as a conscious enterprise. Their endeavour was no longer to show the nobility of the Portuguese, but the vitality of the Brazilian. Such vigour was not imported from Portugal, but inherited from the natives of the land. From the Indians –

or what they imagined the Indians to be – they extracted the necessary ingredients, material and otherwise, in order to brew a nationalist concoction with a unique, non-European flavour.

Yet, in making ample use of the exotic, these writers aroused the reader's imagination not with ethnographic accuracy, but with the equipment which they knew how to handle: European imagery heavily shaded with erotic details, unusual surroundings, or unbelievable displays of bravery. Gonçalves Dias, in his indianist poems, excels in this formula, by mixing female beauty, minuscule women's aprons, grandiose landscapes, and intrepid male courage. It is, in Candido's expression, a 'cocktail of medievalism, idealism, and fantasied ethnography'. His poem, I-Juca Pirama, about the lament of a brave Tupi prisoner facing his own death, is, continues Candido, 'one of these undisputed things which have been incorporated into the national pride, it is the very representation of the country, such as the magnitude of the Amazon, the Ipiranga cry [of Independence], or the national green and yellow colours' (Candido 1969, p. 85). Candido praises Gonçalves Dias as a great poet, 'in part for his capacity to find in poetry the natural medium for the feeling of fascination for the New World of which Chateaubriand's prose had been up until then the main interpreter' (Candido 1969, p. 84).

José de Alencar's O Guarani (1857) is about a Tupinambá Indian, Peri, whose dedication to his white masters saves them from the rage of his own people, warriors and cannibals. He falls in love with the young daughter, Ceci, but, unlike Caramuru, no sanctioned union between them is possible. Interethnic romance is always a one-way affair: white male and Indian female, but never the other way around, white female with Indian male.[5] Heroically, he rescues her from a portentous flood and ends up platonically beside her on the frond of an uprooted palm tree, drifting down the torrent. Almost as strong as the natural elements, Peri is the epitome of abnegation, altruism and strength of character. Yet, he is barred from white society as an equal.

Alencar dedicated two more books – Iracema (1865) and Ubirajara (1874) – to the subject of indianism, in search of a truly Brazilian character and distinct identity. His influence in the national imagination has been considerable, as the following passage by Antonio Candido indicates:

> Just as Walter Scott fascinated Europe's imagination with his castles and knights, so did Alencar establish one of the most cherished models of Brazilian sensitivity: that of the ideal Indian, as developed by Gonçalves Dias, but projected by him onto daily life. The Iracemas, Jacis, Ubiratas, Ubirajaras, Aracis, Peris – who every year for about a century have disseminated the 'genteel bunch of lies' of indianism through baptismal fonts and registry offices – translate the deep will of the Brazilian to perpetuate the convention that gives to a country of mestizos the alibi of a heroic race, and to a nation with a short history the depth of legendary times.
>
> (Candido 1969, p. 224)

From Chateaubriand to Sting

Both the nativistic and the romantic modes use Indian imagery to construct identities, be they of the indomitable colonizer or of the proud nationalist. In the twentieth century we find a rather sardonic version of these trends during the modernist movement of the 1920s. The figure of the Indian Macunaíma, Mário de Andrade's amoral hero (*herói sem caráter*), is a symbol of the self-derision that was often used by Brazilian nationalists to mark them off from European hegemony.

There is also a more recent trend which cuts across national boundaries and focuses on environmental preservation. The present-day ecological movement shares with the nativistic and the romantic discourses two main features: the emphasis on the 'naturalization' of the Indian and the affirmation of his purity. A latter-day edenic discourse in search of a threatened Eden, the ecological movement, at its most naive presentation (although relatively recent, the movement already shows considerable internal differences), takes the Indian as a monolithic figure, the companion-cum-keeper of both beasts and plants; as an integral part of nature, he is also threatened and needs protection. And thus the protector, preferably European, comes full circle in five hundred years: from invader to saviour. Widely publicized international campaigns involving prominent political figures, show-business stars, religious leaders and news media experts cry out for the saving of Amazonia and, as an extension of it, the Amerindians. The 1989 European tour by the rock singer Sting and his indigenous companion, the Kaiapó Chief Raoni, an old man turned into a sort of Bird of Paradise for the media, with his indefectible lip-plug, stirred once again the old romantic feeling of fascination for the New World, this time embedded in a rhetoric of salvation of a Paradise that is being corrupted by the savagery of the whiteman.

The reasoning seems to follow a straightforward exercise in western logic: unspoiled nature is pure; the Indian is part of nature; therefore, the Indian is pure. Such purity then becomes associated with the wisdom that the whiteman once had but has lost on his way to technological progress and with it to the destruction of his environment. Now the whiteman badly needs to recover his lost wisdom in order to preserve, no longer simply a nation, but the planet. The Indian enters this gloomy picture as the unspoiled reservoir of wisdom, ready to be reappropriated by the whiteman. In this trajectory of the edenic discourse going from Paradise Found to Paradise Lost the figure of the immanent Indian has been a crucial instrument to the transcendental white. For it is the whiteman who 'finds' Paradise, transforms it to the point of ruining it, and then, again through his volition, rescues the Earth from his own rapacity. As the sovereign agent of the world the whiteman has reduced the Indians to mere hostages of his economic terrorism.

For all the apparently sympathetic and benign inclinations the environmentalist rhetoric – associated with the less sophisticated side of ecological activism – displays toward the Indians, it conceals an element of paternalism and intolerance that can easily come to the fore whenever the Indians betray its expectations. If a good Indian is a pure Indian – and here, as usual, the definition of purity is given by the whites – an Indian who falls prey to western seduction (selling lumber, making pacts with the military, striking deals with corporations) is denigrated and doomed to fall lower than the white wheeler and dealer. An Indian who has sold out is, in short, much less deserving of understanding or forgiveness than a white in the same situation. Assigned the absurd role of the guardian of humanity's reserves of 'purity', the Amazonian Indian becomes charged with the 'white man's burden' in reverse, whether he wants it or not.

The civilizing discourse

Running parallel to this eulogizing eloquence is the civilizing discourse, a series of images of the Indian with as long a history as the edenic discourse, but which exploits traits that are its precise opposite.

The idiom of direct control and its attendant civilizing rhetoric has as its basic premise the inferiority of the Indians *vis-à-vis* the whites. Here the Indians are not the children of Paradise, but the creatures of barbarism; they are either renegades or ignorant brutes. It took a papal bull from Paul III in 1537, declaring them to be humans – and therefore eligible for Christianity – for the West to begin to consider them as such (Bosi 1989).

From the sixteenth century onward, just a few decades after the discovery of Brazil, the Portuguese soon adopted the Aristotelian attitude that the Indians were 'natural slaves'; they might be human, but they certainly were the whites' inferiors, and more suitable for hard work, if properly managed. As it turned out, Indian slavery did not prosper as expected, but indigenous lands were valuable and justified continuous massacres with the help of microbe dissemination. The treatment of indigenous peoples as pests extended well into the twentieth century. It has been routine to many regional settlers, and represents the crudest manifestation of white arrogance and impunity. The history of Indian–white relations, be it early or recent, is crammed with bloody episodes of white atrocities, most of them left unpunished. As late as the 1960s, a Colombian court absolved a group of whites who tortured and killed several Indian men and women on the grounds that the victims did not have the status of human beings.

More subtle but no less effective, missionary action has sustained the notion that the Indians are helpless without white assistance, their customs being so primitive as to endanger their own spiritual salvation. Of these customs cannibalism became the banner for the church's pious intervention. The civilizing discourse benefited immensely from deploring the man-eating habits of Indians such as the Tupinambá, the Indians who inhabited the eastern shores of South America when the Portuguese arrived in 1500. Cannibalism provided perhaps the most potent weapon for European control. It had the power to construct with a single stroke two of the handiest images for the colonizing of the New World: white martyrs and Indian heathens. While martyrdom justified the political domination of the 'cannibals', paganism justified the right to subject the Indians to Christian indoctrination.

Innocence lost

Once the European conquerors got over their first bewilderment at the delights of the newly found Eden, the job of taming the wilderness began. Hardly thirty years had gone by since Cabral's memorable landing on the coast of Bahia, and early traders and settlers were already waging wars against the Indians, enslaving them, looting their resources, and dislodging them from their lands. The arrival of the Jesuits in the mid-sixteenth century, with the mission of christianizing the savages, had a rather ambiguous result. By gathering large numbers of Indians in densely populated settlements, both to protect them and as a convenient strategy for conversion, they provided the white settlers with a ready reserve of cheap or slave labour. Interested in saving the Indians' souls rather than their physical integrity, the Jesuits within a couple of decades had adopted the policy of force instead of the time-consuming techniques of persuasion. The priests José de Anchieta and Manoel da Nóbrega made their name in the history of Brazil with a reputation for extraordinary fervour and determination to spread the true religion among the savages. Both resorted to the expedient procedure of 'placing them under the yoke'. For the sake of turning the Indians into Christians, Nóbrega wrote:

> I also wish . . . to see the heathen subjugated and placed under the yoke of obedience to the Christians, so that we could imprint on them all that we desire. . . . Nothing can be done with them if they are left at liberty, for they are brutish people.
>
> (Hemming 1978, p. 106)

And Anchieta:

> We now think that the gates are open for the conversion of the heathen in this captaincy, if Our Lord God would arrange that they be placed under the yoke. For these people there is no better preaching than by the sword and iron rod. Here more than anywhere, it is necessary to adopt the policy of compelling them to come in.
>
> (Hemming 1978, p. 106)

Catholic priests closely accompanied the westward expansion of Portuguese–Brazilian dominions. They followed the often devastating assaults on Indian lands by the Bandeirantes, seventeenth-century adventurers in search of precious minerals, and turned the camps strewn along the latter's way into permanent sites of white occupation. The Indians were either dislodged or concentrated in large settlements (*reduçoes*).

The next four centuries presented variations on this same theme: taming the Indians in the name of western values, be these religious, political, economic or social. The civilizing discourse took on new local colours, both in terms of time and space, but the message has been strikingly uniform: Indianness is a temporary, undesirable condition, and must be eradicated from a country that is trying to make it into the community of civilized nations. In this endeavour, church and state have divided the task of civilizing and integrating the Indians; their discourses may differ in tone, from religious to secular, but they are both powerful instruments with which to control unwanted differences.

Olivegreen garb and drab redtape

As an active representative of the state in indigenous affairs, the army came later. In 1910 the first national agency for the protection of the Indians was created by an army officer, Candido Mariano da Silva Rondon, a true believer in positivism as a humanist philosophy.[6] Faithful to the Comtean brand of evolutionism, he was convinced of the need to preserve the lives of the indigenous peoples as a necessary condition for them, sooner or later, to decide to abandon their primitive ways of their own free will and embrace western civilization. As a civilizing strategy, Rondon applied some army devices to Indian villages, such as furnishing titles and olivegreen uniforms to Indian men who often had no local legitimacy. It was the era of the village 'captains'. Official indigenism was thus created and the destiny of the Indians was sealed: slowly but inescapably, they were to relinquish their lifeways and integrate into national society.[7] A special status was given to them; they were now considered 'relatively incapable' by law – the Civil Code of 1916 – along with married women and children, a triad disturbingly reminiscent of Aristotle's inferior categories – slaves, women and children. In 1985 married women were elevated to full citizenship, but not the Indians. They continue to be wards of the state. Their first 'tutor', the Indian Protection Service (later replaced by the National Indian Foundation), was born from the Ministry of Agriculture (Gagliardi 1989). Throughout the decades it passed through several other ministries, such as Labour, Industry and Commerce, back to Agriculture, then to War (as the Army Ministry was then called), Interior and, more recently, Justice. In none of these bureaucratic bodies did it feel easy or comfortable; in none did it command enough respect and interest to be given sufficient attention and funding. From the 1960s onwards, it has been steadily downgraded. Not even the humanism and humanitarian intentions of the early Rondon days have survived the decline of this Indian official 'tutor'.

In the 1980s the National Indian Foundation fell to the lowest levels of competence and legitimacy. It became the epitome of white coercion and the favourite target of irate Indian leaders and indignant whites who joined the

Indian cause. Drowning in redtape, the Indian Foundation has been plagued with corrupt presidents who with impunity have depredated indigenous resources, from the transfer of large plots of land to private hands, to the sale of lumber; or with medical doctors who sit around in town offices while entire Indian villages suffer from white-transmitted diseases, such as tuberculosis, malaria or measles. In short, either through outright criminal action or through omission, the Indian Foundation has been more often on the side of the problem than on the side of the solution.

In 1985 the military passed on the federal government to civilians during what was called the 'New Republic', a civic interlude when the Brazilian people's high hopes for better times were only proportional to their later disappointment. The Indian issue was a sort of microcosm of the national climate: great expectations which, one by one, were dissolved into thin air by the surreptitious manoeuvres of politicians and interest groups (in the mining and lumbering business, for instance) for whom indigenous rights were an inconvenience. Amazonia came to the fore once again as the last frontier; its abundant resources were now envisioned as the remedy to the cancerous foreign debt. Backstage, the military planned grandiose projects, such as the *Calha Norte* (North Watershed, or literally, 'North Gutter'), designed to bring development into the northern region, while controlling the international borders, and containing the indigenous populations within small pockets of their original lands.[8] From behind the scene, the military continued in command of the Indian policy which for them is inextricably tied to the development of Amazonia. From the recess of their National Security Council offices the army in particular directed the most important moves by the Indian Foundation: bureaucratic decentralization, the appointment of top-level personnel, and even the prohibition of anthropological research in the northern Indian areas. Under the New Republic, the Indian Foundation was reduced to a mere puppet of the military.

These same military had their Army Minister play the role of *éminence grise* in the Sarney government. That powerful man in olivegreen, Leônidas Pires Gonçalves, on 19 April 1989, the National Day of the Indian, declared that the indigenous cultures, being so lowly, were not respectable. The barrage of criticism that followed in the media forced some counter-messages from other military, but the Minister's crudeness rang throughout the country as an apology for white obtuseness and arrogance.

The civilizing discourse does not appropriate the Indian as an image, but as an essence. He belongs to the Brazilian nation, and, therefore, the powers-that-be can do with him as they see fit, regardless of what he may want for himself. Here the Indians are not only nature's creatures, but also the nation's children. Their 'special' status as relatively incapable beings under the wardship of the state reveals in no ambiguous terms the disparity of power contained in the civilizing rhetoric. Picturing the Indians as children, an old cliché in the indigenist scene, is nonetheless a potent trope in the discourse of the powerful. In metonymic fashion, it wraps the relationship of the national state with its indigenous peoples in a cloak of established truths about the nature of the Indian as well as the civilized. It has been the most recurrent message sent forth to the Indians as the way things are and should be. With a single stroke it delivers two of the cardinal commandments of the dominant interethnic truth: 1) whites, i.e., adults, know what is best for the infantile Indians; 2) for Indians to reach adulthood they must relinquish their Indianness. With such forceful semantic weapons in their hands, the rulers of the country have been very successful in maintaining the Indians under control with little recourse to other sorts of more literal weaponry.

Out of Eden and back again

Neither the edenic nor the civilizing discourse has any concern for what the Indians might be on their own account. The representation of the Indian as either noble or villain requires that he remains mute about himself, a passive figure to be moulded by European ideologies, conflicting as these may be.

The voice of the Indian, if heard at all, is devoid of timbre, is rendered a vague and incomprehensible murmur attached to no specific language, to no recognizable tradition. The anonymity of indigenous utterances serves as background to the dominating voice of the West. Even when speaking the national tongue, usually with a strong accent and incorrect grammar, the Indian's voice is not willingly heard. Cultural misunderstandings apart, much of white interpretation of indigenous discourses is distorted by the undisputed certainty about the superior western way of thinking. Indian languages are not generally acknowledged as 'real' languages with their own logic and lexical richness. In Brazilian Amazonia, for instance, regionals refer to Indian languages as *gíria*, slang, and seem utterly incredulous when told that those languages are as sophisticated as Portuguese. To learn an Indian language is to lose prestige among one's 'equals'. Rather than risking a change of mind about indigenous inferiority were one to penetrate their world, it is safer to perpetuate the comfortable assurance passed on from generation to generation that the Indian is culturally retarded.

As would be expected, this syndrome of white status, derived from his ignorance of indigenous languages, is not limited to Amazonia:

> The problem [with bilingual interpreters] was that to know enough Algonquian to ensure accurate and reliable interpretation they [Virginia colonists] had to be so steeped in Algonquian culture that their very identity as Englishmen, and therefore their political reliability, became suspect.
>
> (Hulme 1986, p. 142)

As unintelligible literally or ideologically, the Indian is more easily discarded as a legitimate voice. One can then speak for him, one can assume the position of knowing what is best for him, and what is best for him is to do as the whiteman says. Since the whiteman is not a monolith, the colonization of the Indian's worldview takes the shape of the specific colonizer, giving rise to the church Indian, the army Indian, the Indian Service Indian, or, more recently, the non-governmental organizations' Indian.[9] Thus gagged, he is then judged to be naive or pure, ignorant or innocent, treacherous or defenceless, depending on one's inclination toward edenism or integrationism.

There are also those who, after contributing to the impoverishment of indigenous traditional cultures, proceed to lament the loss of authenticity, a phenomenon Rosaldo (1989) has aptly called 'imperialist nostalgia'. And by authenticity they mean the naked Indian with a bow and arrow in his hand, savagely living off what nature alone provides. Such a quest for the authentic – here closely associated with the exotic – is never pitched against the civilizing quest. Why the Indian is now covered in clothes, often rags, why he no longer hunts with bow and arrow, or anything else, for that matter, in his badly shrunk and depleted land, are questions that the nostalgic white invader hardly asks and when he does he never links them to the effects of white missionizing and land usurpation. Rather, these questions are dismissed as the result of the Indian's inability to learn how to be civilized. Missionaries, military men and regional shopowners usually provide examples of this type of double standard.

The anthropological discourse is the only one that defines itself as 'relativistic' to the point of even aspiring to reach that recondite chimera, the native's point of view. It is obviously not exempt from its own ideological load. The commitment to reveal the intelligibility of apparently opaque customs has given anthropologists the opportunity to show that even if the Indians do not compete with whites in the production of material paraphernalia, they are quite capable of constructing intellectual structures so complex as to require a long professional training to detect them. Despite the attempts to keep an aura of objectivity around the practice of the discipline, most images created by anthropology, with some outstanding exceptions, are reminiscent of the edenic discourse dressed in modern and strenuously 'unbiased' attire.

The specific brand of anthropology in Brazil combines the quest for scientific competence with the commitment to be socially responsible toward the people studied.[10] What this means is that the anthropologist working with indigenous peoples cannot afford the comfort of being an impartial observer. Since he is, above all, a social actor, he is called for by his peers, public opinion, and the Indians themselves to take stances on the basis of the knowledge he has accumulated in the field. This activism is not free from prejudices. The charge that anthropologists and other 'friends of the Indians' have been responsible for the creation of artificial leaders is not totally unfounded. As old habits die hard, Brazilian anthropologists tend to favour the ideal of the resilient Indian with incorruptible faithfulness to traditional values regardless of the pressures put upon him. Anthropologists are thus not exempt from the charge of creating latter-day heroes who represent the idealized qualities the whites wish they themselves had, especially when corruption, impunity and collapse of legitimacy plague Brazilian citizenry.

The pure Indian is then called upon to speak up, to spread his voice loud and wide in order to say what frustrated whites want to hear. It is especially useful that denunciations of social injustice and exploitation come in the refreshing accent of an internal outsider. Neither a national – for whom protest speeches tend to get rapidly worn out – nor a foreigner – the suspicious outsider with unfailing ulterior motives – the Indian represents to white liberals the privileged position of being both a native and a stranger. As a native he has the right to criticize the nation's rules and rulers, himself their victim; as a stranger he has the desired distance to convert beaten tracks into fresh meadows of political discourse.

The good, stoic, politicized and yet pure Indian is then veiled with a legitimacy as diaphanous as it is ephemeral, for it can quickly turn into contempt if he missteps the narrow line drawn by his white supporters. For this model Indian no concessions are made. Were he to lose his purity by becoming involved in corruption and other civilized vices, he could no longer count on the support of his previous friends.[11]

There is a growing awareness on the part of anthropologists that the Indians are reaching the point of not wanting white spokesmen, of reacting to paternalism, be it from the government, the church, or academia. Not only that, but in various parts of the country Indians are turning to the very means of colonization used by whites, such as mass media, movies and video cameras, to assert their identity and minority rights. Astonished with the fast pace of events in the interethnic arena, anthropologists have been slow to catch up with the changes. First, they have lost the role of spokesmen for the people they study; second, they have not yet woken up to the theoretical implications of the shift in the position of the ethnographer *vis-à-vis* the Indians. Anthropologists are increasingly being summoned to work for the Indians as their interpreters to the national powers. Topics of research are less and less the exclusive interest of the ethnographer. From the moment the Indians ask you what you will do with all those questions and answers, they are making you accountable for your presence amongst them. They will then file you for future reference. What the profession will do with this is still to be seen.

Notes

1 In this respect Brazil is no different from most New World nations with native populations. The literature on Indian images created by whites is vast, but it is worth mentioning works such as Pearce 1953, 1965, Baudet 1965, Fiedler 1968, Smith 1970, Dudley & Novak 1972, Chiappelli 1976, Arinos de Melo Franco 1976, Sanders 1978, Berkhofer, Jr. 1978, Axtell 1981, Pagden 1982, Stedman 1982, Barker, Hulme, Iversen & Loxley 1985, Hulme 1986, Taussig 1987. The extensive treatment this subject matter has deserved shows that the fascination with indigenous otherness is, like the Indians themselves, far from extinct.

2 See White's (1976, p. 184) analysis of the ideological value of the 'noble savage' for eighteenth-century Europe: 'the spokesmen for the rising classes needed a concept

to express their simultaneous rejection of the nobility's claims to privilege and desire for similar privileges for themselves. The concept of the Noble Savage served their ideological needs perfectly, for it at once undermined the nobility's claim to a special human status and extended that status to the whole of humanity'.

3 Historian Varnhagen (1848) is equally critical of the 'Caramuru myth' (see also Marchant 1943).

4 There are remarkable similarities between Paraguassu's story and that of Pocahontas as analysed by Hulme (1986, pp. 137–73). It is also a Brazilian example of the much cherished image of the Indian Princess marrying into white society (Stedman 1982).

5 Stedman (1982) provides several examples of this pattern in North America.

6 There is a fairly large literature on Rondon's life and expeditions to Brazil's hinterland. Among the most detailed are Viveiros (1958) and Botelho de Magalhaes (1942). Rondon and his comrades were active participants in the army *coup* that overthrew the monarchy and installed the Republican regime in Brazil. For the history of positivism in Brazil see Lins (1964).

7 For the first time in Brazilian history the 1988 Constitution grants the Indians the right to maintain their ethnic identity indefinitely, with no reference to integration into the national society.

8 For a critique of the role of the military in Brazilian Amazonia, with special attention to the Calha Norte Project, see Ramos (1990a).

9 For an overview of various of these images of the Indian in Brazil see Ramos (1991); for specific details about non-governmental organizations see Ramos (n.d.).

10 An appraisal of the Brazilian ethnological enterprise can be found in Ramos (1990b).

11 See, for instance, the outcome of Shavante leader Mario Juruna's political career as a House Representative in the early 1980s in Brasilia (Ramos 1988), or the reaction of a non-governmental organization to Tukanoan Indians who, also in the 1980s, had been involved in agreements with a mining company and the military (Ramos n.d.).

Acknowledgements

My thanks to Angela Gilliam for inviting me to present the original of this chapter at the symposium 'The Social Construction of the Past. Representation as Power', AAA Meetings, Washington, DC, 1989. I also thank Mariza Peirano for a generous reading of an earlier version, and Jeremy Beckett for his comments and kindness in improving its English.

References

Arinos de Melo Franco, A. 1976. *O Indio Brasileiro e a Revolução Francesa*. Rio de Janeiro: Livraria José Olympio Editora.

Axtell, J. 1981. *The European and the Indian: essays in the ethnohistory of colonial North America*. New York: Oxford University Press.

Barker, F., P. Hulme, M. Iversen & D. Loxley 1985. *Europe and its Others*. 2 vols. Colchester: University of Essex.

Barros, J. de 1968. *O Caramuru. Aventuras prodigiosas dum Portugues colonizador do Brasil.* Adaptação em prosa do poema épico de Frei José de Santa Rita Durão. Lisbon: Livraria Sá da Costa – Editora.

Baudet, H. 1965. *Paradise on Earth: some thoughts on European images of non-European man*. New Haven: Yale University Press.

Berkhofer, R. F., Jr 1978. *The White Man's Indian*. New York: A. A. Knopf.

Bosi, A. 1989. Vieira, ou a cruz da desigualdade. *Novos Estudos* (CEBRAP) 25, 28–49.
Botelho de Magalhaes, A. A. 1942. *Impressões da Comissão Rondon*. São Paulo: Companhia Editora Nacional.
Buarque de Holanda, S. 1977. *Visão do Paraíso*. São Paulo: Companhia Editora Nacional.
Candido, A. 1967. *Literatura e Sociedade. Estudos de teoria e história literária*. São Paulo: Companhia Editora Nacional.
Candido, A. 1969. *Formação da Literatura Brasileira*. 2 vols. São Paulo: Livraria Martins Fontes.
Chiappelli, F. (ed.) 1976. *First Images of America*. 2 vols. Berkeley: University of California Press.
Dudley, E. & M. E. Novak (eds) 1972. *The Wild Man Within: an image in western thought from the Renaissance to Romanticism*. Pittsburgh: University of Pittsburgh Press.
Fiedler, L. 1968. *The Return of the Vanishing Native*. New York: Stein & Day.
Gagliardi, J. M. 1989. *Os Indios e a República*. São Paulo: Hucitec/EDUSP.
Hemming, J. 1978. *Red Gold*. London: Macmillan.
Hulme, P. 1986. *Colonial Encounters. Europe and the native Caribbean 1492–1797*. London: Methuen.
Lins, I. 1964. *História do Positivismo no Brasil*. São Paulo: Companhia Editora Nacional.
Marchant, A. 1943. *Do Escambo à Escravidão*. São Paulo: Companhia Editora Nacional.
Mendes de Almeida, C. 1876. Sobre a história patria. *Revista do Instituto Histórico e Geográfico Brasileiro* 39, 5–24.
Morse, R. (ed.) 1965. *Bandeirantes. The historical role of the Brazilian pathfinders*. New York: Alfred A. Knopf.
Pagden, A. 1982. *The Fall of Natural Man: the American Indian and the origins of comparative ethnology*. Cambridge: Cambridge University Press.
Pearce, R. H. 1965. *The Savages of America: a study of the Indian and the idea of civilization*. Baltimore: Johns Hopkins University Press.
Pearce, R. H. 1988. *Savagism and Civilization: a study of the Indian and the American mind*. Berkeley: University of California Press.
Ramos, A. R. 1988. Indian voices. Contact experienced and expressed. In *Rethinking History and Myth*, Hill, J. (ed.), 214–34. Urbana: University of Illinois Press.
Ramos, A. R. 1990a. An economy of waste. Amazonian frontier development and the livelihood of Brazilian Indians. In *Economic Catalysts to Ecological Change*, 161–78. 39th Annual Conference, Center for Latin American Studies, University of Florida, Gainesville, Working Papers.
Ramos, A. R. 1990b. Ethnology Brazilian style. *Cultural Anthropology* 5, 452–72.
Ramos, A. R. 1991. A hall of mirrors. The rhetoric of indigenism in Brazil. *Critique of Anthropology* 11, 155–69.
Ramos, A. R. n.d. The hyperreal Indian. Unpublished ms.
Rosaldo, R. 1989. *Culture and Truth*. Boston: Beacon Press.
Sanders. R. 1978. *Lost Tribes and Promised Lands*. Boston: Little, Brown & Co.
Smith, H. N. 1970. *Virgin Land: the American West as symbol and myth*. Cambridge, Mass.: Harvard University Press.
Stedman, R. W. 1982. *Shadows of the Indians*. Norman: University of Oklahoma Press.
Taussig, M. 1987. *Shamanism, Colonialism, and the Wild Man*. Chicago: University of Chicago Press.
Varnhagen, F. A. 1848. O Caramuru perante a história. *Revista do Instituto Histórico e Brasileiro* 10, 129–52.
Viveiros, E. de 1958. *Rondon Conta Sua Vida*. Rio de Janeiro: Livraria São José.
White, H. 1976. *Tropics of Discourse. Essays in cultural criticism*. Baltimore: Johns Hopkins University Press.

6   *Literacy and power in colonial Latin America*

JOANNE RAPPAPORT & THOMAS B. F. CUMMINS

Runa yn(di)o ñiscap machoncuna ñaupa
pacha quillcacta yachanman carca chayca
hinantin causascancunapas manam cananca
mapas chincaycuc hinacho canman himanam
vira cochappas sinchi cascanpas canancama ricurin
hinatacmi canman.

(Salomon & Urioste 1991, p. 157)

(If the ancestors of the people called Indians had known writing in earlier times, then the lives they lived would not have faded from view until now.

As the mighty past of the Spanish Vira Cochas is visible until now, so, too, would theirs be.)

(Salomon & Urioste 1991, p. 41)

As the early seventeenth-century author of this Quechua manuscript tells us, alphabetic literacy exerted a considerable influence on the reconstruction of a native Andean worldview and historical memory under European domination. In this chapter, we examine the role played by alphabetic literacy and the narrative pictorial image in the process of domination of native Andean peoples during the colonial period: how the power of European institutions was constituted and maintained through the spread of different forms of literacy in indigenous communities. Specifically, we examine the process by which visual and alphabetic literacy within the aboriginal community supplanted the primacy of oral tradition, thus determining new forms, contents and modes of transmission of historical thought; how written documents influenced the definition of new forms of political process within and across native communities; and the role literacy played in compressing a range of cultural domains into an overelaborated political sphere and a range of visual genres into a similarly overcondensed medium.

Alphabetic literacy

The backbone of Andean ethnohistorical investigation is traditionally constituted by a corpus of anomalous documents: chronicles, written in Spanish, Quechua or some combination of the two, by elite, educated Indians, and directed toward a primarily European audience (for examples of such writings see Garcilaso de la Vega [1616] 1962, Pachacuti Yamqui Salcamaygua [1613] 1967, Guaman Poma de Ayala [1615] 1980, Salomon & Urioste 1991). On the one hand, these native treatises have been mined as sources of historical evidence for the reconstruction of Incaic social, political, economic and religious organization (Murra 1980). On the other, they have been analysed as literary texts, as examples of indigenous efforts at communicating native concepts and values using a foreign idiom and medium (Adorno 1982, 1986).

In this chapter we take a different approach, concentrating on legal documents – land-titles, wills, royal decrees, dispute records – as opposed to book-length narrative histories. It is more properly within the legal document, accessible to native authorities and carefully guarded for posterity by them, that the power of history is codified according to Spanish linguistic and legal criteria, filtered through the institution of private property, Spanish notions of heredity, and colonial definitions of the nature of the process of transmission of land, movable wealth, political rule, and prestige. In other words, it is the legal document and not the chronicle that has constituted from the colonial period to the present the major genre of written expression and of communication across the two cultures and of codification and transmission across time of the oral and spatial memory.[1]

Although we perceive literacy as playing a central role in the transformation of native Andean thought and organization, unlike the more evolutionary theorists, such as Goody (1977) and Ong (1982), we do not consider literacy as a neutral technology that moulds thought in predictable ways. In contrast, we look for explanation within the social and political matrix in which specific literacies are employed to comprehend the impact that the written word had on native Andean peoples (Street 1984). It is not so much literacy itself, but the legal idiom in which the contents of documents are cast and thereby legitimized, and the administrative structure through which they are operationalized, that has determined the transformation of Andean society through the domination of the written word. Stern (1982) has asserted that by operating within Spanish legal conventions, even if to secure protection against exploitation for Indians, colonial native authorities relinquished control over their own structures of authority and were forced not only to continue to play by European rules, but also to defend them against challenges to European authority. Similarly, growing native participation in the literate conventions of the Spanish legal world, characterized by its exclusivity and individualization of claims, undermined other modes of expression and of communication, fostering the restructuring and repositioning of formerly oral, pictorial or ritual genres (Gruzinski 1988). Thus, it is not so much the technology of writing, as the impact of its operationalization within a specific colonial context, that is central to our analysis.

Form: orality, literacy, practice

In many ways, colonial-era Spanish writing was fundamentally oral in nature, replicating in space the temporal dimension of oral communication through a refusal to appropriate the economy of expression that characterizes written communication. In other words, colonial writing is constituted, in many cases, by oral communication set down in writing, or by ritual acts described in detail, over and over again.

The clearest example of the orality of colonial-era Spanish writing can be seen in the numerous documents that record the process by which communities were divested of their lands. These documents are especially ubiquitous for the towns around the administrative centre of Pasto, where the native population fell precipitously during the first half-century of conquest, leaving Spaniards with an opening for usurping what they saw as underutilized lands (e.g. ANE/Q 1685; ANE/Q 1693; Padilla, López & González 1977, pp. 40–1). In order that such lands be freed for public auction, public announcement by an Indian crier was necessary. Frequently, the town crier was obliged to repeat his message some thirty times; his words – or a translation into Spanish of them – are reproduced, verbatim, as thirty identical sentences in the documentary record.

Just as orality is reproduced in writing in colonial Latin American documents, ritual practice is relived through its inclusion in the legal record. Once again, Spanish scribes neglected the economy of expression that writing could afford: instead of briefly mentioning that certain rituals took place at designated sites with designated participants, they are described in painstaking detail, over and over again. For example, in the numerous records of disputes over chiefdoms, we are given repeated descriptions of the possession ceremony whereby political authority was bestowed upon a hereditary chief through the ceremonial offering of woven mantles by neighbouring chiefs and the carrying of the chief in procession on a special chair – in Quechua called a *tiyana* – around the plaza (e.g. ANE/Q 1694; ANE/Q 1735a). Spanish holders of tribute-grants called *encomiendas* received their encomiendas in similar ceremonies (ANE/Q 1727a).

What is significant here is that by replicating orality and ritual in writing, Spanish scribes effectively bypassed orality altogether. These texts and ceremonies were originally written, and were later read – or memorized and repeated – in public, only ultimately to be committed to paper again. Here is a situation in which the audience receives the oral text, but knows it will be recorded in writing. The result is that from early on, there is no need to rely upon oral tradition, which begins to lose its validity, and is replaced by written documents. This point will be taken up again later, when we examine indigenous use of written evidence instead of spoken testimony to bolster legal claims.

Furthermore, the replication of selected acts and statements repeatedly in the documentary record would ultimately dictate what future generations would remember about the past. The impact of conventions of documentary writing upon native thought in the colonial period is convincingly recounted by Gruzinski (1988), who details the contents of eighteenth-century community titles fabricated by Mexican Indians, who had used Spanish documents as a model. To jump ahead a few centuries, we should take note of an experience in the indigenous community of Panán, Colombia, where people listening to the anthropologist reading their eighteenth-century land-title listened most carefully when the text of the possession ceremony was read. In nearby Cumbal, the text of the ceremony, which is still practised today, is a central part of oral historians' description of the creation of their reservation (Rappaport 1994). Memory is condensed into those oral and ritual acts that have been set in writing.

Contents: legal documents and social transformation

Colonial-era legal documents codify in the political arena ritual acts that themselves encode political, social and religious referents through the use of geographic and temporal space, experienced through bodily movement (see Connerton 1989). That is, documents reduce multivocal practices to univocal texts by politicizing them, by confining them to the domain of social administration.

A good example of this is the enumeration of boundary markers in the mid-eighteenth century title to the Pasto community of Cumbal (NP/P 1758; NP/I 1758). Cumbal's boundaries, as described in the title, include a number of named boundary markers, as well as natural features of supernatural importance, such as rivers and lakes.[2] The colonial chiefdom of Cumbal, like its twentieth-century counterpart, was organized into a hierarchy of sections, arrayed from north to south in parallel bands of territory. Participation in colonial, nineteenth century, and contemporary political organizations has always been structured according to the territorial hierarchy, with authorities from different sections assuming key administrative positions in a fixed rotational order that corresponds to the path of the sun between the summer and winter solstices, and which also determined participation in festival sponsorship (Rappaport 1988, 1994). Interestingly, the enumeration of Cumbal's boundaries in its title follows precisely the hierarchical order that structures ritual and political life in the community. Nevertheless, in the title, the symbolism of the section hierarchy is condensed into the political domain, and this is how the boundaries have been read by later generations of Indians, who seek ritual referents in other sections of the title, in particular, in descriptions of the possession ceremony whereby land-title was granted to the community, and not in the list of boundary markers (Rappaport 1994).

In other cases, native modes of historical interpretation, aboriginal means of ritually incorporating outsiders into communities, and myths, once encoded in writing, become decontextualized political material that can be reconstituted in the mythic sphere by succeeding generations that have access to documents. Such is the case of the title to the community of Vitoncó, Tierradentro (ACC/P 1708) prepared by the eighteenth-century chief, Don Juan Tama de la Estrella, who legitimized his rule over the community by associating himself in the title with heavenly bodies and with streams, both of supernatural importance in the pre-Columbian period, as well as with conquest-era military leaders, probably themselves participants in shamanic activity. The title to Vitoncó simply states that Don Juan Tama was the 'son of the Star of the Tama Stream', and that he acquired his political authority by triumphing over the neighbouring chief Calambás, taking his head. In an uninformed reading of the title, such information appears extraneous to the central point of the document: the Spanish administration's legitimization of Don Juan Tama's political authority and of Vitoncó's boundaries. The written word has thus politicized formerly multivocal symbols. Nevertheless, these seemingly odd facts probably served as points of legitimacy for Tama in the eyes of his own people. As late nineteenth- and early twentieth-century Páez reread Tama's title, they recontextualized these demythified and politicized symbols within the framework of post-Independence Colombian politico-military leaders, adding to them a mythic flavour that does not correspond to their mythic significance at the time of the writing of the title (Rappaport 1990).

Since these documents are drafted by individuals active in the administration of their communities and are retained and read by them and by their heirs, legal papers exert a great influence on the indigenous community. If we examine the social matrix in which such documents were written, used and transmitted during the colonial period, we will begin to understand how legal writing was so influential in transforming native categories of thought and of social organization.

Legal documents enfranchize the individuals who enjoy access to them. In the colonial-era Pasto Province this meant the hereditary chiefs, or *caciques*, who served as intermediaries between the community and the colonial administration, and who controlled the means of preparing such papers. In the first instance, *caciques* were enfranchized through their monopoly of the technology of writing. In a day and age in which political power was exercised to a great extent through writing, only those who knew how to write, or who were able to communicate with scribes, either in Spanish or through an interpreter, could lay any claim to the reins of power (Phelan 1967, Vidal 1985). Pasto *caciques*, like their Incaic counterparts to the south, were educated in special schools, where they learned to read, to write, and to speak Spanish; such was the case with sixteenth-century *caciques* Don Andrés Guachag y Mendoza of Guaca and Don García Tulcanaza of Tulcán, both of whom were also quite active in the European conquest of the Pacific lowlands (Moreno Yánez 1986). It is no accident that these men produced a greater volume of legal documentation than did their illiterate counterparts and that, correspondingly, their insertion into the colonial political arena impacted so deeply upon their communities.

But it was not only the literate *cacique* who was enfranchized by the legal document. Similarly empowered were those with access to the legal arena through the services of scribes. In some cases, we do not know whether certain *caciques* were literate or not, but we do know that they were able to cement political claims through recourse to writing. Especially interesting evidence in this respect are chiefly wills, which list those objects which their authors perceived as important signs of status during their lives and which, by hereditary transmission, could possibly affect the status of their heirs. Good examples are the testaments of two early *caciques* of Tuza, in what is today Carchi Province, Ecuador. Both Don Cristóbal Cuatin and Doña Catalina Tuza, living at the turn of the seventeenth century, encoded in their wills a series of power objects of Incaic origin, including wooden lacquered drinking-vessels called *keros* (*limbiquiros* in the testaments), silver *keros* called *aquillas* and various types of finely woven cloth called *qompi*, that made it clear to the colonial administration and to their heirs that they had been recognized as authorities by the Incas (ABC/I 1592, f. 1v; ABC/I 1606, f. 2v; both transcribed in Landázuri (n.d.: [Cuatin] 256–9, [Tuza] 282–92)).[3] Here, we must stress the central role played by these Incaic symbols of authority in the process by which the *Spanish* recognized the *colonial* authority of Pasto chiefs, achieved not simply through the possession of such objects, but even more so through their inclusion in a written document. A good indicator of this is the presence in a 1624 will from Túquerres of another pair of *keros*, objects not present in earlier such documents from north of the Inca frontier.[4] The inclusion of Incaic symbols of recognition of political authority in a document written almost a century after the Spanish invasion in a region far to the north of the boundaries of Tawantinsuyu illustrates that it was under European authority that certain Incaic symbols were revalidated and recontextualized in the colonial political arena, and that they were operationalized in part through writing.

Similarly, legal writing revalidated in a new political context certain northern Andean signs of political authority. Thus for example, Don Cristóbal Cuatin's 1592 will lists *caracoles*, or snail-shells, among the objects he valued (ABC/I 1592, f. lv). Even more intriguing is Cuatin's mention of two *mates*, or gourds – similar in function to *keros* or *aquillas* – sold to him by Juan Quaya, principal of Tuza (ABC/I 1592, f. 2r). Quaya is undoubt-edly the same *mindala* or status-trader, cited by Grijalva as having used his special access to trade goods as leverage for usurping political control from an hereditary chief (Grijalva 1937, pp. 81–4; Salomon 1986).

Just as Gruzinski (1988) discovered in his analysis of central Mexican community titles authored by Indians, the northern Andean documentary record contains intriguing references to native-authored documents that bestowed legitimacy upon their owners by virtue of their written character, even if the documents were not recognized as legitimate by the Spanish administration. One example will suffice. Antonio Tandazo Montoya y Minchala, a native of Loja in what is today southern Ecuador, established his legitimacy over the early nineteenth-century Pastos by displaying royal decrees:

> Repreguntado, como dise que todo lo que se le pregunta es falzo, quando resulta de la misma sumaria decia publicamente a los yndios ser casique de muchos pueblos y que traia siete cedulas reales para poder radicarse donde le pareciese y que tambien traia breves pontificios. . . . Dixo: Que es cierto traia consigo siete reales cedulas y que profirio tambien ser casique de muchos pueblos y podia vivir donde mejor le acomodase.
> (ANE/Q 1803, f. 7v)[5]

(Asked again how he could say that all asked of him is false, when the written record states that he publicly told the Indians that he was the *cacique* of many towns, and that he carried seven royal decrees so that he could establish himself where he desired, and that he also carried papal briefs. . . . He responded: That it is true he carried seven royal decrees on him and that he also claimed to be *cacique* of many towns and could live where he was most comfortable.)

Later in the record, we learn that some of these documents were concocted by Tandazo himself:

> Preguntado si eran suyas las bulas viejas que se le han manifes-tado y tambien el papel que empiesa la Asia dibidido y concluye Pasto y doze de mil ochocientos tres, finalizando con la firma que

dice Antonio Montoya y Minchala con su rubrica. . . . Dixo:
Que es cierto que las bulas y pedasos son suyas, y lo mismo el
papel referido y que no lo ha escrito por si sino que se formó de
su orden por un cavallero a quien no lo conose ni sabe su
nombre, porque era pasajero, de quien dice ser la firma y
rubrica, y que el fin fue de poblar el citio de Mataconchoy.

(ANE/Q 1803, ff. 9v–10r)

(Asked if the old bulls which were shown to him were his, and
also the paper that begins with divided Asia and ends with Pasto
12 of 1803, ending with a signature that says Antonio Montoya
y Minchala with its rubric. . . . He responded: That it is true
that the bulls and pieces [of paper] are his, as well as the referred
paper, and that he did not write it himself, but that a man he
does not know, nor does he know his name, formed it under his
supervision, because he was a passenger, and the signature and
rubric are his, and that he did it in order to found a town in the
place called Mataconchoy.)

Despite the fabricated nature of the documentation, the Spanish administration was deeply concerned about the use of the written word to cement
native authority, because they themselves recognized the tremendous force
of authority that the written word wielded within their own system. And
the Indians who responded to these written symbols of political control
had, like the *caciques* who included material symbols of chiefly authority in
their wills, capitulated to a new system of legal legitimization of authority
which, from their perspective as the underdog, crystallized most perfectly
in the symbol of the written word.

Finally, and in a similar vein, officially recognized written documents
bolstered chiefly authority by affording *caciques* the possibility of registering
their control over posts of authority and over community lands in their
wills – in other words, not only the form, but also the contents, of writing
legitimized chiefly status. A number of *caciques* named their political heirs in
their wills (ANE/Q 1736, f. 7r). Don Feliz Quastuza, *cacique* of Guaca,
writing in 1711, stated the following:

Yten declaro que el casicasgo le toca a mi hermano Don Julian de
la Bastida o a alguno de sus hijos y hasta en tanto que parescan
estos que mi hijo Don Bartholome Quastuza lo mantenga como
io lo e tenido.

Yten declaro que para el descargo de mi consiensia que este
casicasgo no le toca a mi sobrino Don Gabriel de la Bastida hijo
de Doña Maria Bastida mi hermana porque su padre fue Don
Joseph Changona Garsia del pueblo de Pimanpiro y asi no le toca

el casicasgo declaro para que conste como tambien lo sauen
todos los principales del pueblo de Guaca.

(ANE/Q 1734, f. 6v)

(I also declare that the chiefdom passes to my brother Don Julian
de la Bastida or to one of his sons and until one of them appears,
my son, Don Bartholome Quastuza, should maintain it as I
have.
I also declare, to ease my conscience, that this chiefship does not
pertain to my nephew, Don Gabriel de la Bastida, son of Doña
Maria Bastida my sister, because his father was Don Joseph
Changona Garsia from the town of Pimanpiro and for this
reason the chiefship does not belong to him. I so declare so that
it is on record and so that all of the principales of the town of
Guaca are aware of it.)

Others, such as Doña Gregoria Chimachanag of Jongovito and Mocondino,
near Pasto, sought out witnesses to prove that at one time there had existed
legal papers documenting her inheritance of the *cacicazgo* (ANE/Q 1765).
Don Ambrocio Fernández Táques declared in his 1713 will that he was
cacique of Taques 'por testamentos de mis antepasados' ('by testament of
my ancestors') (ABC/I 1787, f. 29r). And most telling is the will of Doña
Micaila Puenambas, *cacica* of Guachucal in 1691, who not only refers to legal
documents to ensure that her nephew, Don Juan Bautista Ypialpud, inherits
the chiefship, but also wills him the legal patent of nobility and the royal
provision that she had inherited from her father (ANE/Q 1695, f. 38r).

The increasing centrality of writing in Indians' lives can be traced in these
wills from 1592 to 1759. In the late seventeenth century, *escritorios* or
portable desks begin to appear in testaments.[6] In at least one of these cases,
we even learn what was kept in them, as is outlined in Don Sebastián
Yaputá's 1681 testament, in which the *cacique*'s son is left a locked box:

para que guarde las memorias de las cobransas de los real
tributos.

(ANE/Q 1736, f. 9r)

(So that he keeps [in it] the records of collection of royal tribute.)

Such documents are repeatedly cited in the wills as evidence of ownership of
land; the use of documents to prove land ownership appears to have
depended upon the physical presence of the written word in the hands of the
witness, since possession of title meant possession of the object.[7] A good
example of this is the 1711 will of Don Feliz Quastuza, of Guaca, who was
forced by necessity to deposit title to his land with a Spaniard in Otavalo, in
exchange for a debt and in another instance, was robbed of his titles and,
consequently, of his land:

Yten declaro que tengo otras mas tierras en este Mumiar y
asimesmo en el pueblo de Guaca y como los papeles me los tiene
usurpados Don Gabriel de la Bastida me e quedado yndefenso
mando a mi hijo Don Bartholo si en algun tiempo paresieren con
los mesmos demande y quite las tierras que en ellos mensionare.

(ANE/Q 1734, ff. 3v–4r)

(I also declare that I have other, further lands in Mumiar and also
in the town of Guaca, and as Don Gabriel de la Bastida has
usurped the papers, I am without defences [and] I order my son,
Don Bartholo, that if they should ever appear, he should sue
them and take from them the lands mentioned in [the papers].)

These were expensive papers to prepare: in the early eighteenth century,
Don Mathias Quatimpas of Tusa paid out four mares in exchange for the
cost of preparing an inventory of possessions, a good example of the fact
that access to the written word was confined to the privileged few (ANE/Q
1746, f. 9r).

As we examine the wills, we note that along with the particular brand of
legal writing used by Andean Indians and their Spanish overlords came a
shift in the ways in which land ownership was described. In early testaments, for example, plots were identified by toponyms, sometimes by the
names of the owners of adjacent parcels, but never by a detailed enumeration of boundaries (ABC/I 1592, ABC/I 1787). It is only at the end of the
seventeenth century that the description of boundary markers begins to
appear in the documents, and that they are homogenized so as to comply
with the legal dictates of the dominant society (for the late seventeenth
century: ANE/Q 1747; ANE/Q 1757; for the eighteenth century: ANE/Q
1746; ANE/Q 1734). These transformations are to dominate future readings
of the documents, especially in the nineteenth and twentieth centuries.

Let us turn briefly to how these documents were read by the Indians. For
the most part, they were probably only consulted by a few *caciques* and by
their legal representatives. This is certain in a number of instances in which
the originals have been retained by the community, but are barely legible:

Con la solemnidad nesesaria [Don Simon Mainbas, *cacique* de
Tuza y Puntal] manifiesta vnos ynstrumentos antiquados perte-
necientes a vnas tierras que posee para que de ellas se cirba
Vuestra Merced de mandar que el presente escribano le de vn
tanto de todo lo que se hallare legible porque con las hinjurias del
tiempo se ban consumiendo por lo que so nesesita su refacsion.

(ANE/Q 1757, f. 3r)[8]

(With the necessary solemnities [Don Simon Mainbas, *cacique* of
Tuza and Puntal] submits some ancient instruments belonging

to some lands that he owns, so that Your Honor will order that the present scribe copy over what he finds legible, because with the ravages of time they are being consumed and are in need of repair.)

In other instances, they were read in rituals (ANE/Q 1747, f. 11v). And in others, we know that they were owned by *caciques*, as is evident from the legend of a bound volume of documents held by the *caciques* of Tuza, Puntal and El Angel:

> Contiene este quaderno los ynstrumentos antiquisimos desde el año de quinientos ochenta y seiscientos veinte y nueve, con vna real provision y otros mandamientos de amparo y possecion de las tierras de Mumial en fabor de Don Diego y Don Francisco Paspueles casiques principales de todos tres pueblos de Tusa, Puntal y el Angel: esta en posesion Don Agustin, Don Manuel Tussa: onse fojas.
>
> (ANE/Q 1792)

> (This notebook contains the very ancient instruments [dating] since the year fifteen eighty and sixteen twenty-nine, with a Royal Provision and other writs of protection and possession for the lands of Mumial, in favour of Don Diego and Don Francisco Paspueles, principal *caciques* of all three towns of Tusa, Puntal and E1 Angel: it is owned by Don Agustin, Don Manuel Tussa: eleven pages.)

Legal papers retained by *caciques* were clearly only read in certain legal contexts. And then, their contents were examined for specific reasons, such as to ascertain boundaries or to prove that the chiefdom was inherited properly. In other words, their form and the way in which they were used forced their owners to shift their own vision of space and of time, so that it corresponded more closely to Spanish legal dictates, which emphasized boundaries over (toponymic) essence and chronology over non-linear notions of temporal process.

Printing and the transformation of visual images

On some unrecorded day during the first sixty years of Spanish occupation, an unknown *cacique* from the south coast of Peru was laid to rest according to ancient custom. Although it is one of any number of sixteenth-century anonymous graves and its excavation is a minor footnote in the archaeology of the region, its peculiar contents mark for Andean colonial history one of the principal intersections between historical and traditional forms of knowledge. Along with Andean objects of symbolic importance, a printed papal bull dated 1578 was neatly folded and carefully placed on the *cacique*'s chest (Bird 1943).

There is little reason to believe that the need to possess the document in death meant that the deceased could ever have read it. Nor is there evidence from the burial, apart from the document itself, that the Catholic religion from which the document issued had been fully embraced. Nonetheless, it is highly probable that the document had either been read or explained to the deceased while he was alive. Whatever the case, here, in this burial context, the Andean sense of object and the European sense of text became for a brief moment confused. The bull outlines papal indulgences which could be extended to the deceased to save his soul in the afterlife. But the context in which it was placed indicates that the document did not produce meaning for the dead *cacique* by virtue of its written text, although the text would have been meaningful to any literate person who sought such indulgences. In contrast, the bull was meaningful as a symbolic object which concretely stood for the salvation that it offered.

Certainly, for Indians the papal bull was an exotic thing, like the European glass beads and glazed ceramics which are also found in early colonial native burials. However, just as the European beads and ceramics found a correspondence in Andean culture, thus making them desirable, so too did the written document. In this instance, nevertheless, the correspondence is not so precise because it extends beyond categories of objects to systems of knowledge. The Andean object which could be said to correspond most closely to the document is the *quipu*, a mnemonic device of coloured and knotted strings used in Andean cultures to recall various categories of information and which were also sometimes buried with the dead (Menzel 1976, p. 230). In this burial, then, we can sense the possibility of a confusion between writing and mnemonics in the early colonial period.

The act of writing to communicate presupposes literacy, while mnemonics is based instead on the memorization of facts which are represented in an object. The object itself cannot abstractly communicate knowledge as writing does. Rather, it stands for categories of knowledge which are then specified in relation to memorized data. Thus, the *quipu* and the *quipucamayoc* (the one who has memorized the *quipu*) are not independent of each other in the way that the writer and reader are. The Andean sense of intimacy between object and person generated by this form of recording knowledge also provides a means by which the written European text could be accommodated to Andean sensibilities. A document in this context is not regarded as generic but as specific, and literacy is not a prerequisite for its possession. If the document has been read or its contents explained, then it would continue to signify, not as a written text, but as a visual one which, like a *quipu*, communicates by its form and design information that is already known. In this sense, illiteracy is overcome by applying Andean means of communication rather than European ones. The placement of the papal bull with the deceased thus marks the acceptance of a European object and at some level perhaps the religion to which it referred into the Andean sphere; what is not necessarily accepted at this point, however, is the European understanding of how the form communicates its information.

In this sense the bull does not exactly correspond to the *quipu* because there is no equivalent to writing in the Andes. Hence, its significance is also grounded in Andean notions of the role of other objects in the communication or preservation of knowledge. That is, objects grouped together by virtue of the designs they bore were displayed in tandem on specific occasions to represent events in the past. This is part of the function which the Inca *keros*, *aquillas* and *gompi* textiles listed in the colonial wills filled in the Andean world.[9] The designs on these objects were abstract: the textiles bore chequerboard patterns and the *keros* had geometric incised abstract designs called *tocapu*; the textiles and vessels were gifts presented to the victorious side after battle and the designs on both objects refer to Inca warfare. Thus, specific design elements encoded in objects were used to conjure up specific historical associations, and it is significant that these objects are listed in some of the very early native wills (Albornoz 1967, p. 23).[10]

The papal bull on the dead *cacique*'s chest probably carried a similar sort of meaning for the deceased and as such was in and of itself signified as an object, whether it could be read or not. Its formal appearance as ordered lines of abstract shapes undoubtedly exerted a power within the *cacique*'s communities and then in his tomb.[11]

A much later example demonstrates that documents continued to be perceived in this way by illiterates into the eighteenth century. Written documents continued to be understood as objects in an early eighteenth-century messianic movement among the Páez of Tierradentro, headed by a man who asserted his leadership by virtue of letters he had received from God, but who could not read the letters:

> Estando en la dicha prision el dicho indio dixo sin ser preguntado ablando con este declarante y los demas que auian ydo con Su Merced que si no querian creer que dios le auia ablado le mostraria vna carta que Dios le auia dejado escrita y que le soltasen, la yria a traer y que de lo qual dio noticia a Su Merced dicho señor Gobernador quien mandó lo sacasen de la dicha pricion y que yendo con Su Merced entregase la dicha carta y que pasando con el dicho yndio a otra casa mandó le bajasen vna mochilita pequeña que estaba colgada a la serca de la casa y que abierta la dicha mochila allaron en ella vnos pliegos de papel blanco y que tomando el dicho yndio vno de los pliegos en la mano dixo ser aquel la carta que Dios le auia dejado escrita sobre el altar de la capilla y que asi viesen lo que decia dicha carta

porque el no la entendia y que siendo reconosida por Su Merced
alla era solo vno de los pliegos de papel blanco y que hauienle
dicho [que] no auia en el dicho pliego ninguna cosa escrita lo
pidio y estandolo reconociendo dixo en su lengua señalando la
marca de la imprenta: que aquello era lo que auia quedado
escrito.

(AHT/B 1729, ff. 160r–v)

(While in said prison, said Indian stated in an unsolicited decla-
ration while talking with this witness and the rest of those who
had accompanied Your Honor, that if they did not want to
believe that God had spoken to him, he would show them a
letter that God had written and left for him and if they would
free him, he would bring it. The Governor informed Your
Honor, who sent for him to be taken from prison and, accompanying Your Honor, to deliver the aforementioned letter.
Going with said Indian to the other building he ordered that they
take down a small woven bag which was hanging on the wall.
When the aforementioned bag was opened, in it they found
some sheets of white paper. When said Indian took hold of one
of the sheets he said that this was the letter that God had left him
on the altar in the chapel, and that they would look at what was
written in the letter, because he could not understand it. Once
inspected by Your Honor, it was seen to be simply one of the
several sheets of white paper. When he was told that there was
nothing written on said sheet, he asked for it and examined it
and spoke in his own language, pointing to the water-mark: that
that was what had been written.)

This role as object did not remain static in the colonial world; the power and
meaning inherent in the function of documents and in Andean articles of
symbolic importance such as *keros*, textiles and their designs were not
constant. After 1570, as literacy increasingly became a reality among high-
ranking *caciques*, the concept of the possession of a document moved from
the ritual sphere it occupied in this early colonial burial to the political and
social spheres, in which objects of Andean importance – both land and
symbolic paraphernalia – were legally constituted by their appearance in
documents (Wachtel 1977, pp. 150–1). The written record enfranchised
both the objects and those who possessed them by creating a paper trail by
which ritual action and word were legitimized, as has been documented
above.

   In this context Andean abstract designs, which had supplied part of the
pre-Columbian meaning of the object, were no longer seen as significant
because they could not be transferred from the textiles or the *keros* to the
documents; they could not carry meaning in the written linguistic channel

in the same way that pictographic forms in Mexico did. Perhaps for this reason there is only one Peruvian manuscript that uses Andean forms of representation: Pachacuti Yamqui's *Relación de antigüedades deste reyno del Perú* (Pachacuti Yamqui Salcamaygua [1613] 1967). The main pictorial source for illustrations of the Andes is not Pachacuti Yamqui's opaque *Relación*, but Guaman Poma's *Nueva Cronica i Buen Gobierno* (Guaman Poma de Ayala [1615] 1980), which is consciously based on European book illustrations. On the other hand, Mexican pictorial forms continued to be used in historical and legal documents well into the eighteenth century (Gruzinski 1988).

This is equally true for the information gathered from *quipus*. The historical or statistical information is recorded only in written form in Spanish, based upon a presentation by a *quipucamayoc*, the man who translates the *quipu*. Moreover, all extant records derived from *quipus* are recorded in Spanish; neither an image of the *quipu* nor the language to which it corresponds ever finds its way into a written document. By analogy, all information presented in documents recording testimony of monolingual Quechua speakers is translated into Spanish (Mannheim 1991). Neither the *quipu* nor the original Quechua testimony enters directly into the document as evidence, but is always mediated by the Spanish language. This again is not true in Mexico, where legal documents are written in a number of native languages.

It is this process of translation and writing which impeded any Andean representational form from becoming part of the documentary record, as they did in the documents in the Viceroyalty of New Spain. There, not only are colonial documents concerning land disputes, lineage and inheritance written in both Spanish and native languages such as Nahua, Maya, Mixtec and Zapotec, but also they are sometimes illustrated by modified native pictorial imagery or they are translations of native pictorial forms, glossed in Spanish, Nahuatl, Mixtec and sometimes in all three.[12] These elements allow for the native voice to enter not only into the language of the document, but also into the very structure of the written record.[13] In the Viceroyalty of Peru, in contrast, both Spanish and native legal documents such as land-titles, wills and suits are univocal, all written in Spanish. Only toponyms and proper names of important Andean items are written in a native language, almost always Quechua in both native and Spanish documents.[14] More importantly in terms of imagery, native documents are not amplified or presented through any form of a native representational system, although there had existed an Andean system of representation based primarily on colour and abstract geometric design in which laws, property and history were recorded. But this native system did not enter directly into the documents, as analogous forms did in Mexico: in the colonial Andes, legal documents are not illustrated (Cummins n.d.). The acquisition of literacy in the Andes for conducting colonial political and economic business meant that, unlike in New Spain, there was no longer any place for the native voice. The ability to distinguish word, representational image and symbolic object as separate categories was as important as the acquisition of literacy itself.

The point is that not only did Spanish, as it became the language of Andean colonial documents, replace Quechua, but also the act of literacy did away with Andean forms of representation which were dependent on oral Quechua interpretation. It is perhaps no coincidence, therefore, that the strongest schools of colonial painting developed in the Andes, from Potosí to Popayán. The Andean abstract or schematic representations, which signified in relation to the objects on which they occurred, were completely replaced in the official sphere of colonial native culture by European pictorial representation.

In this new system, an image could operate independently or in relation to a text, but it was not beholden to the text for explanation. Paintings and statues represented almost exclusively religious themes, which in the early colonial period were used as didactic tools to illustrate points of doctrine. But it is also clear that they became important objects in the household belongings of the *caciques*: beginning in the late sixteenth century, chiefly wills record the possession of paintings along with native items such as *mates*, textiles and *caracoles* as valuable items.[15] More importantly the number of paintings increases after the turn of the century, while the native objects such as *keros*, native textiles, *caracoles*, etc. disappear almost completely. At the same time, *caciques* begin to have themselves depicted within the paintings, as the donors.[16] That is, paintings begin to serve as a visual alternative to an important cultural act.

This does not mean that items such as *keros* disappeared from native culture. In fact, they were one of the rare prehispanic forms to continue into the colonial period (Kubler 1961). However, as objects, they were no longer capable of producing meaning in the same way as before the arrival of the Spaniard. It is therefore significant that the decoration on the *keros* changed from abstract geometric designs to pictorial narrative compositions, based on a European style of painting. Moreover, the images depicted the rituals in which the objects were used, in a similar way to the seventeenth-century paintings. The form of decoration was now European, and recorded the act.

Conclusion

Clearly, literacy cannot be understood as a neutral technology, but operates as an instrument of power which impacts native communities differently in relation to specific historical and cultural forms. Complexity of society is not singular; there are multiple forms of complex society, and modern Euroamerican society cannot be taken as the sole model for interpreting the power of literacy in the social process, as our Andean examples illustrate. Moreover, literacy as a colonial instrument cannot be considered exclusively in its alphabetic form; we must also take note of the role played by pictorial literacy in the process of domination, and of the interplay among various literacies within the colonial context. The power of literacy is intimately linked to political and social status: it was the *cacique* who dominated the skills or resources of writing, and it was most often the son of the *cacique* who became a painter.

While literacy in Euroamerican society, as well as in Mexico, has increasingly become a major area of concern for scholars, studies of Andean literacy – and of colonial literacy in most formerly non-literate societies – have not focused on the process and effects of writing on native culture, yet it is in the Andes that we can observe most patently the transformative power of literacy as a colonial tool.

Notes

1 In fact, in both Colombia and Bolivia, Spanish-language colonial documents have provided Indians with evidence for the reconstruction of oral traditions and myths in the present (cf. Rivera 1986; Rappaport 1990).

2 The ubiquity of named boundary markers is especially evident in colonial Pasto wills, which sometimes document the contours of individual plots. See, for example, the late seventeenth-century will of Don Sebastian Calisto, principal mayor of the parcialidad of Yaputa, Carlosama (ANE/Q 1747).

3 The role of gifts, especially cloth, in the expansion of Tawantinsuyu is discussed by Murra (1975). The use of *aquillas* as ceremonial vessels is explained by Grijalva (1923), and their presence in sixteenth-century Otavaleño chiefly wills is mentioned by Caillavet (1982). The presence of *qompi* signified status as a descendant of the Incas; frequently interpreted by the Spaniards as subversive, the symbolic value of the cloth for the Indians was glossed as *worship* of the fabric in Spanish-authored documents (see Espinosa 1989).

4 For an example of the inclusion of *keros* in a northern will, see ANE/Q [1624] 1735b, f. 88r. Earlier wills, which do not contain references to these objects, include the 1589 testament of the *cacique* of Guachucal, Don Diego Aza (ANE/Q 1695, ff. 48r–49v).

5 See Moreno Yánez (1976) and Oviedo (1987) for a more detailed description of Tandazo's movement.

6 For example, the 1681 will of Don Marcos Taques of Tulcán (ANE/Q 1727b); the late seventeenth-century will of Don Sebastian Calisto of Carlosama (ANE/Q 1747); the 1709 testament of Don Mathias Quatimpas, principal of Tusa (ANE/Q 1746).

7 As early as 1606, Doña Catalina Tuza distributed land to her subjects through the use of documents (ABC/I 1606, f. 1v). See also the 1689 testament of Don Francisco Paspuel Guachan de Mendoza, *cacique* principal of Guaca (ANE/Q 1757, f. 12r); the 1713 will of Don Ambrocio Fernandez Taques (ABC/I 1787, ff. 29r–v); the undated will of Jacoba Heznam, a commoner from Tusa (ANE/Q 1792).

8 See also the seventeenth-century will of Andrés Yazam, of Tulcán (ANE/Q 1772, f. 3r).

106   JOANNE RAPPAPORT & THOMAS B. F. CUMMINS

9 Similarly, in the Magdalena Valley of what is today Colombia, Simón ([1627]
   1982, V, p. 245) reported that the victors of war drank out of the heads of their
   victims and that their skins were stuffed and set out as trophies during the
   celebrations in which details of military operations were remembered.
10 Catalina Tuza owned a piece of cloth called *tucllapacha* (probably *ticllapacha*),
   which was a type of weaving done in a chequerboard pattern (ABC/I 1606, f. 4r).
11 Even Guaman Poma de Ayala ([1615] 1980, p. 814), who avails himself of both
   writing and drawing, conflates the idea of writing and the notion of Andean
   image-making. In his depiction of a colonial scribe, who is clearly shown
   writing, the author labels him with a Quechua term, *quilcacamayoc*, which came
   to mean 'el escribano de oficio' (González Holguín [1608] 1989, p. 301),
   although *quellccani* meant both 'dibujar' (to draw) and 'escribir' (to write).
12 For colonial continuance of prehispanic imagery in documents see Smith (1973).
   On the continued importance of such documents into the twentieth century see
   Parmenter (1982). For the use of Nahua as a written alphabetic part of Spanish
   legal documents see Anderson, Berdan & Lockhart (1976), Karttunen &
   Lockhart (1976), Lockhart (1982, 1985).
13 Lockhart (1985, pp. 474–5) notes that there are structural differences between
   Nahuatl and Spanish documents of the same type, for example more direct
   speech in Nahuatl than in Spanish examples.
14 Indigenous items of commercial value are mentioned by their Quechua names in
   both native and Spanish wills and debt obligations. For example an *anaco* or
   woman's dress is listed among other debt items in a contract between Spaniards
   (ANE/Q 1604, ff. 417r–419r).
15 He states that he has 'una imagen de lienzo viejo' and 'un bulto de Santiago para
   mi capilla' (ABC/I 1592).
16 Individual or group portraits in a European format could also be used as a form
   of proof in the same manner as a written document. The earliest extant example
   is the group portrait of Afro-american *caciques* from Esmeraldas sent to Philip II
   in 1587. See also Cummins (1991).

Acknowledgements

The research upon which this chapter is based was conducted by Thomas Cummins
with partial support from the Center for Materials Research in Archaeology and
Ethnography, Massachusetts Institute of Technology, and by Joanne Rappaport
with support from the Fundación de Investigaciones Arqueológicas Nacionales,
Banco de la República (Bogotá) and from the Wenner-Gren Foundation for
Anthropological Research. We would like to thank the directors of the various
archives in which we collected historical data; we are especially grateful to Grecia
Vasco de Escudero, director of the Archivo Nacional del Ecuador. We would also
like to thank Marka, Instituto de Historia y Etnografía Andina (Quito) and its
director, Cristóbal Landázuri, for assistance in data collection.

References

ABC/I 1592 (Archivo del Banco Central, Ibarra, Ecuador). Testamento de Cristobal
   Cuatin, principal del pueblo de Tuza. 1339/244/1/M.
ABC/I 1606 (Archivo del Banco Central, Ibarra, Ecuador). Testamento de Doña Catalina
   Tuza, principal del pueblo de Tuza. 1335/295/1/M.
ABC/I 1787 (Archivo del Banco Central, Ibarra, Ecuador). Demanda que hace Pedro
   Ramon de Rueda . . . en nombre de Bernardo Garcia Tulcanaza y otros, a

Francisco Perez, quien se ha introducido en las tierras que estan a beneficio del comun de los indios. 979/232/3/J.

ACC/P 1708 (Archivo Central del Cauca, Popayán, Colombia). Titulo del resguardo de Vitoncó. Partida 757 de 1883.

Adorno, R. (ed.) 1892. *From Oral to Written Expression: native Andean chronicles of the early colonial period.* Syracuse: Foreign and Comparative Studies, Latin American Series.

Adorno, R. 1986. *Guaman Poma: writing and resistance in colonial Peru.* Austin: University of Texas Press.

AHT/B 1729 (Archivo Histórico de Tierradentro, Belalcázar, Colombia). Tierras de los ocho pueblos . . .

Albornoz, C. de [1582] 1967. "Instrucción para descubrir todas las guacas del Pirú y sus camayos y haciendas." *Journal de la Société des Américanistes* 56, 17–39.

Anderson, A. J. O., F. Berdan & J. Lockhart 1976. *Beyond the Codices.* Berkeley: University of California Press.

ANE/Q 1604 (Archivo Nacional del Ecuador, Quito, Ecuador). Obligacion de Martin Gonzalez y Rogrogo Sanchez de Soto en favor de Antonio Marquez del Pedraca. Notaría Primera, Escribano Alonso Vergara.

ANE/Q 1685 (Archivo Nacional del Ecuador, Quito, Ecuador). Materia seguida por Lucas Falconi, cacique de Botana, sobre licencia de venta de tierras. Fondo Popayán, caja 8.

ANE/Q 1693 (Archivo Nacional del Ecuador, Quito, Ecuador). Autos del Alferes Real Nicolas Gregorio Zambrano sobre el remate de un pedaso de tierra del pueblo de Quina, jurisdiccion de Pasto. Fondo Popayán, caja 12.

ANE/Q 1694 (Archivo Nacional del Ecuador, Quito, Ecuador). Materia seguida por don Ambrosio de Prado y Sayalpud, sobre el cacicazgo de Cumbal," Fondo Popayán, caja 13.

ANE/Q 1695 (Archivo Nacional del Ecuador, Quito, Ecuador). Don Juan Ipialpud contra Rafael Assa, sobre el cacicazgo de Guachocal. Fondo Popayán, caja 13.

ANE/Q 1727a (Archivo Nacional del Ecuador, Quito, Ecuador). Doña Juana de Basuri y Sanbursi, sobre que se le entregue la encomienda de Buesaquillo en Pasto. Fondo Popayán, caja 45.

ANE/Q 1727b (Archivo Nacional del Ecuador, Quito, Ecuador). Patricio Cisneros contra Maria Taques Garcia Tulcanasa, cacica principal de Tulcan, por las tierras de Carampuer. Fondo Indígenas, caja 46.

ANE/Q 1734 (Archivo Nacional del Ecuador, Quito, Ecuador). Autos de Domingo Yaputa, Francisco Paspuel Tuza y demas caciques de Guaca, sobre las tierras nombradas San Bartolome. Fondo Indígenas, caja 53.

ANE/Q 1735a (Archivo Nacional del Ecuador, Quito, Ecuador). Autos de don Reymundo Guaycal sobre el casicasgo de Cumbal. Fondo Popayán, caja 55.

ANE/Q 1735b (Archivo Nacional del Ecuador, Quito, Ecuador). Testamento de Doña Luisa Actasen, viuda de Pedro Queasa, principal del ayllu de Chaytan, en Túquerres. Fondo Popayán, caja 55.

ANE/Q 1736 (Archivo Nacional del Ecuador, Quito, Ecuador). Don Domingo Garcia Yaputa, Gobernador del pueblo de Carlosama, sobre el cacicazgo de Carlosama. Fondo Popayán, caja 58.

ANE/Q 1746 (Archivo Nacional del Ecuador, Quito, Ecuador). Autos en favor de Miguel Garcia Paspuel Tuza por unas tierras que heredó de su abuela. Fondo Indígenas, caja 63.

ANE/Q 1747 (Archivo Nacional del Ecuador, Quito, Ecuador). Autos de Don Visente Garcia Yaputa, governador, y el comun de yndios del pueblo de Carlosama, con Don Mariano Paredes, sobre las tierras nombradas Yapudquer y San Sevastian, en los Pastos. Fondo Popayán, caja 75.

ANE/Q 1757 (Archivo Nacional del Ecuador, Quito, Ecuador). Cuaderno de los instrumentos de la escritura de venta, otorgada por Don Pedro Guatinango a Don Andres Gualsago y testamento de Don Francisco Paspuel Guachan en la causa que siguen

Don Hernando de Cuatinpas y Don Pedro Garcia, principales del pueblo de Tusa, con Don Antonio Luna, sobre tierras. Fondo Indígenas, caja 77.

ANE/Q 1765 (Archivo Nacional del Ecuador, Quito, Ecuador). Autos de Don Manuel Pirtajoa y Chimachanag sobre el cacicasgo de Jongobito y Mocondino en Pasto. Fondo Popayán, caja 114.

ANE/Q 1772 (Archivo Nacional del Ecuador, Quito, Ecuador). Autos de Don Juan Rosero, vecino de la Provincia de los Pastos, con los indios de Tulcan, sobre unas tierras. Fondo Indígenas, caja 97.

ANE/Q 1792 (Archivo Nacional del Ecuador, Quito, Ecuador). Titulos y ynstrumentos de los yndios y casiques del pueblo de Tusa sobre la propiedad de vnas tierras. Fondo Cacicazgos, caja 3.

ANE/Q 1803 (Archivo Nacional del Ecuador, Quito, Ecuador). Expedientes relativos a los autos criminales contra Antonio Tandazo. Fondo Rebeliones, caja 6.

Bird, J. 1943. Excavations in northern Chile. *Anthropological Papers of the American Museum of Natural History* 38, 171–319.

Caillavet, C. 1982. Caciques de Otavalo en el siglo XVI: Don Alonso Maldonado y su esposa. *Miscelánea Antropológica Ecuatoriana* 2, 38–55.

Connerton, P. 1989. *How Societies Remember*. Cambridge: Cambridge University Press.

Cummins, T. B. F. 1991. We are the other: Peruvian portraits of colonial *Kurakakuna*. In *Transatlantic Encounters: Europeans and Andeans in the Sixteenth Century*, Andrien, K. & R. Adorno (eds), 203–31. Berkeley: University of California Press.

Cummins, T. B. F. n.d. Abstraction and representation: the transformation of the image of the Inca in the sixteenth century. Unpublished ms.

Espinosa, C. R. 1989. La masacarada del Inca: una investigación acerca del teatro político de la Colonia. *Miscelanea Histórica Ecuatoriana* 2: 6–39.

Garcilaso de la Vega, El Inca. [1616] 1962. *Historia general del Perú*. 4 vols. Lima: Universidad Nacional Mayor de San Marcos.

González Holguín, D. [1608] 1989. *Vocabvlario de la lengva general de todo el Perv llamada lengua qquicha o del Inca*. Lima: Universidad Nacional Mayor de San Marcos.

Goody, J. 1977. *The Domestication of the Savage Mind*. Cambridge: Cambridge University Press.

Grijalva, C. E. 1923. *Cuestiones previas al estudio filológico-etnográfico*. Quito: Banco del Ecuador.

Grijalva, C. E. 1937. *La expedicíon de Max Uhle a Cuasmal, o sea, la protohistoria de Imbabura y Carchi*. Quito: Editorial Chimborazo.

Gruzinski, S. 1988. *La colonisation de l'imaginaire: sociétés indigènes et occidentalisation dans le Mexique espagnol, XVIe–XVIIIe siècle*. Paris: Gallimard.

Guaman Poma de Ayala, F. [1615] 1980. *El primer nueva corónica y buen gobierno* (critical edition by J. V. Murra & R. Adorno). Mexico: Siglo XXI.

Karttunen, F. & J. Lockhart 1976. *Nahuatl in the Middle Years: language contact phenomena in texts of the colonial period*. Berkeley: University Publications in Linguistics.

Kubler, G. 1961. On the colonial extinction of the motifs of precolumbian art. In *Essays in Precolumbian Art and Archaeology*, 14–34. Cambridge: Harvard University Press.

Landázuri, N. C. n.d. Los curacazgos pastos prehispánicos: agricultura y comercio, siglo XVI. Unpublished manuscript.

Lockhart, J. 1982. Views of corporate self and history in some valleys of Mexican towns, late seventeenth and eighteenth centuries. In *The Inca and Aztec States, 1400–1800: Anthropology and History*, Collier, G. A., R. I. Rosaldo & J. D. Wirth (eds), 367–93. New York: Academic Press.

Lockhart, J. 1985. Some Nahua concepts in postconquest Guise. *History of European Ideas* 6, 465–82.

Mannheim, B. 1991. *The Language of the Inka since the European Invasion*. Austin: University of Texas Press.

Menzel, D. 1976. *Pottery, Style and Society in Ancient Peru*. Berkeley: University of California Press.

Moreno Yánez, S. E. 1976. *Sublevaciones indígenas en la Autidencia de Quito.* Bonn: Estudios Americanistas de Bonn.

Moreno Yánez, S. E. 1986. De las formas tribales al señorío étnico: Don García Tulcanaza y la inserción de una jefatura en la formación socio-económica colonial. *Miscelánea Antropológica Ecuatoriana* 6, 253–63.

Murra, J. V. 1975. *Formaciones económicas y políticas del mundo andino.* Lima: Instituto de Estudios Peruanos.

Murra, J. V. [1615] 1980. Waman Puma, etnógrafo del mundo andino. In *El primer nueva corónica y buen gobierno,* Felipe Guaman Poma de Ayala (critical edition by John V. Murra and Rolena Adorno), xiii–xix. Mexico: Siglo XXI.

NP/I 1758 (Notaría Primera de Ipiales, Colombia). Expediente sobre los linderos del Resguardo del Gran Cumbal. Escritura 997.

NP/P 1758 (Notaría Primera de Pasto, Colombia). Expediente sobre los linderos del Resguardo del Gran Cumbal. Escritura 228 de 1908.

Ong, W. J. 1982. *Orality and Literacy: the technologizing of the word.* London & New York: Methuen.

Oviedo, R. 1987. Antonio Tandazo. *Revista Obando* 3, 47–50.

Pachacuti Yamqui Salcamaygua, J. de Santacruz [1613] 1967. Relación de antigüedades deste Reyo del Pirú. In *Crónicas peruanas de interés indígena,* 281–319. Madrid: Biblioteca de Autores Españolas.

Padilla, S. M., L. Lopez & A. L. González 1977. *La encomienda en Popayán (tres estudios).* Sevilla: Escuela de Estudios Hispano-Americanos de Sevilla.

Parmenter, R. 1982. *Four Lienzos of the Coixtlahuaca Valley.* Washington, DC: Dumbarton-Oaks Studies in Pre-Columbian Art and Archaeology.

Phelan, J. L. 1967. *The Kingdom of Quito in the Seventeenth Century.* Madison: University of Wisconsin Press.

Rappaport, J. 1988. La organización socio-territorial de los pastos: una hipótesis de trabajo. *Revista de Antropología* 4, 71–103.

Rappaport, J. 1990. *The Politics of Memory: native historical interpretation in the Colombian Andes.* Cambridge: Cambridge University Press.

Rappaport, J. 1994. *Cumbe Reborn: an Andean ethnography of history.* Chicago: University of Chicago Press.

Rivera, C. S. 1986. *"Oprimidos pero no vencidos": luchas del campesinado aymara y quechwa, 1900–1980.* La Paz: HISBOL.

Salomon, F. L. 1986. *Native Lords of Quito in the Age of the Incas.* Cambridge: Cambridge University Press.

Salomon, F. & G. L. Urioste (trans. & eds) 1991. *The Huarochirí Manuscript: a testament of ancient and colonial Andean religion.* Austin: University of Texas Press.

Salvat Editores Ecuatoriana. 1985. *Arte colonial de Ecuador, siglos xvi–xvii.* Quito: Salvat.

Simón, Fray P. de [1627] 1982. *Noticias historiales de las conquistas de Tierra Firme en las Indias Occidentales.* 8 vols. Bogotá: Banco Popular.

Smith, M. E. 1973. *Picture Writing from Ancient Southern Mexico: Mixtec place signs and maps.* Norman: University of Oklahoma Press.

Stern, S. 1982. *Peru's Indian Peoples and the Challenge of Spanish Conquest.* Madison: University of Wisconsin Press.

Street, B. V. 1984. *Literacy in Theory and Practice.* Cambridge: Cambridge University Press.

Vidal, H. 1985. *Socio-historia de la literatura colonial hispano-americana: tres lecturas orgánicas.* Minneapolis: Institute for the Study of Ideologies and Literatures.

Wachtel, Nathan. 1977. *The Vision of the Vanquished: the Spanish conquest of Peru through Indian eyes, 1550–1570.* New York: Barnes & Noble.

The social construction
of antiquity

The construction of antiquity and the egalitarian principle: social constructions of the past in the present

WILLIAM A. SHACK

Let me introduce this commentary with a personal vignette. It is one that came to mind after having read the chapters in this section of the volume on the social construction of antiquity. I was reminded of early childhood, a black lad growing up in Chicago. I was terrified of white folks, especially white men. On the happy occasions when my mother would take me along on her journeys downtown, she always warned me to be on my best behaviour. And when boredom or tiredness led me to become fidgety, like most children 3 or 4 years of age are wont to be, my mother would threaten that if I did not behave she would give me to the Bogey Man. To emphasize that the threat was not an idle one and to strike terror in my young heart, she would point out the Bogey Man: the nearest white man. To me the world of downtown Chicago seemed full of Bogey Men. There were white men everywhere; fifty-odd years ago black folks were rarely seen downtown, even performing menial, low-paid occupations. That to this day in momentary flights of fantasy I still harbour the thought that some – though not all – white men are in fact Bogey Men is not the point here. In terms familiar in the discourse on the social construction of the past, the sociological meaning underlying that personal vignette is that my mother had deconstructed the conventional form of black–white relationships perpetuated in oral and literary genre; a view to wit – black: evil and white: good. As the chapters make clear, the construction of black–white relationships, that is a dominant–subordinate relationship, has a long history set in antiquity of informing particular genres of humanistic and sociological literature. By representing to me white men as Bogey Men, my mother created a mechanism of social control by using a secular symbol of evil creatures in the here and now, not in some biblical land in the bye and bye. And though I confess never to have seen the Bogey Man commit an act of ritual cannibalism, that is eating little black children which my mother asserted with stern absolute authority and with a straight face was the fate of those who were naughty, I was thoroughly convinced this was fact, not fancy.

I am inclined to think that my mother's deconstruction of the conventional worldview of black folks and white folks was not unique: that she and numerous other black mothers shared a common cultural construction of the Bogey Man; that it was a representation of white folks that required no decoding to be understood within the social milieu of Black Metropolis. Black protest literature crafted by such writers as Langston Hughes, Richard Wright, James Baldwin, Ralph Ellison, Chester Himes and others makes plain the universality of white image-making in black communities from New York's Harlem to Chicago's Bronzeville.

What I have described above might be called 'Mother Hits Back'. This would paraphrase accurately the title of Julius Lips's (1966) study of the representation of white people in the paintings and sculpture of non-white artists. Some examples he presents date back to the artists' initial contact with whites. First published in 1937, Lips's study would be considered old-fashioned by contemporary standards of social anthropology; indeed the Foreword was written by Bronislaw Malinowski. But as the publisher's note states, Lips 'was far ahead of his time' in seeing the white man through native eyes, a picture that was not flattering.

The personal vignette I related and the observations recorded by Lips represent the obverse side of the chapters in this section. Bernal (Ch. 8) discusses how the transformation of the image of Ancient Greece became a tool for imperialism and European hegemony; a similar theme is developed by Rowlands (Ch. 9) in his treatise on how the growth of anthropological archaeology has tended to encourage the colonization of the prehistory of others; knowledge and domination at the level of gender and the division of labour continues the previous theme in Gero's contribution (Ch. 10); Rao (Ch. 11) illustrates how the malleability of the archaeological record contributes to the political volatility between Hindus and Muslims.

Bernal's chapter (Ch. 8) contributes to the scholarship of what the late St Clair Drake called the vindicationist tradition in black American sociological and historical literature. Such writers as DuBois (1939), Snowden (1970) and Drake (1987) himself, like Bernal, have attacked the bias that persists in the study of black folks from white perspectives. This perspective has persistently relegated to insignificance the contribution of black folks in antiquity to the shaping of western civilization. Bernal labels this bias the Aryan Model of Ancient Greece because it denies the African/Asian elements which helped to shape the Greek civilization. However, Bernal expands further the boundaries of his thesis in arguing that the Aryan Model of Ancient Greece was necessary for European hegemony over African and Asian peoples.

Perhaps Bernal sums up best what I take to be the underlying theme of this volume on the social construction of the past when he writes that 'the notion that the colonists possessed a deep civilization going back to Plato and Aristotle was essential to both their own sense of categorical superiority and the acceptance of this European cultural domination by local elites' (p. 126). The first part of this thesis is hardly debatable, namely that the colonists created their own sense of categorical superiority, racial and cultural. As to the second part of the thesis, I have seen no compelling evidence to support the

view that local elites accepted unquestioningly European cultural dominance.[1]
Here I am reminded of a period of social history in the not too distant past
when some African Americans who were biologically white but sociologically
black 'passed' as members of a dominant group. Crossing the colour line, as it
was then called, did not represent the acceptance by blacks who passed of
white cultural dominance; rather it was a strategy utilized by black folks for
maximizing limited economic opportunities in a situation of political domination and extreme racial oppression. Studies of this phenomenon reveal that
blacks who crossed the colour line in the 8 a.m. to 5 p.m. daily round of work
despised both whites and their culture (Drake & Cayton 1945). This would
seem to be borne out in a more recent study by Mayer of urban blacks in South
Africa. Mayer wrote that 'according to popular black thinking in Soweto,
whites are not well endowed with such qualities as kindness, gentleness,
humility, respect and love' (Mayer 1980, p. 25). Further, those interviewed
said that 'in South Africa the whites are the worst enemies of civilization'. And
they went on to add that 'the civilized are true Africans who still have respect
and love for their fellow beings' (Mayer 1980, p. 25). Similarly, ethnographic
evidence of the rejection by local elites of European culture are to be found in
the study of Zionist independent African churches in South Africa and other
regions of the continent, as well as in some religiously inspired Melanesian
movements, the so-called 'cargo cults'.

Rejection of cultural domination and its attendant biases in the construction
of knowledge is not limited to racial categories in social situations. Gender
plays a role in the construction of archaeological knowledge. Patriarchical
bias in the practice of archaeology, as Gero (Ch. 10) argues, restricting
women's scholarship to 'low-status, low-technology, theoretically irrelevant'
(p. 151) positions, effectively imposes on the construction of prehistory a
gender version of Bernal's Aryan Model. Men appropriate women's labour,
that is, the products of women's analysis of archaeological materials, thereby
reinforcing a male construct of knowledge about the ancient past.

Archaeology and history share common features of malleability, continually
recreating the past, a principal function of which past is to socially construct
the present. The recreated past is increasingly being used to legitimate claims
to land, to political title, etc. as Rowlands (Ch. 9) reminds us, thrusting
archaeology into the debate of nationalism and ethnicity. The impulse to
preserve the past is part of the impulse to preserve the self, an impulse that is
given 'legitimacy' when grounded in objects from the past. As cultural symbols, such objects of the past that create the basis for communities of shared
memory are often outside museum settings, the easy access to which fuels the
imagination of myth-making. And when social constructions give rise to
myth, as Rao (Ch. 11) argues, myth 'lends sanctity and rightness to a course of
action. Thus, creating a myth in the image of the present legitimizes and
sanctifies actions undertaken in the present' (p. 160). In India, the domain of
Rao's research on the conflict between Muslim and Hindu over rightful claims
to sacred space, symbols from both myth and history and archaeology may be

interpreted differently by different groups in the competition for control of power and authority. Fact becomes fancy. That too is irrelevant if in the course of time the hegemonic struggle for dominance is affirmed; the process of reconstructing the past on the assumption of truth asserts itself.

These cursory examples of reconstructing the past to accommodate hegemonic social practices of the present suggest two relevant observations which I draw from the work of the Haitian anthropologist, Trouillot. In writing about peasants and capital in Dominica, Trouillot (1988, p. 27) says that 'social scientists always inherit the colonizer's path'. Among other possible interpretations, I take this statement to mean that social scientists have too often accepted without question the colonizer's social construction of the colonized, but the obverse has not entered social anthropological discourse. On the second point, Trouillot (1988, p. 27) writes that 'power precedes scholarship: one engenders delineations, the other inscribes them'. In this sense, nowadays it appears to be fashionable in some circles of social scientists to believe that scholarship precedes power; that notion is perpetuated in anthropological writings, many of which are unintelligible and which are usually read by other anthropologists, rather than by the people who are the subjects of their studies. The argument is that these anthropological writings become the icons which give symbolic legitimacy to power structures. Perhaps, but I have not seen the evidence, and I am hard put to imagine that the power structures of the past, let alone those of the present which produce the patterns of domination in the cultures mainly studied by anthropologists, were guided by the writings of social scientists. Certainly this is not the case if the concept of power is used in the conventional sense in political anthropological discourse. Political domination is clearly a manifestation of power. 'Power', as Smith (1968, p. 193) wrote, 'is the capacity to take autonomous action in the face of resistance from persons, groups, rules or material conditions. It is the ability to pursue one's will effectively, if necessary by imposing it on others.' However, the presumption of authority in writings about other cultures is not the same as power, either representational or instrumental.

Social anthropological discourse on the social construction of the past often confuses two intellectual processes for which the chapters in this section of the volume offer a constructive correction. One process is represented by Bernal (Ch. 8) and indeed in the engaging overview of anthropology and history outlined by Drake (1987). Each writer delivers a clarion call for a reassessment of the representation of peoples of colour as depicted in European historiography. Clearly this is the vindicationist role represented in a certain kind of African American scholarship (see Drake 1987). The second process concerns the assumptions about domination, power, authority and the like, which all too often are smuggled into discussions by and about anthropologists and the people they study. Ramos (Ch. 5) comes close to what I have in mind when she writes that anthropologists are not exempt from the charge of creating latter-day heroes who represent the idealized qualities the whites wish they themselves had (p. 85). I would go further to say that for the most part anthropologists have excluded from the discourse on the social construction of the past the verbal and written images of culture history created by those for whom we claim to speak. And in the few instances when the 'native' voice is allowed to be heard, it is usually as a foil for the anthropologist's own representation of himself or herself, a reflection of the fieldwork situation, as it is called.

These chapters suggest to me what George Bond has said elsewhere, that 'the critical voices of indigenous scholars are usually absent from the field of academic discourse' (Bond 1990, p. 288). I would add that the critical voice of the indigenous common folk is also absent from the field of academic discourse. And until the indigenous voice is heard in the first person, including the voice muffled by gender bias, and not filtered through various editions of fieldnotes and self-reflective queries, anthropologists will continue to misconstrue representations that mothers of colour construct of the Bogey Man.

Note

1 Indeed, the movement *Presence Africain* developed precisely as a counter-force rejecting European, especially French, cultural dominance.

References

Bernal, M. 1994. The image of Ancient Greece as a tool for colonialism and European hegemony. In *Social Construction of the Past: representation as power*, Bond, G. C. & A. Gilliam (eds), 119–28. London: Routledge.

Bond, G. C. 1990. Research in past occurrences. In *Fieldnotes*, Sanjek, R. (ed.), 278–90. Ithaca: Cornell University Press.

Drake, St Clair 1987. *Black Folks, Here and There*. Los Angeles: Center for Afro-American Studies, University of California at Los Angeles.

Drake, St Clair & H. Cayton 1945. *Black Metropolis*. New York: Harcourt, Brace & Co.

DuBois, W. E. B. 1939. *Black Folks, Then and Now*. New York: Henry Holt & Co.

Gero, J. M. 1994. Gender division of labour in the construction of archaeological knowledge in the United States. In *Social Construction of the Past: representation as power*, Bond, G. C. & A. Gilliam (eds), 144–53. London: Routledge.

Lips, J. [1937] 1966. *The Savage Hits Back*. New York: University Books.

Mayer, P. (ed.) 1980. *Black Villagers in an Urban Society*. Cape Town & New York: Oxford University Press.

Ramos, A. 1994. From Eden to limbo: the construction of indigenism in Brazil. In *Social Construction of the Past: representation as power*, Bond, G. C. & A. Gilliam (eds), 74–88. London: Routledge.

Rao, N. 1994. Interpreting silences: symbol and history in the case of Ram Janmabhoomi/Babri Masjid. In *Social Construction of the Past: representation as power*, Bond, G. C. & A. Gilliam (eds), 154–64. London: Routledge.

Rowlands, M. 1994. The politics of identity in archaeology. In *Social Construction of the Past: representation as power*, Bond G. C. & A. Gilliam (eds), 129–43. London: Routledge.

Smith, M. G. 1968. Political anthropology. In *International Encyclopaedia of the Social Sciences*, 189–202. New York: Macmillan.

Snowden, F. 1970. *Blacks in Antiquity: Ethiopians in the Greco-Roman experience.* Cambridge, Mass: Harvard University Press.

Trouillot, M.-R. 1988. *Peasants and Capitalism: Dominica in the world economy.* Baltimore: Johns Hopkins University Press.

8   The image of Ancient Greece as a tool for colonialism and European hegemony

MARTIN BERNAL

It is widely believed that 'classics' is the academic discipline furthest away from modern politics. It is not merely supposed to inhabit the ivory tower but to be in its topmost storey. I attempt to challenge these assumptions. In my book (Bernal 1987), I argue that far from being detached and peripheral, the German academic discipline of *Altertumswissenschaft*, transposed into England and the United States as 'classics', has been central to northern European culture in the nineteenth and twentieth centuries and that it has usually been highly 'political'. Classics has incorporated social and cultural patterns in society as a whole and has reflected them back, to provide powerful support for the notion of Europe possessing a categorical superiority over all other continents, which in turn justifies imperialism or neo-colonialism as *missions civilisatrices*.

Two models for the origins of Ancient Greece

In order to analyse these scholarly and political developments, I have found it useful to distinguish between two schemes of the origins of Ancient Greece which I have called the 'Ancient' and 'Aryan' models. Most of us have been educated in the framework of the latter model, according to which Greek culture developed as the result of one or more invasions from the north by Indo-European speakers. The invaders conquered the native population, who were supposed to have been sophisticated but soft. As so often in myths or histories of conquests, there are strong connotations of gender here. The image is clearly one of the 'masculine' Aryans seizing and dominating the 'feminine' natives. Apart from their having been white or Caucasian and definitely not Semitic or African, conventional wisdom can say very little about these pre-Hellenes, except for what can be reconstructed from what are supposed to be the many linguistic traces of their culture in Greek language and proper names.

No one questions the fact that although Greek is an Indo-European language, it contains an extraordinarily high proportion of non-Indo-European elements. It is also clear that this pattern can be explained by the 'Aryan Model', the non-Indo-European elements being attributed to the pre-Hellenes. This linguistic pattern makes it impossible to claim that Greek as a language was homogeneous or that the Greeks were pure Indo-Europeans or Aryans. Instead, the Aryan Model proposes that while there was linguistic mixing, both invaders and natives were 'racially pure' but that the conquest was by a superior branch of the white race. In this way, the picture produced is different from that of the Aryan conquest of India, because the aborigines of the Subcontinent were 'dark'; thus in the long run the conquest there led to 'racial degradation' of the conquerors. The origin of Greece was pictured as having been more like the Germanic destruction of the Roman Empire, in which (according to the nineteenth-century view) the Teutons infused a vigour into the Celtic and Roman European population.

The Aryan Model for Greece has been of obvious advantage to nineteenth- and twentieth-century racists, but this fact does not automatically falsify it. Nevertheless, while the Germanic invasions were historical events – and there is strong legendary evidence that there were Aryan conquests of north India – such a tradition is completely lacking in the case of Greece.[1]

> The true home of the Greeks before they won dominion in Greece
> had passed clean out of their remembrance, and they looked to the
> east, and not to the north, as the quarter from which some of their
> ancestors had migrated.
>
> (Bury 1900, p. 75)

What the early twentieth-century classicist Bury saw as their faulty memory, I call the Ancient Model. This historical scheme is referred to by Aeschylus, Euripides, Herodotus, Socrates, Diodorus Siculus, Pausanias and others (Bernal 1987, pp. 88–112). It was omitted by one or two and denied only by Plutarch in what is generally seen as an outburst of spleen against Herodotus. In other writings, Plutarch admitted Greece's deep cultural debts to the Near East. He took it as axiomatic, for instance, that Greek religion came from Egypt (Bernal 1987, pp. 112–14, 117–19).

According to this Ancient Model, Greece had once been inhabited by primitive tribes – Pelasgians and others. It had then been settled by Egyptians and Phoenicians, who had built cities and civilized the natives. The Phoenicians, for instance, had introduced the alphabet, while the Egyptians had taught the Pelasgians such things as irrigation, the names of the gods and how to worship them.

The Ancient Model was not seriously challenged until the end of the eighteenth century and was not overthrown until the 1820s, when northern European scholars began to deny the colonizations and play down Egyptian and Phoenician cultural influences on Greece. These historiographical devel- opments cannot be linked to the availability of any new evidence, because the great discoveries took place later in the nineteenth century; the first archae- ology of Bronze Age Greece by Schliemann and the decipherment of cuneiform took place many decades after the change of models, and Champollion's decipherment of hieroglyphics was not accepted by most classicists until the 1850s. Therefore, the reasons for the overthrow of the Ancient Model have to be looked for not in internal developments within the disciplines, but in the *Zeitgeist* or intellectual milieu of the time.

In northern Europe, the years from 1815 to 1830 were outstanding for their political reaction and their religious revival. Thus, the reaction against Ancient Egypt should be seen in the light of Egypt's centrality to the beliefs of the Freemasons – see *The Magic Flute*. The Freemasons were seen by reactionaries to have been at the heart of the French Revolution and specifically to have been behind its anti-Christian 'religion of reason'. In the long run, however, the Ancient Model was destroyed not because of any threat it posed to Christianity but because of the predominance in the nineteenth century of Romanticism, racism and the concept of progress. Romanticism was important because in its attack on the Enlightenment, it emphasized local peculiarity and the importance of place and kinship in the formation of cultures. Romantics preferred small communities, which were supposed to promote virtue, to the broad empires like those of Rome, China and Egypt, which had been admired in the Enlightenment. The Romantics also believed that virtue was produced by demanding or stimulating environments, particularly the cold ones of mountains and the North like Scotland and Switzerland. Thus, the Greeks, who were now beginning to be seen as particularly virtuous, were required in some way to have been northern, because they could not have derived their civilization from the luxurious and decadent South and East.

Moreover, by the end of the eighteenth century the Ancient Greeks were felt in some way to represent the childhood of Europe. This notion came from Plato's description of Solon's interview with Egyptian priests who told him 'you Greeks are always children. There is no such thing as an old Greek' (*Timaeus* 22B). From Antiquity to the Renaissance, such a description was a damning condemnation of cultural shallowness. After the eighteenth century, it became an accolade. Childhood as a qualitatively distinct period of life was a new discovery of the mid-eighteenth century. It came at the intersection of Romanticism and the new paradigm of progress, and was perceived as a period with a paradoxical combination of free imagination and asexual purity. Thus, the traditional view of Ancient Greece as the ethnic melting pot of the eastern Mediterranean became increasingly distasteful.

Still worse was the fact that the most significant conquerors of Greece were seen to have been Egyptians and Phoenicians who were becoming categorized as Africans and Semites. Such a picture was utterly offensive to racism which was sweeping all before it, at the turn of the nineteenth century.

The triumph of racism, of course, was influenced by the northern European need to denigrate the peoples they were exterminating, enslaving and exploiting in other continents. European expansion and the arrogance and optimism that flowed from it were also important in the new predominance of the notion of progress, which itself affected attitudes towards the Ancient Model.

Previously, the greater antiquity of the Egyptians and the Phoenicians had given them a reputation for cultural superiority. Now, however, the idea that 'later is better' benefited the Greeks who were seen as the epitome of the newly desirable qualities of youth and dynamism.

In the new period, the image of the Greeks changed from one of intermediaries, who had transmitted *some part* of the civilization and wisdom of the East to the West, into one of them as the creators of civilization. At the beginning of the eighteenth century, Ancient Greeks were admired because of Homer and the later poets. In the middle of the century, led by the founder of academic art history, Johann Joachim Winkelmann – who had himself never seen any classical Greek art – cultivated Europeans began to see Greek art as the highest form ever created. Finally, in the 1780s, historians of philosophy came to agree that there had been no philosophy before the Greeks. The new Romantic historians began to see history as the biography of 'races'. The apparent double achievement of the Greeks in poetry and art associated with youth and wisdom which generally came with the maturity of a 'race' gave the Ancient Greeks a superhuman status as the models of balanced and integrated humanity.

This feeling was particularly strong in Germany, where for other reasons neo-Hellenism had become extraordinarily passionate in the eighteenth century. In 1793, at the peak of the French Revolution, the brilliant young aristocrat and polymath, Wilhelm von Humboldt, sketched out a plan for a new education which would reintegrate men and women who were being spiritually torn apart and alienated by modernity through the study of the most perfectly integrated people of the past, the Ancient Greeks. Fourteen years later, in panic after its defeat by Napoleon, the Prussian government instituted widespread reforms and Humboldt was put in charge of national education. In this way, he was able to implement many of these ideas and establish the humanistic education of the *Gymnasium* and the university *Seminar* focused on *Altertumswissenschaft* (the 'study/science of Antiquity'), and upon the Greeks in particular.

This new education had clear meritocratic tendencies and was thus a threat to the aristocracy, many of whom opposed the new ideas. Similarly, its English offshoot, 'classics', was seen as a middle way between reaction and revolution. However, this apparent balance is misleading because in the beginning, the chief purpose of those advocating a humanistic education focused on Ancient Greece was to forestall or avoid revolution and in fact it served very effectively to maintain the *status quo*, despite some minor trouble from the radicals associated with the philhellenic movement in support of the Greek War of Independence.

In this atmosphere of popular and institutionalized philhellenism, which naturally intensified after the outbreak of the Greek War of Independence against Turkey in 1821, it is remarkable that the Ancient Model survived as long as it did. However, it was a very tough nut to crack. Connop Thirlwall the first writer of a history of Greece in the 'new' way wrote in the 1830s:

> It required no little boldness to venture even to throw out a doubt
> as to the truth of an opinion sanctioned by such authority and by
> prescription of such a long and undisputed possession of the public
> mind.
>
> (Thirlwall 1835, I, p. 63)

The man who did this was one of the first products of Humboldt's new educational system, the brilliant polymath Karl Otfried Müller. Claiming a base in 'science' which his predecessors had lacked, Müller maintained that the later reports about the Egyptian and Phoenician settlement and civilizing were the result of liaisons between the Egyptian, Phoenician and Greek priesthoods of later times and were, therefore, untrustworthy. Furthermore, as none of the legends that made up the Ancient Model could be proven, they should not be believed. There were two sleights of hand here. The first was the requirement of 'proof' in an area where the best that can be hoped for is competitive plausibility. The second was placing the onus of such proof on those who accepted the massive ancient testimony rather than on those who challenged it (Bernal 1987, pp. 308–16). The unspoken basis for Müller's claims was the new axiom that Europe was and had always been categorically separate from and superior to Asia and Africa. Thus, proof was required to justify something as 'unnatural' as the Ancient Model.

The rapid general acceptance of Muller's discrediting of the Egyptian colonization shows how well attuned it was to his times. His denial of Phoenician influence on Greece was not so easily accepted. It is for this reason that during most of the nineteenth century, the predominant image of the origins of Greece was one that I call the 'Broad Aryan Model' which denied the Greek traditions concerning the Egyptians but accepted those about the Phoenicians. Indeed the best-known colonization of Greece from Egypt – that of Danaos in Argos – was now attributed to the Phoenicians. In fact, in the middle of the nineteenth century there was a boom in British interest in and admiration for them. Men like the prime minister Mr Gladstone – who wrote extensively on early Greece – clearly felt a sympathy for an upright manufacturing and trading people, who spread civilization while selling cloth, and carried on a little bit of slaving on the side.

This identification of the Phoenicians with the English was shared by the French and somewhat later the Germans, who therefore detested them. It seems to have been from the Roman stereotype of the bad faith or 'perfidy' of Phoenician Carthage that the common French term and image of *Perfide Albion* arose. Nevertheless, the Phoenicians were then, as they had been at least since the Renaissance, chiefly associated with Jews – with whom indeed they shared a common language, Canaanite, as well as many religious and other customs. Thus, the peak of the Phoenicians' reputation in the writing of history tallies well with the years of relative tolerance for Jews, between the dwindling of the traditional Christian religious hatred of Jews and the development of 'racial' anti-Semitism.

In some ways it is useful to see anti-Semitism as a luxury. Northern Europeans could only afford it when the rest of the world was utterly crushed. Thus a major cultural factor behind the rise of anti-Semitism in the 1880s and 1890s was the extraordinary arrogance associated with the triumph of imperialism. It was during these decades that belief in the Phoenicians' formative role in the creation of Greek civilization plummeted. They saw not only the peak of imperialism and the peak of anti-Semitism around the Dreyfus case but also the publication of very influential articles denying that there had ever been any significant extra-European influence on the formation of Greece (Bernal 1987, pp. 370–7). The Broad Aryan Model survived, however, until the decade 1925–35, when the 'Semites', both Jews and Phoenicians, were firmly put in their place, outside European civilization. At one level, this was clearly linked to the perceived and actual importance of Jews in the Russian Revolution and world communism. At another it was the result of supreme self-confidence mentioned above.

While I maintain that the 'externalist' or ideological forces described above provided the chief impetus for the shift of models and the only one for the destruction of the Ancient one, there was an important 'internalist' impulse behind the creation of the Aryan Model in the 1830s and 1840s. This was the working out of the Indo-European language family and the plausible belief that there must at some time have been a single proto-Indo-European language which was probably spoken to the north or north-east of the Black Sea. Thus, if Greek was an Indo-European language, at some stage it would have had to have been introduced from the North. It was on this basis that it was possible to postulate an 'Aryan invasion' despite the absence of any archaeological evidence or ancient authority and thus satisfy the externalist demands for a northern origin.

The situation has changed since 1945 with the moral revulsion at the consequences of anti-Semitism seen in the holocaust. Even more important has been the simultaneous rise of the Third World and of Israel as a bastion of imperialism or 'western civilization'. All of these changes have led towards the reacceptance of Jews as Europeans. Among Jews themselves, increased self-confidence has been largely reflected in Zionism and religious revival. However, there has been a much smaller movement to restore the reputation of the Phoenicians, led by men who could accept neither of the more orthodox expressions of identity. Thus, since the 1960s there has been a battle to bring back the Broad Aryan Model. Resistance by the 'extremists' seems to come largely from inertia and respect for authority, which is naturally very high in such traditional disciplines as classics and historical linguistics. Despite this, the defenders of the Extreme Aryan Model have been weakened both by the changing intellectual climate and by increasing evidence of Egyptian and Levantine influence in the Aegean during the Late Bronze and Early Iron Ages. The Broad Aryanists – led largely by Jewish scholars – are now gaining ground and will almost certainly succeed by the end of the century. The restoration of the Ancient Model, in a slightly revised form, will take somewhat longer.

Even if one accepts the argument put forward here that the Aryan Model was conceived in what we should now consider to be the 'sin' and error of racialism and anti-Semitism, this does not in itself invalidate it. Many extremely fruitful theories – such as Darwinism – have been developed for what would later seem to have been very dubious reasons. However, there is no doubt that the Ancient Model was discarded not because of any inherent defects but because it did not fit the *Weltanschauung* of the nineteenth century. The Aryan Model had the advantage that it made Greek history conform to what was seen as the universal historical principle of unequal races. It was this external 'surplus explanatory value' – to use the term of the philosopher of science Imre Lakatos – that allowed the Aryan Model to supersede the Ancient one. Thus today, while there are not sufficient grounds to abandon the Aryan Model without further ado, there does seem to be a good case for reopening competition between it and the Ancient Model, as revised in the light of some of the discoveries made since 1825, to see which of the two has superior heuristic value.

This competition is made in terms not of certainty but of competitive plausibility and is judged in the light of evidence from contemporary documents from the Late Bronze Age, archaeology, language, place-names, divine and mythological names and religious ritual. In some cases – such as the documents and archaeology – the evidence merely tends towards the Ancient Model. In the others, it supports the latter strongly.

There is absolutely no doubt of the achievements of the early Indo-European linguists or that despite the many foreign aspects and elements mentioned above, Greek is fundamentally an Indo-European language. Thus, I would argue not for a complete restoration of the Ancient Model but for the establishment of a synthesis, incorporating the linguistic advances of the nineteenth century and adjusting some traditional dates in the light of archaeological evidence from the twentieth century. Nevertheless, I believe that the new scheme should be closer to the Ancient than to the Aryan Model, in that it accepts that there were Egyptian and Phoenician settlements and that there were massive and fundamental cultural influences on the Aegean from the Near East.

Models of Greek history and anthropology

Here we should leave the attempt to reconstruct historiography or even worse historical reality and turn to something which anthropologists are clearly happier with, the structure and function of myth, in this case the myth of Aryan Greece.

> When one examines what the general function of the concept civilization really is, and what common quality causes all these various human attitudes and activities to be described as civilized, one starts with a very simple discovery: this concept expresses the self-consciousness of the West. One could even say: the national consciousness. It sums up every thing in which Western society of the last two or three centuries believes itself superior to earlier societies or 'more primitive' contemporary ones. By this term Western society seeks to describe what constitutes its special character and what it is proud of: the level of its technology, the nature of its manners, the development of its scientific view of the world and much more.
>
> (Elias 1978, pp. 3–4)

The Aryan Model for Greece has been essential to this appropriation. It requires both its two facets, that Ancient Greece was the first true civilization and that it was exclusively European. Specifically it was necessary to nineteenth-century colonialism. The French were explicit in justifying their rampages and excruciating exploitation as a *mission civilisatrice* and in some ways the Portuguese theoretical encouragement of *assimilados* was a use of the same fig leaf. Because of their intense and systematic racialism after 1850 the English, Dutch, Germans and Belgians were unable to maintain that they could bring racially inferior peoples to this standard, though the creation of 'brown Englishmen' proposed in Macaulay's Minute in the 1830s survived the Indian Mutiny and the horrors of the late nineteenth and early twentieth centuries. However, even when they emphasized 'pacification' and 'establishing law and order' rather than assimilation, the notion that the colonists possessed a deep civilization going back to Plato and Aristotle was essential to both their own sense of categorical superiority and the acceptance of this European cultural dominance by local elites.

It is interesting to note that this superstructural hegemony has survived the collapse of old colonialism and has become even more important to neo-colonialism. The native elites required to mediate western economic control have to be imbued not only with western civilization but also with the idea that it is the only civilization. The centrality of this can be seen in the violence of the attack on Unesco, which threatened to challenge this monopoly.

At home, however, the situation is not so secure. Relativism backed by ethnic minorities in Europe and North America as well as such subversive groups as anthropologists has established a firm foothold. This insecurity is best illustrated by outlining the development of western civilization courses. These were originally created in the First World War to cement America as a nation of European immigrants against German, 'Hunnish' or semi-Asiatic barbarism. These also contained a strong liberal bias against the German authoritarian 'Spartans', and gained a new nature and impetus from anti-communism, which was seen as a struggle against non-European forces.

This anti-communist thrust in western civilization courses, with their strong emphases on the Persian Invasions of Greece and the Peloponnesian War, intensified in the 1940s with the congealing of the Cold War. However, an interesting development took place as the emphasis on Ancient Greece came closer to the German Romantic conception of Greece and what had been the originally anti-German courses became a celebration of German neo-Hellenism. This coincided with the extreme right's appropriation of western or European civilization at a higher level, seen both in the deconstruction of De Mann and the vulgar work of Allan Bloom. In this way, 'western civilization' became western *Kultur* in the sense that Germans distinguished between the superficial and sophisticated *civilisation* of the French and their own deeper, ineffable nature. While 'civilization' was linked to the 'West' and pinko-grey peoples, it claimed universality. *Kultur*, on the other hand, was by its very nature the possession of a particular people or race for whom purity was important. Although the word 'civilization' has been retained there has been an increasing use of such terms as 'heritage' and 'legacy' in connection with it. 'Heritage' has a double message; first, that there are some people who are genetically not entitled to receive it. This is the tragedy of conservative Jews like Allan Bloom who champion the western 'heritage' while being denied a part of it by the reactionaries they admire. The second mesage is that those who do genetically *belong* to western civilization must conform to its canons and not defy or subvert them with original thought or actions.

As mentioned above, since the creation of the Aryan Model, Ancient Greece has served two functions. It is seen as the first universal civilization and at the same time as the cultural ancestor of the Europeans. This gives Europe a universal character as the continent that is not merely the vanguard of world progress but is the essence of the world itself. With the increase of right-wing influence and pessimism in the face of non-Europe, we are seeing an increase of the ancestral function at the expense of the universal.

It is in this context that I believe it is essential to attack the Aryan Model not merely because it is heuristically fruitless but because it is politically and culturally pernicious. For both of these reasons, I argue that there is need for a radical reassessment of the image of Ancient Greece and that we should turn from one of a civilization which sprang – like Athena from the head of Zeus – virgin and fully formed, to one in which Greece grew up at the intersection of Europe, Africa and Asia as a thoroughly mixed and eclectic culture. The greatness and extraordinary brilliance of Greek civilization in antiquity was not the result of isolation and cultural purity but of frequent contact with and stimulus from the many surrounding peoples on the already heterogeneous natives of the Aegean. It was from this type of fruitful confusion that all the great cultures of Greece – Mycenaean, Classical, Hellenistic, Byzantine and modern – were formed.

Note

1 The so-called 'Dorian Invasion', more commonly called 'the Return of the Heraclids' in antiquity, represented a tribal movement from north to south within Greece. Very few scholars indeed deny that the 'pre-Dorian' population of southern Greece was Greek-speaking – to do so means not merely to reject the extremely plausible reading of the Mycenaean script, Linear B, as Greek but also to make the Homeric heroes, who lived before the Return of the Heraclids, non-Greeks. This is a sacrifice that few philhellenes or classicists have been prepared to make.

References

Bernal, M. 1987. *Black Athena: the Afroasiatic roots of classical civilization*. Vol. I. *The Fabrication of Ancient Greece 1785–1985*. London & New Brunswick: Free Association Books & Rutgers University Press.

Bury, J. B. 1900. *A History of Greece to the Death of Alexander the Great*. London: Macmillan.

Elias, N. 1978. *The History of Manners: the civilizing process*. Vol I. New York: Urizen Books.

Thirlwall, C. 1835–44. *A History of Greece*. 8 vols. London: Longman.

9 The politics of identity in archaeology

MICHAEL ROWLANDS

In 1973, David Clarke published a paper in *Antiquity* entitled 'The Loss of Innocence in Archaeology'. He was alluding to a naivety in archaeological practice as part of a more wide-ranging attack on the subjectivism and parochial forms of empiricism that, he felt, pervaded the subject. His purpose was to advocate greater rigour in the development of explicit theory and method that would build a sustainable body of archaeologically derived generalizations.

Naivety of course does not represent ignorance. It refers to an unreflexive mode of practice that takes for granted the axioms on which established work predetermines the value of future knowledge. By encouraging a common-sense, taken-for-granted conviction in the obvious rightness of simply getting on and 'doing archaeology' rather than discussing the ideological bases of interpretation, a natural defence is formed against accusations of bias. By contrast with some current postmodernist claims, the issue of truth is not an issue for naive claims to knowledge. Sources and criticism of evidence are as much the methodological underpinnings of common-sense knowledge as explicitness is a priority for positivistic claims.

Yet the dilemma of disciplinary confusion is a more widespread phenomenon. Everywhere the foundations of expert knowledge are being undermined and this reflects a more general crisis in the relationship between intellectuals and society in the late twentieth century. The rapid movement of people, goods, information and money in the modern world system makes it increasingly difficult for any one group of intellectuals to maintain monopolies in ideas. Scepticism is rife of authority claims from professionals whose impersonal knowledge appears either irrelevant or dangerous – scientists endanger the environment, doctors are bad for you, lawyers are incompetent, professors have nothing to say. At the most fundamental level, it is the claim to science (loosely defined here as an externally validated system of knowledge) that is doubted, coinciding with movements in different disciplines to subvert the traditional division between the thinking subject and passive social object, and replace it with a more engaged and equal relationship.

Archaeology suffers from a particular version of this dilemma. One of its claims is that social and personal identity depends on a secure sense of past which archaeologists produce through objective knowledge and the acceptance of its findings in the established structures of academic bureaucracy. Another has been a populist argument that it produces a knowledge open and available to all; that it forms an ethical discipline through its engagement directly with people in society. The politics of archaeological claims to both objective and subjective knowledge have recently become more central to understanding the formation of the discipline. Nationalism and ethnicity (Kohl 1993, Kristiansen 1993), gender and class (Gero & Conkey 1991) and power/knowledge claims (Miller & Tilley 1984, Shanks & Tilley 1987) are some examples of how bias in archeological knowledge has been exposed. The ideological role of archaeological interpretation was exposed with a second, political, loss of innocence in the furore over the first World Archaeological Congress in Southampton in 1986. That particular event, in fact, demonstrated both the politics of doing academic work as well as the political implications of archaeological representations of alternative pasts. What was striking about this challenge to archaeological naivety was the role of non-European archaeologies in challenging the metanarratives of principally European- and North American-dominated global archaeology. The convenient forgetting of the political construction of European prehistory was challenged more by the experience of 'writing prehistory' in the periphery as resistance to colonial constructions of indigenous pasts than by political events in the archaeological heartlands of Europe and North America.

This was in spite of the fact that Europe has been the site of some of the greatest controversies in the representation of collective identity in the twentieth century. The search for cultural origins has successfully organized much archaeological writing in the West until recently precisely because of the appeal of collective identity.

> The impulse to preserve the past is part of the impulse to preserve the self. Without knowing where we have been it is difficult to know where we are going. The past is the foundation of individual and collective identity, objects from the past are the source of significance as cultural symbols.
>
> (Hewison 1987, p. 45)

For cultural heritage to be significant it must therefore be unifying and transcendent and be constitutive of a sense of personal and group identity. Moreover, the possession of a collective heritage puts the fragmentation of modern society firmly in its contingent and ephemeral place by placing identity within a sense of enduring time and place. The discovery of cultural origins has become one of the principal means of doing this and as a trope that authenticates a diverse range of archaeological writings from the academic to the popular, it has arguably been more powerful than naturalization as a metaphor in modernist ideological formation (cf. Rowlands 1987). However, an essentialist line of argument only gains any credence because of a naive, unreflexive adherence to the belief that neither person nor group exists without a sense of identity. But what is identity and why do we need one?

Identity and categories of the person

We can scarcely do without the word identity these days to describe an almost inviolable right to existence. Usually this requires an adjective that specifies the identity; this provides a singularity which of course is precisely what the term is meant to convey. Yet academic concern with identity, at least, has displayed a considerable growth in attention over the last few decades. The *International Encyclopaedia of Social Sciences* published in 1968 carries two substantial articles on the subject, one on the psychology of identity and the other on the political dimensions of identification as a process. By comparison, the first edition of the same encyclopaedia in the early 1930s does not mention the word. Such a significant shift in the usage of the term, I suggest, can also be correlated to the development of concepts such as cultural heritage and ideas about national character in general intellectual discourse from the 1940s onwards. In anthropology, the work of Margaret Mead and the Culture and Personality school was a particularly important element in developing a concern for building national character through an understanding of the transition from 'traditional' to 'modern' societies (see Gleason 1983). The development of a concern with identity has therefore been consistent with the recognition of the problem of the individual in mass society (from de Tocqueville to the present). Modernization produces identity as a problem precisely because it evokes a sense of loss and nostalgic desire (Robertson 1990). Whether it is the effect of an experience of emigration and immigration in the twentieth century or fears of the threat of cultural homogenization or the doubts cast on the unity of the self due to fears of anomie, alienation and loneliness, identity has become the keyword to describe a sense of loss.

The word identity comes from the Latin root *idem*, the same, and evokes a principle of endurance and continuity, usually in essentialist terms. The *Oxford English Dictionary* (OED) definition conveys much the same meaning:

> the sameness of a person or thing is itself and not something else; individuality, personality. Personal identity (in Psychology) the condition or fact of remaining the same person throughout the various phases of existence; continuity of the personality.

Both the above usages are consistent with the empiricist philosophy of the individual derived from John Locke's *Essay concerning human understanding* (1690) and David Hume's *Treatise on Human Nature* (1739). For them, the unity of the self was not a problem until the traditional Christian notion of the soul gave way to doubt as to the original unity of the person (Langbaum 1977, p. 25). Both Locke and Hume used the word identity to express doubt as to the naturalness of the self and therefore the necessary unification of mind and body. The possibility of losing identity or the fact that uprootedness, alienation and loneliness could seriously affect secure possession of a sense of identity was the logical outcome of this position.

Once posed as a question of doubt, broadly speaking, there have been two kinds of response to what forms an identity. The term identification was introduced by Freud to describe the process by which the infant internalizes external persons in the process of socialization. Developed by Melanie Klein and popularized by Erikson (1959), the term identity or identity crisis described a process by which the core of the individual and the core of his/her communal culture become one and the same. This situating of ego formation in the historical context of a particular cultural history meant that the elements of interiority and continuity were indispensable to the development of a secure sense of self. Regardless of change and crisis in social and historical context, identity as a sense of inner sameness and continuity would be reproduced and survive, as a template, to structure new cultural forms. An alternative sociologizing tradition has consistently maintained that identities are labile and contingent, reflecting particular social circumstances. Symbolic interactionists such as Goffman (1967) and Berger & Luckman (1967) popularized the sociological understanding that social interaction, mediated through symbolic structures, shaped the self-consciousness of the individual. There was no inner core but instead a sense of self, derived circumstantially from processes of socialization. The view that identity is a product of the interaction between the individual and society means that the self is not some inner, historically constituted and unchanging core, but is constantly altered by changes in social situation. Primordialists therefore see identity as deep, internal and permanent whilst interactionists see it as shallow, external and contingent on social circumstance.

The models and theories of identity developed in archaeology share elements of both these paradigms. Whether this represents the projection of a modernist concern with unified identities on to the past where such entities never existed remains a significant question. But archaeology, as with other disciplines, has been part of the explosive growth of concern with identities in the last few decades. Partly it constitutes a response to the growing recognition of the capacity of ethnic, national and minority groups to generate disorder when their sense of integrity is threatened and partly it is due to the growth of mass consumerism and fears about the coca colonization of global culture (Robertson 1990). In response to these anxieties, identity as something perduring and consistent has become a key value that archaeology, due to its access to the long term, is credited with being particularly well situated to exploit. The manipulation of archaeology in the shoring up of identities is now far more widespread than in the 1930s when Kossinna-like racial arguments stalked the archaeological landscape. Whether in the form of cultural heritage, where the production of archaeological identities might be seen as admirable in empowering local groups and indigenous rights or in cases of ethnic nationalism where archaeological accounts of the past may be distorted to serve political goals that most would find distasteful and objectionable, identities are produced as categorial imperatives to serve political ends. This is far removed from the naive, unreflexive 'good old days' of empiricist archaeology but is consistent with the general relation of intellectual work to society.

Archaeology and nationalism

Nations without pasts are a contradiction in terms and archaeology has been one of the principal suppliers of the raw material for constructing pasts in modern struggles for nationhood. Hobsbawm (1992) has written ironically that the historian is to the nationalist what the poppy-grower is to the heroin addict. Archaeology, especially in its modernist form, has been formed on the premise of a sense of loss, its subject matter conceived to be the recovery of tradition and a sense of community in contrast to the feeling of disenchantment for the world in which they live (Robertson 1990). For nationalists, the 'imagined community' is often portrayed as an idealized entity that once existed or was under threat and whose demise must be fought against and recovery sustained. Alternatively, much of the recent writings on nationalism have been elaborately concerned with demonstrating the fictitious element of such reconstructions of the past – the invention of tradition in the building of new worlds (Hobsbawm & Ranger 1983). Handler writes of the attempts by the Quebecois to construct bounded cultural objects as 'a process that paradoxically demonstrates the absence of any such objects' (Handler 1988, p. 191). One of the purposes in seeing the past as a strategic resource to serve current political purposes is to avoid the central issue of historical primordialism. By excluding the passions from this sense of identity, they erupt instead elsewhere as various kinds of personal, often non-academic practices.

Whatever the relative success of the traditionalism that so marks a nation – the battles, flags, great dynastic events – it depends less on claims to possess historical symbolic value and more on how they constitute a community of shared memory.

Anderson (1981) has stressed that where the imagination of collective identity is constituted in memory, nationalisms are shaped as communities of shared feeling or passion. Understanding the construction of British identity after 1870, for example, would be inseparable from understanding how the class politics of the early industrializing period were displaced into the construction of a unified national identity based on custom, tradition, and the creation of royal rituals (Canadine 1983). Custom versus history, as Hobsbawm & Ranger (1983) remind us, is really the politics of timeless inevitability versus social rupture and the politics of change. It is also the difference between a self-knowledge created through writing and an unreflexive sense of self based in the imagination. This is why the battle for custom to become identified with history (or vice versa) is basic to educational practice in the building and preservation of a nation. After Italy had been politically unified Massimo d'Azeglio said 'We have made Italy, now we have to make Italians' (quoted in Hobsbawm 1992, p. 4).

The real issue is whether the archaeological pasts that archaeologists do or should produce are or should be those wanted by nationalists. Clearly there is one view that all contestatory pasts are equally mythological and are simply desirable or undesirable at any particular moment in time. Another, with which I am more in sympathy, claims to detect error, to show not only how things have become but also how they might have been otherwise. Hobsbawm makes this point by repeating the words of Ernest Renan in his famous lecture 'What is a Nation?' in 1882:

> Forgetting history, or even getting history wrong (*l'erreur histori-que*) are an essential factor in the formation of a nation, which is why the progress of historical studies is often dangerous to a nationality.
>
> (Renan quoted in Hobsbawm 1992, p. 3)

So an archaeologist who writes within a national or ethnic framework cannot help but take a critical stand as to how his/her work is used. There seems little doubt that this is a growing dilemma for archaeologists. However, it is significant that the rise of contestatory archaeological narratives of the past has found its most virulent form in places where the discordance between colonial master narrative and local indigenous identities has been greatest. Perhaps it is particularly significant that such clashes have been most prominent in regions with immigrant population settlement and where appeals to prior origin by minorities will depend on archaeologically derived pasts. Of course the call for contestatory histories in the West – working-class histories, gender, race, etc. – has emphasized struggle in the narrative at home as well, but in a curious way it has also served to neutralize its impact. As Joan Scott has written, 'proliferation of others' histories has not so much politicized the discipline (a charge usually levelled by the defenders of orthodoxy) as it has exposed the politics by which one particular viewpoint established its predominance' (Scott 1989, p. 690, quoted in Dirks 1990). By absorbing these biases it becomes possible still to claim that there are timeless truths 'transcending accidents of class, race and gender, that speak to us all' (Scott 1989, p. 683, quoted in Dirks 1990).

The debate between Ucko and Cunliffe on the lessons to be drawn from the exclusion of South African academics from the World Archaeological Congress rehearsed similar lines. Ucko claimed that the inexorable conclusion of the 1986 World Archaeological Congress was that academic work cannot be separated from politics, whilst Cunliffe argued that the controversy was a clear justification that objective archaeological truth was all-important and should transcend local politics (Ucko 1987, pp. 139–41).

Ironically, what makes a sense of past constitutive of a nation is its link with modernity. In the eighteenth and nineteenth centuries history became part of the enactment of modern nationalisms. From the writing of chronicles and annals of kings and dynasties, history progressed to the narrative of the formation of the nation-state as a community of shared memory. To paraphrase a point made about history by Dirks (1990), archaeology is one of the most important signs of the modern. We are modern because we are historically conscious, and historically conscious because we are modern. But equally, to cite Habermas (1987), we are modern in the belief that we already live in the future. Our present therefore is constituted in the irony of having transcended a sense of the traditional whilst achieving a future as the triumph of reason. History and Reason have therefore always been in tension with each other and yet dependent upon each other as mutually constituted creations of modernity.

In the Third World, each new nation created by independence from colonial rule had in turn to create its own narrative of possessing an authentic pre-colonial past, suffering the rupture of colonial possession and reachieving authenticity through its struggle for freedom. The master narratives of nineteenth-century European nation-states were appropriated by the subjects of colonial rule and turned against the master narratives of imperial history. But in the process what has come to be realized is that although defined in opposition, the shape of that historical narrative is still that of the colonizer. If the subject voices were constituted in resistance to colonial rule, then it is not surprising that a sense of past has been colonized as well and frequently gives form to idealized futures.

> Nationalism produced a discourse in which, even as it challenged the colonial claim to political domination, it also accepted the intellectual premises of modernity on which colonial domination was based.
>
> (Dirks 1990, p. 26)

Behind this claim are of course familiar constructs for modelling change. A familiar pattern would be the way in which homogeneous, undifferentiated social solidarities of the past have given way to the fragmentation of modern society – a belief in alternative paths to modernity, in which fragmentation of the western societies will be avoided by sustaining continuity with an authentic past. The double helix of homogenization and heterogenization is twisted on the axis of historical change such that social fragmentation and cultural homogenization become opposed to each other in temporal succession. As Hobsbawm (1992, p. 6) argues, classical nineteenth-century liberal nationalism was organized on opposite principles to those of contemporary ethnic politics in former Yugoslavia, Georgia and elsewhere. It aimed to unify and extend the scale of human social and cultural units by inclusion (via language and education primarily) rather than by separation and exclusion. This is one reason why Third World regimes have found nineteenth-century European traditions so congenial to their problems of integration and unification, whilst in the same period the exporters of these models have been involved in reinventing local ethnic or regional loyalties as categorical imperatives of the modern bureaucratic state.

Heritage in this setting has diversionary potential in the sense that the aim is to substitute the promotion of local identity for active engagement in national politics. The reason why modern nationalism often means monuments is surely this. The past as property means ownership of what constitutes unity in a chosen sense of place. Whether at national or local levels, the objectification of national spirit and the recognition of the people or races as embodiments of that spirit takes an enduring form that emphasizes long-term continuity. Symbols of transcendence are chosen from the rubble of cultural history in line with their capacity to displace attention from political conflicts. It is not surprising, therefore, that archaeologies have contributed more to the primordialist view of identity, since by escaping the deceit of historical writing, the production of past material cultures has the spontaneity of a kind of unconscious speech, a taken-for-granted, common-sense existence that simply demonstrates that a people have always existed in that place. The origins of naivety in archaeological interpretation can now be properly contextualized within a nineteenth-century nationalist mode of thought.

Archaeologists and development

Archaeologists, of whatever political persuasion, are involved inevitably as producers of expert knowledges. How are claims to control the materiality of the past defined by expertise, legalization and the rights of higher authorities to know better? Such disputes hinge on the question of whose expert knowledge carries authority. In a controversy over a sacred site in Hawaii (Spriggs 1989), Kenneth Emory of the Bishopsland Museum claimed that his concern was to protect the integrity of the knowledge that has been passed down by scholars, Hawaiians and otherwise (that is real knowledge). In this manner he justified his scepticism over the 'springing up of sacred sites' everywhere and the claims by followers of an Hawaiian revivalist cult that the information in museum books is often in error because it is gathered by whites to whom Hawaiian informants did not tell the truth. Could expert archaeological knowledge in Hawaii ever really cope with the Christian revivalist idea that the Hawaiians were the one of the lost seven tribes of Israel that migrated to the Pacific via the Red Sea and Indonesia?

Clashes between archaeologists as local experts and carriers of 'local knowledges' have been fought out on the terrain of 'who can speak with authority versus who can speak with authenticity'. Trying to be both is not necessarily any more successful. The Nigerian archaeologist Nwanna Nzewunwa has documented how becoming an archaeologist estranged him from his own ethnic group, in the way that expert knowledge, education and the city opposes the rural, the traditional and the village (Nzewunwa 1990, pp. 193–7). Here the historical axis is twisted on a geographical scale to create the urban/

rural divide with the village as repository of ancestral knowledge, of craft, folk knowledge and tradition in tension with modernity identified with urban living and formal education as the fountain of rational expertise – primary health care, literacy, development and aid technologies. In other words, academic archaeology acquires authority due to its association with the signs of urban modernity, whilst an indigenous sense of past retains veracity due to its association with orality and tradition. The capacity to have a past, either historically or archaeologically constituted, comes with development and is symptomatic of progress.

Of course the fact that the state is concerned only with certain kinds of representations of the past and not others has implications for defining what is conceived to be legitimate archaeology rather than treasure-seeking and the evaluation of memory as a cultural resource versus museums and archives. Inventing tradition is therefore a product of the codes creating cultural knowledges, i.e. inclusion:exclusion, sameness:difference, writing:memory. In other words, a tradition that aspires to emphasize what makes a group, community, nation different is somehow immediately suspected of being contrived, self-conscious, and false in the eyes of others. In order to protect them from others, the rituals of distinct traditions have to be bracketed and displaced into some safe place where their performance can be held unhindered and consumed without discomfort. Invented folklores, craftlore, Scottish ballads, festivals, etc. are all well-known features of this kind of privatized traditionalism whatever the scale. The only problem with this anodyne view of tradition – either of the invented or discovered kind – is that in much of the world tradition as we know it today was created through contact with modernity in the context of colonialism. In Africa, for example, such timeless features of African society as divine kingship, tribalism, segmentary lineages and fetishism can all be shown to have been produced or transformed in meaning through encounters with colonial rule. The British and other colonial powers were therefore drawn into the production of those components of African tradition that in the postcolonial era have been widely cited as the principal impediments to full-scale modernity. Headlines which despair of the current plight of Africans illustrate a current view that modernization has failed in Africa because of insuperable, indigenous, cultural blockages rather than because of contemporary, external, political realities.

The belief that the colonizers had history and the colonized had custom and tradition sustained and in part still does sustain an anthropology/archaeology dualism (Asad 1979). Mignolo (1992) has described the complicity between alphabetic writing and history in the Renaissance view of knowledge and how this denied Amerindian understanding of their own history since how could the memory of past events be preserved without writing. It is striking that archaeology was least developed in those parts of the colonized periphery where British anthropology in particular was most powerful. We still know virtually nothing in fine-grain detail of the archaeology of vast tracts of west central Africa, for example, whereas ethnographically it formed the backbone for British structural functionalist anthropology. What Dirks (1990) calls the policing of tradition by which he means the ways in which tradition is codified, controlled, reformed and suppressed, became not only the discourse of anthropology but also the justification for fieldwork by providing a more controllable access to custom than did objects and museums. It would appear that anthropology and archaeology were in competition to provide a disciplined account of traditional society, the one based on oral tradition, the other on material culture and both opposed by the official written histories made by European observers. Ironically, the growth of anthropological archaeology has tended to encourage this colonization of the prehistories of others by judging their significance in terms of how well they illustrate some general benchmark in human progress such as the origins of farming, or of metallurgy or the state. For an African archaeologist, the need to have a suitable piece of generalizable academic capital in order to be invited to conferences in the archaeological heartlands of Europe and North America was and is of great importance since jobs and promotion depend on external validation of this kind.

But the very success archaeology has had in evaluating and subsuming local prehistories by the contributions they make to universal comparative projects of western origin has also revealed the limitations of the archaeological project on a global scale. Such universalizing goals were suitable in the context of colonial ideologies where a clear separation existed between Us and Them – where the colonized Other could be domesticated and made an example, however crudely, of some more grandiose paradigm. In this sense classical evolutionism may have changed in substance since the nineteenth century but its basic role as a framework for hierarchically ordering societies on a single scale of values has not changed much. But the fear that the growing transnationalization of capital and developments in communication and transport has created a global culture that will extinguish local identities in a gigantic wave of mass consumerism, has undermined the desirability of archaeology's older generalizing goals. One response as a counter to global homogenization would obviously be to claim expertise in local knowledges which archaeology could claim as its own constituency. Local prehistories are particular and irreducible by the very method of their excavation and recording, and simply denying the need to abstract and generalize has produced the 'thick description' that provides a localized sense of past. The idea of thousands of local archaeology societies producing their own accounts of local pasts simultaneously on a global scale is not at all far-fetched. If the European experience is anything to go by, this is what follows from a successful creation of a sense of nationhood usually in the guise of the creation of a national museum followed by local museums to re-present subordinated identities.

An alternative to this would be for archaeology to break out of the simplicity of such a scenario by investigating the global processes and forms themselves. An archaeology of colonialism, for example, is barely acknowledged as existing and yet an archaeological version of Eric Wolf's (1982)

Europe and the People without History is certainly both feasible and probably more relevant than that based on the ethnohistory and ethnography available to him. Immanuel Wallerstein's three volumes on *The Modern World System* (1974–89) provide the most overall account of contemporary and historical processes of globalization since the sixteenth century. The accounts offered so far, however, are still produced within an ambience that evaluates the pasts of others by their closeness or otherwise to that of the 'Europeans' providing the account. Whilst in an evolutionist past, an Old World archaeology would describe Africa or the Americas in terms of what they lacked (writing, true religion, cities, markets, money or history), now it would be a question of how much they have lost, measured as an absence of otherness itself. Taussig has described this sense of loss as 'This infernal American identity machine . . . composing a mosaic of alterities around a mysterious core of hubridity seeth-ing with instability, threatening the First World quest for a decent fix of straightforward Othering' (Taussig 1993, p. 143).

Archaeology and the postmodern

Just as there seemed to be a growing acceptance of a value-committed archaeology and a willingness to debate the kind of archaeological objectivity required to discern between alternative pasts, the whole archaeological enterprise seems beset by the current slippage of historicity announced as a predominant feature of the postmodern. Jameson (1984), in one of the most well-known formulations of the culture of postmodernism, described it 'as an era experiencing a new depthlessness and a consequent weakening of histori-city representing an inability to unify past, present and future . . ., leaving a rubble of distinct and unrelated signifiers' (Jameson 1984, p. 79), the reduction of experience to a series of pure and unrelated presents in time and a 'general waning of effect with a general accompanying sense of consumer euphoria' (Jameson 1984, p. 79). In the shift from the modern to the postmodern we witness the replacement of angst about the alienation of the subject by the fragmentation of the self. Such a breakdown in the temporal ordering of things also gives rise to a peculiar treatment of the past – postmodernism abandons memory and sense of historical continuity while simultaneously developing an incredible ability to plunder history and absorb whatever it finds there as some aspect of the present. Moreover, archaeology seems willing to provide a postmodern access to the Other that anthropology once promised through primitivism but which is now no longer possible. The likelihood that a primitive Other is now only possible either as science fiction, or by archae-ology providing mythical alien pasts to experience personally in museums and theme parks, reveals the true hunger for wholeness and unity which anthro-pology was always a little inadequate in providing. But these are not tempor-arily experienced pasts – as would be sequence-explored in some kind of time machine or as an exploration of the collective identity of shared memory.

Instead they are rhizome pasts (Deleuze & Guattari 1977) – pasts constructed out of a multiplicity of events that cannot be understood by reference to origin or genesis or deep structures but as social networks of power and desire that nonetheless have trajectories and futures to be understood.

But who is served by this view of the past? The majority of people who visit museums and art galleries are educated, middle-class and obey Bourdieu's (1984) principle that length of time in higher education determines who visits museums. By comparison the main consumers of postmodern imagery are anything but the educated middle class. As Eagleton (1985) has argued, postmodernism in historical effect is conservative – not only in terms of the complacency it generates in creating perfect consumers but also because the images it produces are consumed by those whose historical voice would not be heard anyway. Postmodern art forms and cultural artefacts have also been described as self-embracing and incapable of referring to conditions outside of the problem of image creation (Harvey 1989, p. 323). We have no means of distinguishing class or gender relations in the differential consumption of such images. Instead, the postmodernist collapse of metanarrative – in its decon-structionist sense – was celebrated precisely as play on tropes, privileging writing over language and as a radical approval of the loose play of difference in the creation of individual realities. Totalizing concepts such as class, race, society, etc. had no prior existence, nor could they be deemed to be the hidden determinants of postmodern identities. In fact, identity itself becomes a fictitious and doubtful concept based on the heady modernist desire to deny Lockean doubt and assert a common-sense acceptance of a unified self.

If identities are not given, then the politics of postmodernism must deny that relevance of a sense of past and replace it with a temporarily indeterminate consumption of the past as image. In this respect the point made by Harvey (1989) that postmodernism is a movement within modernity is well made. Little has changed in the sense that the seeking of coherent narratives of the past is still the major legitimation of elite status in advanced capitalism. Sub-categories, such as gender, class and race, have a potential historical consciousness to be realized rather than repressed through the unsettling disorder of the loose play of difference. However, even if we allow alternative narratives of how things came to be, the postmodern as a dominant ideology which proposes the existence of a plurality of archaeological voices is ac-companied by the suspicion that some of these are more authentic than others. The aestheticization of politics to stifle social aspirations and revolutionary movements has happened before. However, it is a new twist to promote alternative historical voices whilst at the same time making clear that some are not to be taken as seriously as others. This is not because the deconstructionist approach threatens an open play of meaning unchecked by the realities of the archaeological record (Hodder 1992, p. 166), but precisely because eventually the latter has to be introduced to rank the relative claims made by minority voices. Shanks & Tilley (1987, p. 192) have made much the same point in criticizing Habermas's naive faith that debate and discussion in a liberal society will make any difference in a subject like archaeology where the system only allows certain people to do or write archaeology. Probably few will have the courage to pursue the poststructuralist argument in archaeology this far and instead a revisionist faith will be expressed, confirming the objectivity of the archaeological record and its independence and capacity to resist any account imposed upon it (cf. Hodder 1992, p. 166). This clearly does not go far enough since achieving objectivity still relies on meaning, text and 'ideas in people's heads' which are precisely the subject of the deconstructionist critique. Such an intention requires what Bourdieu has called 'methodological objectivism', a necessary moment in all research, by which he meant 'the break with primary experience and the construction of objective relations which once accomplished, demands its own supersession' (Bourdieu 1977, p. 72). It must also assume the existence of a more dialectical relationship between past and present in which answering 'how things might have been otherwise' requires equal understanding of the play of structure that escapes human consciousness and effectively prohibits certain kinds of action either to enter historical consciousness or to be stifled in the event.

Conclusion

The social construction of archaeological pasts is more than personal values getting involved in the academic enterprise. In the differing contexts of nationalism, development and the postmodern, we encounter the silences and gaps in archaeological explanations that determine which sites are excavated, what kinds of artefacts are privileged in the legitimizing of expert archaeological knowledges. The fact that the materiality of the archaeological record can resist these selective pressures or that silences can be exposed does not deny the obvious effects of such value commitment in archaeological practice. What I would suggest has been the key value motivating archaeological work is the notion of identity employed. If archaeology has tended traditionally to be on the primordialist side, current interest in notions of agency and the individual suggest a late but necessary move towards the interactionist perspective. Pushed to its limit, a postmodern denial of identity, except as temporary and fleeting refusal of anxiety, would have more serious implications for a future demand of archaeological narratives.

Of the motivations considered in this chapter, the expansion of archaeology's relation to nationalism and ethnicity in the construction of collective identity seems certain to continue. Partly the materiality of the archaeological record will assure this. Partly also the creation of alternative pasts is increasingly being used to legitimate land claims, ethnic territories, and access to economic resources. Representations of communities of shared memory are diversifying, often outside the museum into settings that are more immediately graspable and open to appropriation. What seems clear is that whilst the relation of archaeology to nationalism has been the dominant force historically in Europe and for new nations creating themselves out of the exigencies of colonial rule, the wider issue is that of the construction of communities of shared memory. From the standpoint of modernity, every age is thus judged to attain the fullness of its time not by being but by becoming.

Acknowledgements

I am particularly grateful for Chris Tilley's comments on this chapter and to Bruce Kapferer for his insights on the subject of identity.

References

Anderson, B. 1981. *Imagined Communities*. London: Verso.
Asad, T. 1979. Anthropology and the end of ideology. *Man* 14, 607–28.
Berger, P. & T. Luckman 1967. *The Social Construction of Reality*. New York: Doubleday.
Bintliff, J. 1992. Postmodernism, rhetoric and scholasticism at TAG: the current state of British archaeological theory. *Antiquity* 65, 274–8.
Bourdieu, P. 1977. *Outline of a Theory of Practice*. Cambridge: Cambridge University Press.
Bourdieu, P. 1984. *Distinction*. London: Routledge.
Canadine, D. 1983. The context, performance and meaning of ritual: the British monarchy and the invention of tradition. In *The Invention of Tradition*, Hobsbawm, E. & T. Ranger (eds), 101–65. Cambridge: Cambridge University Press.
Deleuze, G. & F. Guattari 1977. *Anti-Oedipus*. New York: Viking.
Dirks, N. 1990. History as a sign of the modern. *Public Culture* 2, 25–33.
Eagleton, T. 1985. Capitalism, modernism and postmodernism. *New Left Review* 152, 60–73.
Erikson, E. H. 1959. *Identity and the Life Cycle: selected papers*. New York: International Universities Press.
Frank G. 1993. Was there a Bronze Age world system? *Current Anthropology* 34, 3.
Gero, J. & M. Conkey 1991. *Engendering Archaeology: women and prehistory*. Oxford: Basil Blackwell.
Gleason, P. 1983. Identifying identity: a semantic history. *Journal of American History* 69, 910–31.
Goffman, E. 1967. *The Presentation of Self in Everyday Life*. London: Allen Lane.
Habermas, J. 1987. *The Philosophical Discourse of Modernity*. Massachusetts: Massachusetts Institute of Technology Press.
Handler, R. 1988. *Nationalism and the Politics of Culture in Quebec*. Madison, Wis.: University of Wisconsin Press.
Harvey, D. 1989. *The Condition of Postmodernity*. Oxford: Basil Blackwell.
Hewison, R. 1987. *The Heritage Industry*. London: Methuen.
Hobsbawm, E. 1992. Ethnicity and nationalism in Europe today. *Anthropology Today* 8, 3–13.
Hobsbawm, E. & T. Ranger 1983. *The Invention of Tradition*. Cambridge: Cambridge University Press.
Hodder, I. 1992. *Theory and Practice in Archaeology*. London: Routledge.
Jameson, F. 1984. Postmodernism or the cultural logic of late capitalism. *New Left Review* 146, 53–92.
Kohl, P. 1993. Nationalism, politics and the practice of archaeology in Soviet Transcaucasia. *Journal of European Archaeology* 2, 179–86.

Kristiansen, K. 1993. The strength of the past and its great might; an essay on the use of the past. *Journal of European Archaeology* 1, 3–33.

Langbaum, R. 1977. *The Mysteries of Identity: a theme in modern literature*. New York: Oxford University Press.

Merriman, N. 1989. Heritage from the other side of the glass case. *Anthropology Today* 5, 14–15.

Mignolo, W. 1992. On the colonization of Amerindian languages and memories. *Comparative Studies of Sociology and History* 34, 301–34.

Miller, D. & C. Tilley 1984. *Ideology, Power and Prehistory*. Cambridge: Cambridge University Press.

Nzewunwa, N. 1990. Cultural education in West Africa: archaeological perspectives. In *The Politics of the Past*, Gathercole, P. & D. Lowenthal (eds), 189–202. London: Unwin Hyman.

Robertson, R. 1990. After nostalgia: wilful nostalgia and modernity. In *Theories of Modernity and Postmodernity*, Turner, B. (ed.), 31–45. London: Sage.

Rowlands, M. 1987. Repetition and exteriorization in narratives of historical origins. *Critique of Anthropology* 8, 43–62.

Scott, J. 1985. *Weapons of the Weak*. New Haven: Yale University Press.

Scott, J. 1989. History in crisis? The others' side of the story. *American Historical Review* 94, 688–700.

Shanks, M. & C. Tilley 1987. *Reconstructing Archaeology: theory and practice*. London: Routledge.

Spriggs, M. 1989. God's police and damned whores: images of archaeology in Hawaii. In *The Politics of the Past*, Gathercole, P. & D. Lowenthal (eds), 118–29. London: Unwin Hyman.

Taussig, M. 1993. *Mimesis and Alterity: a particular history of the senses*. New York: Routledge.

Ucko, P. J. 1987. *Academic Freedom and Apartheid*. London: Duckworth.

Wallerstein, I. 1974–89. *The Modern World System*. New York: Academic Press.

Wolf, E. 1982. *Europe and the People without History*. London & Berkeley: University of California Press.

10   Gender division of labour in the construction of archaeological knowledge in the United States

JOAN M. GERO

This discussion begins at some distance from archaeology, and indeed from gender divisions of labour, whether in research communities or in other cultures of interest. I want to open by reiterating Karin Knorr-Cetina's epilogue, in which she quotes Dorothy Sayers:

> 'My lord, facts are like cows. If you look them in the face hard enough, they generally run away.' Dorothy Sayers' analogy between cows and facts [contains] both a philosophical and a methodological point. . . . The philosophical point is that facts are not something we can take for granted or think of as the solid rock upon which knowledge is built. Actually their nature is rather problematic – so much so that confrontation often scares them off. The methodological point is that the confrontation has to be long, hard and direct. Like cows, facts have become sufficiently domesticated to deal with run-of-the-mill events.
>
> (Knorr-Cetina 1981, p. 1)

In order to look at the construction of archaeological knowledge, this chapter takes as its starting point the 'constructivist' interpretation of how knowledge is produced.

A non-discovery model of knowledge, or knowledge as creative construction

Most models of how science is done operate with an idea of scientists using various strategies and devices in order to pull back a curtain on pre-given truths which had previously been concealed (Latour & Woolgar 1979, p. 129). Scientists themselves employ language that conveys the misleading impression that the presence of objects, facts, sometimes even laws, are pre-givens and that such facts and laws merely await the timely revelation of their existence by scientists (Latour & Woolgar 1979, p. 128). We note that archaeology is particularly prone to an objectivist 'discovery' view of science because, quite apart from the relational facts and conceptual objects we produce, our data are often underground, literally covered up, and we must in fact UNcover it up, or DIScover it up. Thus, archaeologists intuitively believe that they 'discover' knowledge more directly than scientists in other fields. In the constructivist view, however, science is not about discovery but about creativity and construction (Latour & Woolgar 1979, p. 129), about making order out of disorder, about the fabrication of statements that reduce noise in data, about chains of decisions and negotiations and selections that can only be made on the basis of previous selections (Knorr-Cetina 1981, p. 5). In this view, science is highly internally structured through the process of production, rather than being descriptive of a disarticulated, external reality.

In the words of Latour and Woolgar (1979, p. 170), 'having an idea represents a summary of a complicated material situation' and results from a particular historical sequence of events and interpersonal exchanges. Facts themselves are not simply recorded as they are observed; they are crafted out of a welter of confusing and conflicting observations, modified and reformulated out of knowledge of what other scientists are working on, and accepted more readily if their proponent has good credentials. Once a 'fact' is arrived at, it is quickly freed from the circumstances of its production and loses all historical reference to the social and contextual conditions of its construction (Latour & Woolgar 1979, p. 106). Thus, the processes that account for and produce scientific facts or knowledge are always invisible since practitioners themselves use language and concepts as though the knowledge they produce had no history, no social life, no culture . . . and no gender.

To view scientific investigation as constructive rather than descriptive, and to see scientific products – knowledge – as highly internally constructed in terms of the selectivity it incorporates (Knorr-Cetina 1981, p. 7) presents a serious challenge to an objectivist view of science. It has led to a research programme that observes science close at hand, demystifying the 'facticity' of science and calling into question other scientific claims. For example, the constructivists' sociology of science gives grounds to doubt the purported independence of discovery and validation which is a prime feature of mature science. Observing science close at hand shows that the 'discovery' or fact production phase of research is actually inseparable from the validation phase; in practice, scientists constantly relate their decisions and selections to the expected responses of specific members of the community of 'validators' (their colleagues), or to the dictates of the journals in which they wish to publish. That is, discoveries are made with a very explicit eye toward potential criticism or acceptance, as well as with respect to potential allies and enemies (Knorr-Cetina 1981, p. 7) and do not set out neutral propositions to be assessed independently by supposedly non-interested 'other' parties. In a similar vein, constructivist science questions the ability of science to filter out bias and to self-regulate truth claims, recognizing that admission into, and ongoing practice within, the scientific 'community' directly depends on adopting and embracing that same 'community's' starting assumptions, its research agenda, its accepted methodologies and its standards. Thus, the truth-testing system is at once closed, internally structured to ensure compatibility, and self-serving.

A constructivist view of science with its internal observations of scientific practice has yet to be applied in archaeology. A sizeable literature does exist to show how archaeological knowledge is conditioned by and responds to ideo-logical factors – that is, how archaeology underwrites and records the prevail-ing sets of beliefs to which researchers also subscribe. Very little work, however (perhaps only that by Kelley & Hanen 1988), has been offered to illuminate constructivist processes at other levels of social conditioning in archaeology, in terms, for instance, of career determination – and here we mean the conditioning that occurs in terms of where a researcher stands in his/her career at the time that particular work is undertaken and promoted, or taking institutional factors into account, such as reputations of institutions with which researchers are associated, or local institutional traditions and priorities in research. And what is finally and ultimately missing is a study of the micro processes of research – 'the idiosyncratic, local, heterogeneous, contextual and multifaceted processes of scientific practice' (Knorr, cited in Latour & Woolgar 1979, p. 152) in archaeology, which would quickly bring us to an ethnology of archaeological research.

Although this close ethnographic work is just getting under way in archae-ology (see Gero & Goodwin 1992) and results are not yet available for analysis, the rest of this chapter suggests that archaeological knowledge and fact are nevertheless amenable to a constructivist analysis, and that archaeology can be demonstrated to be a social, political and, more specifically, gendered insti-tution. Where the sociologists of science such as Latour & Woolgar (1979) or Knorr-Cetina (1981) have failed to address gender as a significant factor in the manufacture of knowledge, this becomes the very centre of the following investigation: what role does a gender division of labour play in archaeological research and in the construction of archaeological knowledge?

The role of gender in the construction of archaeological knowledge

That science is patriarchal and a profoundly male endeavour has been demon-strated (Jordanova 1980, Merchant 1980, Rose 1983, Bleier 1984, Keller 1985, Bleier 1986). The thrust of the feminist critique is several-fold: it shows that women are routinely ignored as a serious subject of study, that male is taken as the norm against which success and deviance are measured, and that flawed research results are used to reaffirm sexist presuppositions about the inevita-bility of women's subordination. Moreover, as Wylie, Okruhlik, Thielen-Wilson & Morton (1989) state, feminist analysis shows that the modern position of women depends on their exclusion and depreciation as knowers. Thus to include and appreciate women's experience – as objects of enquiry and as active scholars – requires 'analysing and challenging the politics of control over knowledge and epistemic authority' (Wylie, Okruhlik, Thielen-Wilson & Morton 1989, p. 379) which we can identify with knowledge construction.

Women do archaeology and, although we 'do' it in smaller numbers than men – women constitute approximately 20 per cent of fully employed archaeologists (Kramer & Stark 1988, p. 11) – we are well represented in the analysis of archaeological materials (Gero 1983, 1985, 1988). The question I now ask is this: do women archaeologists construct a different kind of knowledge – or construct knowledge by a different process – from male archaeologists? And finding differences, how do such differences reflect back on the entire enterprise of producing and accumulating a body of selected observations that we call 'knowledge', and ultimately on the past as we know and tell it? What do such differences tell us of the organization of scholarly labour?

Lithic studies

Let me start with lithic analysis, an area that is generally associated with male activities but in which a relatively large number of women archaeologists have built reputations and made significant contributions. (I need only mention names like Ruth Tringham, Robin Torrence, Ruthann Knudson, Anta Montet-White, Emily Moss, Lucy J. Johnson or Helle Juel-Jensen for this to ring true.) Indeed, in the 1989 American Anthropological Association *Guide to Departments*, women list themselves as lithic analysts at a slightly higher ratio to men than their overall representation in the profession – just over a quarter of the people listing themselves as lithic analysts are women, while women only comprise one-fifth of the full-time professional archaeologists (Kramer & Stark 1988, p. 11).

But a closer look reveals that studies undertaken by women are not representative of the full range of interests in lithics, and entire areas of modern lithic studies include virtually no women investigators at all. Most strikingly, flint knapping, where archaeologists replicate lithic production techniques, is exclusively a male arena (see Gero 1991). Although women archaeologists have often learned to knap, there is virtually no published literature by women as flint knappers. We note too that the tools reproduced by modern (male) flint knappers duplicate a narrow range of standardized tool forms dominated by the projectile point (especially the fluted point) and including only a small suite of other elaborately retouched or heavily worked kinds of knives, core and blade technologies, polished celts and axes.

It is also exclusively male archaeologists who experimentally use these replicated, standardized tools in modern, analogical activities, with an overwhelming emphasis on exaggeratedly 'male' activities: felling trees, making bows or arrows, hunting, spear-throwing, butchering, and note particularly the research on throwing projectiles into, and carving up, modern analogies to big game (mostly elephants or rhinos) to translate male researchers directly into pleistocene hunters. Often this literature draws a fine line between replicative science and macho-drama; shooting arrows into newly killed and (very importantly!) still-warm boar strung up in wooden frames (Fischer, Hansen & Rasmussen 1984) illustrates a particularly lurid kind of research design in which only males participate.

In contrast to the male-dominated areas of lithic studies, a very different line of investigation asks how tasks were carried out with stone tools. It is female investigators who, in disproportionate numbers, have worked from a functional perspective to study expedient, non-standardized tools, at the level of micro-wear analysis, macro-wear analysis, or by means of studying the composition of assemblages. In contrast to the 100 per cent sample of males in flint-knapping research, the ratio of women:men involved in micro-wear studies, for instance, is approximately 1:1, again very disproportionate to the overall ratio of 1:5 women:men employed as full-time archaeologists in the profession. Moreover, in contrast to males' experimental programmes, women's experimental lithic studies focus on nutting (Spears 1975), leatherworking (Adams 1988) and woodworking (Price-Beggerly 1976), all of which are done with unelaborated and non-standardized stone tools.

Thus, male archaeologists interact with lithics, and appear in lithic research, in profoundly and significantly different ways from female archaeologists. The tools that males make and report on making, and the lithic-using activities that they re-enact experimentally, create a discrete sphere of lithic activity from the sphere of lithic production and utilization in which modern women archaeologists are involved. From the modern archaeological research community, 'male' lithics emerge as arrowheads and spearpoints, axes and adzes, while 'female' lithics are flake tools and nutting stones. Archaeological networks of male lithic analysts construct and put forward a substantially different notion of the forms and functions of prehistoric 'stone tools'. Moreover, there is some suggestion that their work goes into collected volumes that are edited by males and dominated by male contributors: compare collected volumes on lithic analysis edited by males (a rapid survey reveals five volumes, published between 1976 and 1989) where an overall average of only 14 per cent of the contributors were women, against volumes on lithics edited by females (two volumes, published between 1985 and 1989), of which 39 per cent of the contributors were women.

At the same time, female lithic analysts push forward with an agenda and a literature on non-standardized tools; lithic sessions organized by women, and volumes on lithic studies edited by women, are more likely to include higher proportions of women contributors. For instance, during the five years of SAA Annual Meeting programmes canvassed (1983, 1985, 1986, 1988 and 1989), there were only four organized sessions specifically on lithics: three organized by males and one by a female. This albeit scant sample suggests that female lithic researchers are more than four times as likely to be asked to participate in a national SAA session organized by a woman (46 per cent women in the woman-organized session) than in a session organized by males (average 11 per cent women in male-organized sessions). Note too that in the selected five-year sample of SAA meetings, women contributed 'voluntary' papers on lithics at a rate of 37 per cent of all volunteered papers on lithics, suggesting that their overall visibility improves when females organize sessions on lithics, but that organized sessions by males do not significantly enhance the visibility of female work.

There is some suggestion too that the functional work on lithics by females also circulates more heavily among women readers. This was shown recently when male graduate students commented that the class readings were 'mostly by women'. Though in fact far from true, the complaint reflected the fact that the syllabi, set by a female, included a higher proportion of female-authored works than students were accustomed to. This had happened, unintentionally, because the works that circulated through the hands of the teacher, and which she found exciting and important, were often the work of women colleagues!

Palaeoethnobotany

Such radical divisions of research labour – and of archaeological knowledge – are repeated in other specialized areas of archaeology. Palaeoethnobotany, widely recognized as a women's research area, is given as a research speciality in the American Anthropological Association *Guide to Departments* by an almost equal number of women and men, 12 compared to 14, although women represent only 20 per cent of the population of archaeologists. From inside the field as well, researchers report a heavily female representation (Gail Wagner & Christine Hastorf *pers. comm.*).

The botanical interests of archaeologists can be distinguished, generally, into camps that focus on large programmatic issues ('the origins of agriculture' or 'palaeoenvironmental reconstruction'), and those that emphasize localized identification of plant remains and their cultural significance. This division, together with its gender loading, is clearly reflected in the 1986 *World Directory of Ethnobotanists* (Jain, Minnis & Shah 1986), which lists 26 female and 37 male North Americans together with their self-reported areas of concentration. While females are underrepresented by a ratio of 4 females to 15 males in putting 'the origins of agriculture' as their first area of speciality, and while 'prehistoric environmental reconstructions' is mentioned only half as often for females as for males, the proportion is very different for those ethnobotanists listing palaeoethnobotany as a first speciality: 16 females and only 15 males. While women identify seeds, note that the seminal (yes, seminal!) volume edited by Stuart Streuver in 1971 on *Prehistoric Horticulture* contained 33 articles, only two of which had females as co-authors!

This suggests that it is males who synthesize the overview, abstract the environment, generalize the adaptation and theorize the origins, while women identify the seeds. Males construct the facts of prehistory – from women's data.

Palaeozoology

Finally, we can glimpse a third area, zooarchaeology, from yet a different perspective. Again, males and females analyse archaeological fauna, females at a somewhat higher representation than their overall representation in the field. That is, males' dissertations on faunal analysis run approximately twice as high as females', in contrast to the overall male:female dissertation-writing ratio of 3:1. In the American Anthropological Association *Guide to Departments*, the same over-representation is maintained in the self-listed palaeozoology specialization: women label themselves palaeozoologists almost half as often as men (18 listings for women compared to 39 for men) although they make up only one-fifth of the population.

If the gender effect in faunal analysis is not very revealing at this scale, we must again peer inside the faunal numbers to find that males completely control the study of some fauna, namely large mammals and, within these, particularly the Pleistocene mammals, a distribution verified by the *American Antiquity* articles that treat elk, caribou, mammoth and mastodon – these remains are studied almost exclusively by males! A very tight North American research network can be traced from the early 1970s through to the present, dedicated to the study of bison bones at bison kill sites – virtually all male – and to Pleistocene mammal studies – virtually all male – in contrast to the palaeo-zoological work that identifies diverse and generalized animal species or that assesses minimal numbers of individuals out of sometimes large faunal samples, work that is shared by both genders but in which women are again over-represented.

This division, like the others discussed above, ramifies further into other knowledge constructs. Big-game hunting, considered among the 'great events of prehistory', is privileged as socially pivotal, nutritionally vital and all-male. Reconstructions of Pleistocene hunting, with all the awe and reverence ascribed to them, then create a high-prestige research niche for studying events from which women are excluded, prehistorically and in contemporary re-search. Women are reaffirmed as secondary citizens, in the past for not being hunters, and in the present, as archaeologists, for being outside the big-bone circle.

Women's containment in faunal analysis, then, is intrinsic to, and necessary for, the bison–mammoth knowledge construct, and is brought about by preselected, pre-erected gender constructs, by sociological, gender-influenced networking in the formation of research groups, and finally by the manipu-lation and practice of power extensions in knowledge construction.

Interpretation of gender as a social construct in research

From this preliminary review, we can characterize the gender/sex system in research as a complex mix of gender ideology, gender sociology and gender politics. The work that women regularly take on in archaeological research is painstaking, labour-intensive and methodologically explicit. It is supported by other female researchers in symposia and in published volumes while it illuminates an exclusion from male-dominated areas of research. It emerges as low-status work that often lies in appendices to important 'synthetic' articles, and, significantly, it is work that represents a low capital investment in equipment, using a mode of production closer to what has been called 'scientific craft production' (Rose 1983, 1986).

The intolerable part of this scenario is not that the sexual division of labour in research produces a sexual division of knowledge. Rather, what is intolerable is the recognition that a sexual division of labour is actually a hierarchy of labour, part of a shift toward a new scientific mode of commodity production where the products of women's analysis are expropriated by men in their synthetic overviews. Women identify seeds, but men construct the power-laden 'origins' of agriculture. Female and male 'facts' are unequal in status, and the facts that matter in archaeology, in science, originate with men because, as Mackie (1988, pp. 7–8) reminds us and Marx and Engels wrote, 'the ideas of the ruling class are in every epoch the ruling ideas'.

The perplexing part of this scenario is whether and how it can continue to operate. How long can men researchers insist on the centrality of bison and Pleistocene mammals in the human experience, or on defining the category of 'tools' on the basis of the small fraction of lithic remains that exhibit extensive retouch? Strathern's (1987) 'awkward relationship' of feminism to traditional disciplinary methods and goals is relevant here: women's research, fundamentally and perhaps unconsciously feminist in its approach to the construction of knowledge, constitutes a fundamental challenge to disciplinary frameworks and, if allowed to persist, necessarily presents a serious challenge to the categories, divisions, assumptions and meanings attached to knowledge. Perhaps the knowledge, the sets of facts that archaeology has already put in place, have so internally structured and pre-ordained our enquiry that archaeology will continue to contain women's scholarship in a low-status, low-technology, theoretically irrelevant position. But the 'competitive premises' (Strathern 1979, p. 284) that characterize women's and men's scholarship suggest that a massive reorganization of knowledge may be necessary and inevitable.

Finally, the exhilarating part of this scenario is the recognition and reclaiming of women's social and intellectual experiences in the construction of archaeological knowledge. The areas of research here identified with women focus on the everyday, common, redundant archaeological materials that make up the overwhelming preponderance of items recovered from the archaeological record. Through these emerge the social lives of prehistory, reinforced and negotiated by interactions with the material world; it is this endless and fascinating playing out of social and gender roles that eclipses palaces, pyramids, origins and bison – and that is often made visible through women's research areas.

Note

An earlier version of this chapter is published in *The Archaeology of Gender: proceedings of the 22nd annual Chacmool Conference*, Walde, D. (ed.). Calgary: The Archaeological Association of the University of Calgary. 1991.

Acknowledgements

I have Melanie Cabak to thank for the observations on both the Streuver (1971) volume and the *World Directory of Ethnobotanists*.

References

Adams, J. L. 1988. Use-wear analysis on manos and hide processing stones. *Journal of Field Archaeology* 15, 307–15.
American Anthropological Association 1988–9. *Guide to Departments*. Washington, DC: AAA.
Bleier, R. 1984. *Science and Gender*. New York: Pergamon Press.
Bleier, R. (ed.) 1986. *Feminist Approaches to Science*. New York: Pergamon Press.
Fischer, A., P. V. Hansen & P. Rasmussen 1984. Macro and micro wear traces on lithic projectile points. *Journal of Danish Archaeology* 3, 19–46.
Gero, J. 1983. Gender bias in archaeology: a cross cultural pespective. In *The Socio-Politics of Archaeology*, Gero, J. M., D. Lacy & M. L. Blakey (eds), 51–7. Amherst: University of MA Department of Anthropology.
Gero, J. 1985. Socio politics of archaeology and the woman-at-home ideology. *American Antiquity* 50, 342–50.
Gero, J. 1988. Gender bias in archaeology: here, then, there, now. In *Feminism within the Science and Health Care Professions: overcoming resistance*, Rosser, S. V. (ed.), 33–43. Oxford: Pergamon Press.
Gero, J. 1991. Genderlithics: women's roles in stone tool production. *In Engendering Archaeology: women and prehistory*, Gero, J. M. & W. M. Conkey (eds), 163–93. Oxford: Basil Blackwell.
Gero, J. & C. Goodwin 1992. The practice of seeing paleoindians. Paper presented in the session 'Envisioning the Past' at the 91st Annual American Anthropological Association Meeting, San Francisco.
Jain, S. K., P. Minnis & N. C. Shah 1986. *World Directory of Ethnobotanists*. Lucknow: National Botanical Research Institute.
Jordanova, L. 1980. Natural facts: a historical perspective on science and sexuality. In *Nature, Culture and Gender*, MacCormack, C. & M. Strathern (eds), 42–69. Cambridge: Cambridge University Press.
Keller, E. F. 1985. *Reflections on Gender and Science*. New Haven: Yale University Press.
Knorr-Cetina, K. 1981. *The Manufacture of Knowledge*. Oxford: Pergamon Press.
Kramer, C. & M. Stark 1988. The status of women in archaeology. *Anthropology Newsletter* 29, 1.
Latour, B. & S. Woolgar 1979. *Laboratory Life*. Beverly Hills: Sage Library of Social Research.
Mackie, M. 1988. Sexism in sociological research. In *Gender Bias in Scholarship*, Tomm, W. & G. Hamilton (eds), 1–23. Calgary: Calgary Institute for the Humanities.
Merchant, C. 1980. *The Death of Nature*. New York: Harper & Row.
Price-Beggerly, P. 1976. Edge damage on experimentally used scrapers of Hawaiian basalt. *Lithic Technology* 5, 22–4.

Rose, H. 1983. Hand, brain and heart: a feminist epistemology for the natural sciences. *Signs* 9, 73–90.

Rose, H. 1986. Beyond masculine realities: a feminist epistemology for the sciences. In *Feminist Approaches to Science*, Bleier, R. (ed.), 57–76. London: Pergamon Press.

Spears, C. S. 1975. Hammers, nuts and jolts, cobbles, cobbles, cobbles: experiments in cobble technologies in search of correlates. In *Arkansas Eastman Archaeological Project*, Baker, C. (ed.) with contributions by C. Spears, C. Classen & M. Schiffer, 83–110. Fayetteville: Arkansas Archaeological Survey.

Strathern, M. 1987. An awkward relationship: the case of feminism and anthropology. *Signs* 12, 276–92.

Streuver, S. (ed.) 1971. *Prehistoric Horticulture*. Garden City, New York: American Museum Sourcebooks in Anthropology.

Wylie, A., K. Okruhlik, L. Theilen-Wilson & S. Morton 1989. Feminist critiques of science: the epistemological and methodological literature. *Women's Studies International Forum* 12, 379–88.

11 Interpreting silences: symbol and history in the case of Ram Janmabhoomi/Babri Masjid

NANDINI RAO

The past is created from and in the image of the present. History and archaeology are entirely malleable, depending as they do on interpretive reconstruction. Since they are perpetually reconstituted in the present, they emerge in a predominantly symbolic dimension. There is a very fine line between historical/archaeological 'fact' and myth, with the distinction being made essentially in relation to contemporary issues and in the contemporary context. The past is thus continually recreated. This chapter examines how pasts are being created in one particular situation in India, in which the rival groups involved have both appealed to 'historical/archaeological facts' and tradition to legitimize their claim to the monument under dispute. These claims have led to violence and carnage, the like of which was seen before only in 1947, when the country was rent apart into the separate states of Pakistan and India. The issue is politically volatile and extremely sensitive. It has been used by various political parties in attempts to further their power and control.

Colonial domination for nearly two centuries (ending in 1947) resulted in the diminution of Indian identity. A recreation and resurgence of this identity was seen through the freedom struggle and in the postcolonial era.[1]

Postcolonial India was (is) marked by chaos and disarray. At such a time, in order to assert a postcolonial 'Indian' identity, it was found necessary to emphasize tradition. The Indian past was reached out for,[2] and Indian customs and culture were proclaimed to be unpolluted by external (especially the colonial) influences. Continuity was vehemently stressed despite centuries of contact with a diversity of cultures whose contributions were largely negated.

Indian reaction to the colonial past is marked by ambiguity and polyvalence. Hatred, xenophobia, awe and envy are all apparent. The attitude of the state, while being similarly polyvalent, has largely emphasized the obliteration of overt expressions of the colonial experience from daily life. Colonial monuments celebrating and commemorating events of importance in the combined past of imperial Britain and India have often been dismantled. For instance, statues commemorating events in the lives of Queen Victoria and King George have been uprooted from the central squares of several cities and lie abandoned today. In their place are statues of members of today's postcolonial power groups. In some instances, squares, streets and monuments have been renamed.

Such has not been the case in the Mozambican postcolonial context (see Sinclair 1986). Here, the view taken is that the colonial past cannot be negated and is an important part of Mozambican history, as it provides an example of the determination of a colonized population to free itself. Thus, the monuments remain:

> it is important . . . to preserve as a symbol of tenacity and determination of our people and as a memory of their humiliation and foreign domination, all historical remains referring both to the creativity and struggle of the Mozambican people as well as the colonial presence in Mozambique.
>
> (cited in Sinclair 1986, p. 82)

In Korea, quite the reverse has occurred. Almost anything bearing signs of the Japanese occupation has been demolished and overt evidence of a Japanese past destroyed.

While some African nations (e.g. Zimbabwe and Botswana) have reacted strongly against archaeological evidence and perspectives that reveal the antiquity of ethnic pluralism, other nations (e.g. Nigeria) find such evidence to be useful for the strategy that promotes unity and have consciously and actively used it to this end (Lane 1990). These are clearly attempts at coming to terms with a (colonial) past that has a direct bearing on contemporary identity.

In India, despite claims by the state to secularism (enshrined in the constitution),[3] the postcolonial re-creation of identity has meant largely and perhaps inevitably (since Hindus number over 80 per cent, with Muslims, the second largest group, numbering only 16 per cent) the re-creation of the Hindu identity. The creation of Muslim Pakistan has in some ways legitimized this quiet but emphatic Hindu stand. Hindu factions have recently emphasized that the ancestors of Indian Muslims too were 'foreigners', having come into India only around the eleventh century AD. They also insist that the Muslims must remember that most of them are converts and, therefore, 'originally' Hindu. Another factor that might explain the aggressive, even militant stance of the Hindus despite their large numbers, is the result of what is seen as the 'pampering' of the minorities by those in the political arena, through the protection of minority rights in exchange for their votes. In fact, this has often meant that governments have taken regressive decisions and stances in order to keep the largely defensive minority populations happy.[4]

It is in the nature of the validating and reaffirming of identity that one also simultaneously denigrates the 'other'. Thus, in re-creating and reaffirming Hindu identity as the 'Indian' one, the majority group (with increasingly overt fiat) has simultaneously found itself in the position of negating the Muslim identity. This has led, inevitably, to conflicts and carnage which have recently focused and telescoped on what has come to be known as the 'Ram

Janmabhoomi/Babri Masjid controversy'. Briefly, the controversy has arisen because Hindus and Muslims have both been claiming a particular territory to be theirs by (historic) right.

The controversy

A mosque in the city of Ayodhya in northern India, in which Muslims offered prayers from the mid-1500s to 1949, and which was erected during the reign of the first Mughal Emperor, Babar, is claimed by the Hindus to be the site of an ancient temple to the god/king Rama. It is contended, by the militant Hindu factions, that Babar destroyed a temple that stood on this site (claimed to be the birthplace of Rama) and constructed the Babri Masjid on its ruins. Both Hindus and Muslims have reached for textual and oral traditional evidence to strengthen, validate and legitimize their claims.

The Hindus maintain that according to one of the Indian epics, the *Ramayana* (which tells his story), Rama was born in and ruled from Ayodhya. This god/king is taken by Hindus to be an incarnation of Vishnu (one of the Hindu Trinity). They also maintain that a 'miracle' occurred in 1949. On the night of 22/23 December, idols of Rama, his wife Sita, brother Lakshmana and faithful servant Hanuman appeared miraculously within the precincts of the mosque at the climax of a nine-day vigil held by Hindus outside it. In addition to quoting from the epic poem and referring to the miracle to demonstrate the validity of their claim to the site, the Hindus also rely on some colonial documents (specifically Carnegy 1870, Nevill 1905, Beveridge [1922] 1969).

The Muslims quote textual, historical and archaeological data to prove that no temple existed on the spot where the mosque is today. Further, they perceive the 'miracle' of 22/23 December completely differently, and use police records to support their view. According to a First Information Report (FIR), made at the Police Station in Ayodhya by the Hindu Sub Inspector of Police on duty (in 1949), a group of Hindus broke into the mosque on the night of 22 December 1949 and installed the statues (see Srivastava 1991 for a translation of the FIR). The Muslims insist that this is the truth and the miracle claimed to have occurred by the Hindus is false. Archaeological excavations (Lal 1976–7, pp. 52–3) in the area have revealed no evidence of a Hindu temple.[5] They have revealed, instead, that Jainism and Buddhism flourished in the area prior to Islamic influence. Early Buddhist, Chinese and Jain texts corroborate this. The texts also reveal that Ayodhya did not become an important religious centre for Hindus until the eighteenth century, by which time the Mughals and, finally, the British had already gained political power.

Interpreting silences

The authors of the three colonial documents that the Hindus present as evidence hold the view that since Babar was a good Muslim, and as the duty (as they interpreted it) of a good Muslim is to build mosques, Babar must have razed a temple to build a mosque in its place. None of the three investigated the validity of this conclusion.[6] Texts of Babar's reign and those immediately succeeding have no record of the razing of a temple by Babar for the building of a mosque.

Contemporary Muslims and some historians maintain that Babar would certainly have mentioned the razing of a temple, since he mentions the building of a mosque in Ayodhya. Even if the fundamentalist Hindu view of Islam is used, i.e. that to gain merit, Babar destroyed a kafir monument, they insist that since such an act is thought to add religious merit and power, Babar ought (by the fundamentalist Hindus' own logic) to have mentioned the deed. They also insist that Tulsidas, a poet who retold the Ramayana and lived during the reign of Akbar (Babar's grandson), would surely have mentioned the fact that a temple of such great significance (commemorating Rama's birth) had been destroyed by Babar. Akbar, too, they claim, secular and progressive in his views, would certainly have made some mention of it.

Archaeological 'facts' are silent about the existence of a temple below the Babri Masjid. As discussed, texts too are silent on this issue. And it is this silence that is being interpreted differently by Hindus and Muslims. The Muslims, Hindus and British have 'read' into the characters of Babar, Tulsidas and Akbar in order to legitimize their different claims.

Some historians, in defending the rights of the oppressed minority group,[7] have appealed to 'facts' to support their view – no material evidence in the archaeological record of the civilization described in the epic poem; in fact, no evidence at all of a Rama cult centre in Ayodhya for several centuries after Babar's reign. They also point out that the British authors reveal far more about their own attitudes towards the Muslims in their analysis of Babar's duties and deeds.

But what has given rise to the controversy?

Symbol and history in the case of Ram Janmabhoomi/Babri Masjid

It is not uncommon for those in power to legitimize their position by claiming descent from the gods. Identification of a ruler with a god was (and continues to be) a pattern.

We see in contemporary India how those in power (both the rulers and the opposition) assume god/saint-like forms. The national (state-controlled) television network recently serialized the two epic poems, the *Mahabhrata* and the *Ramayana*. In both, the protagonists are gods or men with god-like qualities. Krishna in the *Mahabharata* and Rama in the *Ramayana* are incarnations of

Vishnu, come to save the world from evil. Both are extremely potent and powerful symbols. They connote all that is good, right, dutiful and powerful.[8] Those in power used the serialized epics and the symbols within them (such as chariots, various weapons, devotional songs, etc.), and the actors (dressed in full costume) to campaign for votes. The state has thus overtly legitimized the use of religion for power and control. Muslim groups in turn use the green flag and crescent moon and star to whip up religious and communal feelings.

In Maharashtra, a Hindu fundamentalist group bought a chariot used by the television network during the serialization of the *Ramayana* to use in a subsequent election campaign. The *ratha* (chariot) is just as much a powerful symbol as the persons who played the parts of Rama and Hanuman. Characters dressed as Rama (with crown, bow, etc.) and Hanuman (monkey mask, mace, etc.) have often been used by political parties (see, for instance, *Times of India* 1989a).[9] The fundamentalist Hindu political party co-opted the actress who played the role of Rama's wife, Sita, in the serialized *Ramayana* to its great advantage. Sita is a symbol of, and epitomizes, the pure unsullied/ unsulliable 'Indian woman'. Similarly, in south India, an actor-turned-chief minister underwent a third mutation and turned himself into a sadhu.[10] Dressed in ochre robes, the chief minister ruled for several years. To campaign for a second term in office, he had posters of himself playing the roles of various gods in his films displayed around the country. Large cardboard cut-outs of Rama and Krishna, with the chief minister's face, were a common feature (see *Times of India* 1989b, Laxman 1989). These symbols are extremely emotive.

It is contended here that a similar *symbolic legitimization* of power was undertaken in the past. Today, an attempt is being made to understand this by appealing to history. It is further contended that symbolism, being extremely powerful and emotive, cannot be countered with an appeal to historically valid/invalid 'facts'. Such symbolism can perhaps only be countered with equal or more powerful symbolism.[11]

Symbols at Ram Janmabhoomi/Babri Masjid

Valmiki's *Ramayana* states that the events described occurred in the Treta Yuga. It also mentions that at the end of this epoch, Ayodhya (Rama's capital city) disappeared. This epoch is believed by Hindus to have ended in *c.* 3000 BC.

The contemporary epoch (Kali Yuga) witnessed the rise of Jainism and Buddhism in the Indian subcontinent to the extent that the first Indian emperor (Ashoka Maurya) converted to Buddhism. Following the downfall of this empire, northern India seems to have disintegrated into small principalities until the rise to power of the Gupta dynasty, (*c.* AD 300–700). With the Guptas, it is often thought, a Hindu resurgence was experienced in the Gangetic regions. This was the period, historians believe, in which Hinduism was firmly established (see Thapar 1985).[12]

The Guptas emerged as powerful rulers from a rather dubious and obscure background. It is believed that they were originally landed gentry who married into royal families and so acquired status and simultaneously strengthened their holdings into what later became a powerful kingdom with its capital at Pataliputra.

One of the Guptas, Skanda Gupta, who took the title of 'Vikramaditya' (Sun of Prowess), is thought to have shifted his capital from Pataliputra to a town which had been important in the preceding Buddhist period – Saketa, on the banks of the River Sarayu. Skanda Gupta is thought to have renamed Saketa Ayodhya in c. fifth century AD.[13] The two acts of assuming the title of 'Sun' (Rama's lineage is believed by Hindus to have been the 'Surya Vamshi', i.e. the 'line of the sun'), and renaming his capital city after Rama's, gained Skanda Gupta prestige, power and simultaneously a legitimate position of authority and control. Hindu legends reveal the liminal[14] space and time that Rama's Ayodhya occupied.[15] The symbolic equations of Saketa with Ayodhya and Skanda Gupta with Rama are of prime importance here (see Pandey 1989).

Although symbols are ambiguous and malleable, they are used to express concisely what people believe and the way they think, feel and act. If we are to negate the *symbolic* equations (of Saketa-Ayodhya and Skanda Gupta-Rama) and claim these to be 'factual', the then available archaeological and historical evidence ('facts') negate the existence of the god/king Rama's Ayodhya. However, the power of this symbol remains, despite the lack of 'factual' evidence and today, Ayodhya connotes Rama and thus also connotes Hinduism.

Similar symbolic equations occur every year when the Ramlila, or the story of Rama, is played out in the town of Ramnagar, over an area of 25 km (see Kapur 1988). Different parts of the town 'become' Ayodhya, the Dandakaranya forest, the ocean, Lanka and the present Maharaja of Ramnagar, a contemporary of both Rama and of the present. The boy who plays the part of Rama entirely absorbs the character of Rama and is accorded the deference paid to a god. For the thirty days that it takes to perform the entire Ramlila, Ramnagar and its inhabitants enter a symbolic, liminal space.

Such a situation appears also to have occurred in nineteenth-century Awadh with Wajid Ali Shah, the Nawab. Wajid Ali Shah wrote poetry which was sung at his court. He identified himself (and was identified) with Rama, Krishna and Indra. He often used symbols to connote the deities and equated his capital, Awadh, with the various places/spaces that symbolize these figures: Akhtarnagar as the 'city of the sun', and 'Indralok' as Saketdham or Ayodhya (V. Rao *pers. comm.*, in prep.).[16]

It is suggested that a similar symbolic equation might have been established at Ayodhya/Saketa in the past. This would explain the strength of the belief as also the lack of what is termed 'historical evidence'.

Making historical 'facts'

In the case of Ram Janmabhoomi/Babri Masjid, it is abundantly clear that the symbolic equation once made has been negated and/or forgotten.[17] Hindus insist that the *Ramayana* is 'fact' and that Rama ruled Ayodhya/Saketa. They firmly believe that a temple existed at the Babri Masjid site, which was destroyed by Babar. Muslims in turn believe that no temple existed there and that Saketa/Ayodhya is not Rama's Ayodhya. Both groups involved are attempting to reify the symbol and to convert it into a given historical/ archaeological fact.

The issue must be seen in the wider context of the assertion of identity among the communities. Inevitably, this assertion of identity requires a symbol which brings diverse, segmented and fragmented parts together, albeit superficially, as a unit. In expressing identity, Hindus and Muslims have made references to the Indian past and to tradition. The past, as previously emphasized, is reconstructed, but it is done so in selective ways and in the image of the present. This is the rewriting of history selectively and symbolically and has resonances of myth-creation. I use the word 'myth' here to imply that which lends sanctity and rightness to a course of action. Thus, creating a myth in the image of the present legitimizes and sanctifies actions undertaken in the present. The symbolic view of Ram Janmabhoomi had removed it from the domain of what is viewed as 'rational' history and placed it squarely in an a-historical realm that was spaceless and timeless – a liminal space.

Clearly, a symbol is a device which triggers off highly charged emotions. Symbols derived from history (or history, which is in and of itself symbolic and malleable) are often invoked in times of tremendous upheaval and social change. The past presents itself as a sanctuary, a knowable and comprehensible base from which a world submerged in chaos can be understood (i.e. the past, when made to conform to contemporary categories of 'reason' and 'order', provides these when juxtaposed against contemporary 'chaos'). Ayodhya, as the birthplace of Rama, until recently a matter of complete indifference to most Hindus (as it represents no continuity in the various traditions of, for instance, the North-east and South) has been made into an important symbol of a precious past and of a 'continued link' in the form of 'tradition' with it. It has become an important means of expressing Hindu identity in the contemporary postcolonial world in which events have brought about immense change in social, political, cultural and economic spheres.[18] To the state which has labelled itself 'secular' but has unleashed and harnessed communal and religious forces, the (rewritten) past is similarly known and comfortable. Symbols and cues taken from this past have, therefore, gained currency. Simultaneously, to the Muslims in India, the Babri Masjid has become a symbol of Muslim unity in the face of majority Hindu (and increasingly less covert) aggression. The Babri Masjid was not an important mosque until the controversy came to a head, but today few Indian Muslims would allow the building of a temple at a site such as that proposed by the militant Hindu groups who have recently catapulted into popularity.

In conclusion it might be stated that it is clear that history and archaeology are entirely malleable and that their reconstruction is based in large measure on the context within which that reconstruction occurs. In India, where myth and what 'rationalists' would term 'historical/archaeological facts' are conflated, both history/archaeology and myth are simultaneously continuous and discontinuous. Symbols from both myth and history/archaeology, interpreted differently by different groups, are used in widely differing situations to legitimize power and control. In the situation discussed above, historical 'fact' is irrelevant and invoking it will not cause the 'irrational' anger of either group to subside. The boundary between history/archaeology and myth, already flimsy, has collapsed and quite evidently the wrath of the people cannot be cooled by presenting them with so-called historical verities. Both groups are today recreating separate pasts, those that are more in consonance with their contemporary world – a world in which, being insecure, they feel the need to crush any overt expressions of the identity of the 'other'.

Notes

1 It must be emphasized, however, that disharmony resulting from the expression of different identities is not a recent trend in India. It has existed for centuries and even nostalgic, romanticized evocations of what is seen as the glorious past cannot but come face to face with the fact that gruesome horrors have been perpetrated in the names of 'community' and 'religion'. Even a cursory view of the Indian epics and other, historically more 'valid' documents reveals violence and xenophobia to be prolific. Such communal disharmony was harnessed by the British colonialists and it was on a foundation cemented with divisive attitudes that the British retained control for nearly two centuries. After Independence in 1947, India was (and continues in some measure to be) ruled by Oxbridge-educated elites who did not dismantle the colonial (and therefore inherently exploitative) administration. 'Divide and Rule', the basis of British imperialist prowess, while not overtly emphasized in independent India, was certainly the more discrete foundation upon which slogans expressing the identity of a United India were foisted. The 1970s and 1980s have witnessed the coming of age of communalism and the communalization of Indian politics.

2 It needs no emphasis that an appeal to the past is itself a symbolic strategy. Numerous types of reversionisms had sprouted throughout the period of the Freedom Movement in India, the more well known among these being Mahatma Gandhi's 'Ram Rajya', Tilak's Aryanism, Vivekanand's Vedanticism and Saraswati's Vedicism. All these merely reveal the fragmentation (or ambiguity?) of Hinduism and underscore the specific eco-political forces responsible for the 'success' of only two of these – the Gandhian and the Hindu Right versions (R. Hoskote pers. comm.).

3 I shall not enter into the debate on 'secularism' here. With regard to the Indian situation, suffice it to say that while I agree in part with Rai's (1989, p. 277) analysis, that secularism appears increasingly to be 'historically linked with the process of capitalist transformation', I do not agree that the state in India has been unhypocritical when it has used the slogan of secularism. As Miller (1987, p. PE–61) points out

162 NANDINI RAO

'the state, whatever its intentions and desires, is indubitably a *political* machine. It creates conflicts, interests, frustrations and heightened consciousness. . . . No legislation, or lack of can constitute neutrality, uniformity, evenhandedness'. I would suggest that those to whom power was transferred in 1947 were aware of the need to retain divisive, communal attitudes under the veneer of secularism, so as to retain power and control.
Secularism is also problematic in that it largely ignores minority groups by spreading a single allegedly egalitarian mantle across all groups.

4 For example, the infamous Shah Bano Case in which the Supreme Court of India passed an enlightened and progressive judgement which angered the fundamentalist cadres of the minority group. Stepping in, the Indian Government revoked the judgement and gave in to the fundamentalist lobby (see Engineer 1985).

5 Contemporary archaeological/historical analysis requires material archaeological/ historical remains or 'evidence' to prove the occurrence/existence of an event/ monument.

6 In Beveridge's translation of the *Babar Nama*, the crucial passage reads as follows: 'By the command of the Emperor Babur whose justice is an edifice reaching up to the very height of the heavens, the good hearted Mir Baqi [a nobleman of Babar's court] built the alighting place of the angels' (Gopal *et al.* 1989, p. 45).
The authors have also drawn attention to the fact that Beveridge further states that '*Presumably* the order for building the mosque' was given by Babar and that he 'would regard the substitution of a temple by a mosque as dutiful', being a dutiful Mussalman. Thus, colonial administrators (such as Carnegy 1870) assumed that the Mughal emperor was bigoted and that Ayodhya '*must at least have possessed* a fine temple' which '*it seems* that Babar had destroyed'. The language used ('Presumably', 'must have possessed', 'it seems') is revealing. Clearly, the colonizers viewed Babar and his deeds through their idea of what a good Mussalman *would* do (Gopal *et al.* 1989).

7 Muslims have been marginalized in India covertly and discreetly for many years. Today, this discrimination is far more visible. In addition over 60 per cent of Muslims live below the poverty line.

8 It needs no emphasis that symbols are extremely powerful and emotive. Rama and Krishna are symbols of purity, righteousness and power. Often Rama and Krishna are themselves represented by symbols – the bow for Rama, a peacock feather crown or discus for Krishna. Similarly, certain colours are emotionally charged symbols: ochre for the Hindus, representing saint-like qualities, green for the Muslims.

9 It might be added, however, that these representations have been achieved through the oversimplification of very complex characters.

10 A sadhu is a saint or holy/god-man who has renounced the 'material' world and in doing so, has achieved spiritual gain. Sadhus are often seen as possessing supernatural powers such as vision into the future.

11 In fact, the fundamentalists have since clearly maintained that the lack of archaeological evidence makes little difference to their desire to build a temple on the ruins of the mosque. They claim to be responding to people's 'faith' and religious 'sentiments'.
While a 'solution' to the situation is not the focus of this chapter, I do support the idea put forward by Gandhi (1989), that a *Ram Rahim Darwaza* be built – a symbol with connotations of unity and openness.

12 It might be stated, however, that the category 'Hinduism' serves little purpose in a Gupta context. In this period, with the recension of the old texts to allow for new gods and cults, the old Vedic Brahminism yielded to a Pauranicism with Roman, Zoroastrian, Mahayana and chthonic elements (cf. Zimmer 1948, Campbell 1962). It is suggested that the received truth of Gupta Hinduism/Nationalism be critically

re-examined: 'It is not the Guptas who revived nationalism . . . [but] nationalism which revived the Guptas' (Kosambi 1956). Further, there is a deep and wide chasm between Guptan and contemporary Hindu Right versions of Hinduism (R. Hoskote *pers. comm.*).

13 There is some controversy regarding which Gupta king moved to Saketa from Pataliputra. Kalidasa, who lived during the reign of Skanda Gupta's grandfather, already used the names Ayodhya and Saketa interchangeably in his texts. Other (numismatic) evidence indicates that it was Skanda Gupta who shifted. Evidence also reveals that Skanda Gupta often identified himself with Rama (See Gopal *et al.* 1989).

14 I use the word 'liminal' here not to mean 'marginal' or peripheral', but in the way of Turner (1979) to mean a space (spacio-temporal, socio-cultural, political, etc.), that is not bound by empirical co-ordinates, one that is 'betwixt and between', a 'magical space' where 'normal' rules of place/time/society/culture do not apply (see Rao 1990 for such a use of the word in the analysis of music).

15 It appears that when Skanda Gupta set out to find Rama's lost city of Ayodhya, he was advised by Prayaga, king of pilgrimages, to look for the city on the banks of the Sarayu which holds a shrine to Shiva (another god of the Hindu Trinity). Skanda Gupta found the spot, marked it, but was subsequently unable to locate it. While attempting to find it once more, he came across a yogi (a holy man) who told him to let a calf loose. He advised that the spot on which milk would begin to flow freely from the calf's udders would be Ayodhya. When this occurred, Skanda Gupta set up his new capital, and built several temples to Vishnu (of whom Rama is an incarnation). (A similar legend is recorded in Gopal *et al.* 1989). Evidently, the Guptas were legitimizing their position by claiming descent from the line of Rama. It is also abundantly clear that the location of Ayodhya falls into the supra-human domain. Another local legend has it that 'Saketa' is the name of the house in which Rama was born, thus implying that Saketa and Ayodhya are essentially the same.

16 Today, after the fixing of the boundary firmly between the Hindus and the Muslims – a result of the encounter with colonialism – it seems bizarre that a Muslim king would undertake such an identification. Viewed in the context of nineteenth-century India, it would not seem so bizarre. Hindus were in a majority, while the ruler was Muslim. Wajid Ali Shah would require their support to remain in power. To use the symbols of the local people in order to legitimize his position would only be politically expedient.

The same space, i.e. Saketa/Ayodhya/Awadh/Fyzabad, has the seeds of two alternative histories: 1) that of perceiving Babar as *breaking* into a pre-Islamic (liminal) space and imposing an alien order of reality; or 2) that of perceiving Wajid Ali Shah as *bridging* the pre-Islamic space with the contemporary one by locally expressing a local order of reality. Unfortunately the ideologues of the Hindu Right prefer the former reading for purely political reasons (R. Hoskote *pers. comm.*).

17 A 'rational' and, therefore, perhaps more easily acceptable political strategy could be the 'lifting' of such 'amnesia', and the reconstruction of the production of such a symbolic equation.

18 It might be suggested that the attempt to focus Hindu attention on Ayodhya as the birthplace of Rama is the result of the insecurity of the Hindu Right in the face of their perception of Muslims as a homogeneous group and Islam as monolithic and unambiguous. Ayodhya has never really occupied the absolute position in the Hindu mind that Mecca, for instance, does in the Muslim. Liminality and ambiguity are a part of the Hindu *Weltanschauung*. Diverse regions claim that events described in the Epic occurred within their boundaries; the very episodes described therein are represented as having taken place in different areas: Bastar, the Nilgiris, Thailand, etc. Encountering unambiguous Islam has perhaps led to apprehension about the ambiguous nature of Hinduism (R. Hoskote *pers. comm.*).

Acknowledgements

I thank the following persons for the discussions we had together and the comments they made on the manuscript which foreshadowed this chapter: G. Chambers, P. Chikarmane, A. Dave, Professor S. Gopal, R. Hoskote, K. P. Jayasankar, A. Manjeshwar, V. Mathrani, A. Monteiro, and V. Rao. I also thank A. Thadani for undertaking to type it.

References

Beveridge, A. (trans.) [1922] 1969. *Babur Nama*. London: Luzac & Co.
Campbell, J. 1949. *The Masks of God: oriental mythology*. New York: Viking Press.
Campbell, J. 1962. *The Masks of God*. London: Penguin.
Carnegy, P. 1870. *A Historical Sketch of Tahsil Fyzabad, Zilla Fyzabad including Haveli-Oudh and Pacchimrath, with the Old Capitals Ajudhia and Fyzabad*. Lucknow: Government of India.
Engineer, A. A. 1985. *The Shah Bano Controversy*. Hyderabad: Orient Longman.
Gandhi, R. 1989. A design for Ayodhya. *Indian Express* 3 December.
Gopal, S., R. Thapar, B. Chandra, S. Bhattacharya, S. Jaiswal, H. Mukhia, K. N. Panikkar, R. Champakalakshmi, S. Saberwal, B. D. Chattopadhyaya, R. N. Verma, K. Meenakshi, M. Alam, D. Singh, M. Mukherjee, M. Palat, A. Mukherjee, S. Ratnagar, N. Bhattacharya, K. Trivedi, Y. Sharma, K. Chakravarti, B. Joshi, R. Gurukkal and H. Ray 1989. The political abuse of history. *Seminar* 364, 44–6.
Kapur, A. 1988. Thinking about tradition: the Ramlila of Ramnagar. *Journal of Arts and Ideas* 16, 5–32.
Kosambi, D. D. 1956. *An Introduction to the Study of Indian History*. Bombay: Popular Book Depot.
Lal, B. B. 1976–7. *Indian Archaeology: a review*. New Delhi: Archaeological Survey of India.
Lane, P. 1990. Archaeology and development in Africa: present dilemmas and future prospects. Paper presented at the Pan-African Association of Anthropologists Conference, University of Nairobi.
Laxman, R. K. 1989. Cartoon in *Times of India*, 16 November.
Miller, D. 1987. Six theses on the question of religion and politics in India. *Economic and Political Weekly* 22, PE 57–63.
Nevill, H. R. 1905. *District Gazetteer of Fyzabad*. Allahabad, Government of India.
Pandey, G. 1989. Ayodhya and the state. *Seminar* 364, 39–43.
Rai, A. 1989. Addled only in parts: the strange case of Indian secularism. *Economic and Political Weekly* 24, 2770–3.
Rao, V. 1990. Thumri as feminine voice. *Economic and Political Weekly* 25, WS 19–31.
Rao, V. In prep. Performances at the Court of Wajid Ali Shah.
Sinclair, P. 1986. Archaeology, ideology and development: Mozambican perspectives. *Archaeological Review From Cambridge* 5, 77–87.
Srivastava, S. 1991. *The Disputed Mosque: a historical inquiry*. New Delhi: Vistaar Publications.
Thapar, R. 1985. *A History of India*. Vol. 1. London: Pelican Books.
Times of India 1989a. Photograph of Mr Bal Thackeray surrounded by supporters, 8 November.
Times of India 1989b. Photograph of cardboard cut-out of Mr N. T. Rama Rao as Krishna with the discus, 15 November.
Turner, V. 1979. *Process Performance and Pilgrimage*. New Delhi: Concept Publishing House.
Zimmer, H. 1948. *The Art of Indian Asia*. New York: Pantheon Books.

The scholarship
of inequality:
the South African case

12 Lifting the veil of popular history: archaeology and politics in urban Cape Town

MARTIN HALL

It is common cause that interpretations of the past have played an important role in re-enforcing white hegemony in South Africa (Cornevin 1980, Hall 1988, 1990). Within the framework of apartheid education, generations of schoolchildren have been taught that history began when Jan van Riebeeck splashed ashore in Table Bay in 1652. After heroic struggle, the almost empty land was settled by pioneers who defied the treachery of native tribes to bring civilization to the interior. Diamonds and gold brought prosperity to the new cities and homelands were created to preserve the ancestral rights of native tribes, who could thus live separately while enjoying the benefits brought by migrant labour (Smith 1983, Stewart & Mazel 1986). It is also common cause that revisionist historians and archaeologists have demonstrated the mendacity of such settler constructions of the past. Far from being a land sparsely peopled by primitive bands, it has been shown that hunter-gatherers have a history of hundreds of thousands of years in South Africa, and that their cosmology (expressed, for example, in the thousands of paintings on the walls of rock shelters) had a complexity that seems often beyond the lexicon of western intellectual concepts (Lewis-Williams 1981, Deacon 1984). Far from being empty, the interior is shown to have been peopled by farming communities for centuries before the rather seedy Dutch garrison was established beneath Table Mountain. Complex precolonial states thrived for many years in the interior (Hall 1987). Homelands had little or no historical continuity and, linked with migrant labour, were a mechanism for depressing wages to the barest minimum and elevating profits (Stadler 1987).

In recent years, popular constructions of the past have become more sophisticated. Some school textbooks acknowledge the evidence of archaeology. But precolonial history is still not part of the syllabus and, more often than not, this far more substantial past is simply not mentioned – implying, of course, that it is a domain of uncertainty and speculation. More insidiously, ethnic diversity remains the touchstone of popular historical constructions, implying a historically validated continuity of identity. It is too soon to see how current changes in South African politics will bring about a shift in popular perceptions of the past, but the indications are that history and archaeology will become symbols in the construction of new nationalisms. Inkatha has long made use of symbols of Zulu history to ratify its claim as the dominant black party in South Africa (Klopper 1989). As this organization squares up to the African National Congress, it is probable that Inkatha's popular history will become more evident. Chief Mangosuthu Buthelezi is fond of appearing in a complex array of feathers and skins which claim an ancestral authority to govern (Klopper 1989). Similarly, white nationalist icons will be pushed into the forefront by those powerful groups fighting for white control. Carel Boshoff, chairman of the neo-fascist Afrikaaner Volkswag, likes to be photographed in front of his motorized ox-wagon, used in 1988 in the symbolic re-enactment which celebrated the 150th anniversary of the Great Trek (Anon. 1990, Shepherd 1990).

In contexts such as these, archaeology is clearly politicized, and consequently has a progressive political role to play. The purpose of this chapter is to show the close connection between archaeological theory and archaeology's political domain.

Textual archaeology

The proposition that there can be a close connection between the way in which archaeologists construct the past intellectually and the manner in which they engage in their political environment requires an account of the way in which we have approached the archaeology of urban Cape Town. The main theoretical inspiration for our research has been poststructuralist semiotics. By viewing the past as a set of complex texts, intertwined to form a discourse, we have avoided privileging written documents over the archaeological record, or artefact assemblages over travellers' accounts, probate records and paintings. Rather, they are all different views on a past which is revealed through comparison and, particularly, contradiction. This approach provides detailed texture without sacrificing interpretation (Hall 1992).

The point can be illustrated by considering the semiotic role of fish in mid-eighteenth-century Cape Town. A contemporary written text contains marked ambiguities in its author's account of the place of fish in the diet of Cape Town's population. Some passages refer to the large catches of common Atlantic shoal fish that were dried or salted and distributed widely in the town. But elsewhere the author insists that the only fish to be had in Cape Town were Indian Ocean line fish (Mentzel 1921, 1925, 1944). But an archaeological text – faunal assemblages from elite kitchens and an adjacent slave doss-house – shows that both were part of the diet. Indian Ocean line fish were eaten at the tables of Dutch East India Company officials while Atlantic shoal fish were cooked by slaves around open hearths (Hall 1992). Turning back to the written text with this information, we discover a homologous ambiguity in the author's accounts of slavery. In some passages slaves are described in bucolic terms, content around their fires after a hard day's work. Elsewhere they are satanic – lazy and threatening, hair smeared with coconut oil and teeth stained by betel juice (Mentzel 1921, 1925, 1944). By setting a detailed part of a verbal text against a detailed part of a material text in this way, we can find the central tension in eighteenth-century Cape Town – between slaves and their masters – in everyday lives. Archaeology interprets the document and the document interprets the archaeology (Hall 1992).

This textual analysis can be placed within a Marxist concept of class. Class – as a set of relationships – focuses on discordance and contradiction and interprets them in terms of domination and opposition (De St Croix 1981). Thus food can be seen as rich in meaning and aquatic resources can be set alongside the preparation of game birds and cuts of beef, pork and mutton in showing how the merchant elite of the Dutch East India Company signified, in everyday terms, how they were different from common soldiers and slaves.

For the early nineteenth century there is still debate about the class structure in Cape Town. But without doing too much violence to different positions, Cape Town society can be seen in three tiers. The smallest and dominant class was made up of the wealthiest merchants, who were mostly wholesalers with strong connections with British capital. Beneath them were the petty bourgeoisie – mostly retailers of imported commodities, foodstuffs and locally manufactured goods. Local industry, however, was poorly developed and so there was no urban proletariat in the formal sense. Rather, there was a broad underclass comprising porters, poorer fishermen, labourers, domestic servants, washerwomen and others. Until 1838 this underclass also included slaves (Bickford-Smith 1988, Bank 1991).

Interpreting the past in this way – as a series of texts – has a further advantage: it allows us to tease apart the continuum of connections between past and present – the manner in which the past is constantly reinterpreted to serve changing political circumstances. Chief Buthelezi's Inkatha and Carel Boshoff's Afrikaaner Volkswag both mobilize texts from the past in the context of the present. Similarly, images of Cape Town in the early nineteenth century have an important political role in the present.

Cape Town in the early nineteenth century

Although the merchant princes and petty bourgeoisie of Cape Town were anxious to build an image to the contrary, life in Cape Town in the early nineteenth century could be rough. One insight into this world is through reports written by wardmasters in 1840, in response to a smallpox epidemic. Some areas, such as the streets to the north of the commercial centre of the city, were described favourably, although there were always some houses crammed with people living in poverty. Other areas clearly shocked the wardmasters, even though they were themselves long-time residents of the same town. In the waterfront area, between Strand Street and the bay, they found up to fifty people living in small, three-roomed hire houses, occupants so numerous that they could not be counted huddled in cellars and in the cavities under the steps of ornate town houses and back yards crammed with shacks. Because the wardmasters were concerned with the circumstances that propagated smallpox, they commented on hygiene. Some yards were clean, but many were filthy. The wardmasters described some situations where excrement and other waste from a house was disgorged onto people living lower down the hillside. Everywhere, rubbish was left to rot in piles on the streets.

Many members of Cape Town's underclass were black: 'prize negroes', slaves from Madagascar or Indonesia and Khoi from the interior of the Cape. But the coincidence of race and class was by no means exact, and the private yards and backstreets also housed white labourers and indigents (Judges 1977). Contemporary perceptions of divisions within the underclass underline its cosmopolitan character. Writing in 1836, the Attorney General of the Cape noted that 'Malays', although barbarian, were generally respectable and well behaved. Similarly, the special wardmasters had commented that there were many respectable 'Mohomadens' who made every effort to keep their houses and yards clean. The Attorney General's full contempt was reserved for the 'lower Irish'.[1]

These documentary texts are supplemented by the texts of archaeological assemblages (Figure 12.1). Our programme of excavation has been concentrated in three parts of the city. Near the northern margins of the earlier Dutch town we have excavated a well, dug in the back yard of a house in Barrack Street (Hall, Halkett, Klose & Ritchie 1990). On the opposite side of the town, we have recovered a large assemblage from a back yard in Bree Street (Hall, Halkett, Klose & Portuesi 1993). In the waterfront area, we have excavated the yards of four hire houses in Sea Street (Hall 1991a). Although these assemblages have been passed through the usual taphonomic filters that make archaeological interpretation difficult and challenging, they provide compelling evidence of the conditions of the underclass so briefly glimpsed through documents such as the special wardmasters' reports and the comments of the Attorney General.

The Bree Street back yard reveals two distinct patterns of refuse disposal. In the first place there are a number of small pits, beneath the floor of a present outbuilding, containing dense domestic rubbish, principally Asian ceramics that may have been dumped when they ceased to be fashionable in the early nineteenth century. More relevant for the purposes of this discussion is the dense scatter of material across the back of the property. Today truncated by a more recent wall, this area was, in the early nineteenth century, a more extensive lot bordered on all sides by the houses that faced outwards on to Buitenkant and Hout Streets, Hottentot Square and Bree Street. It is likely that this was a 'private yard'. The waste in this area contains highly fragmented sherds of ceramics, broken clay tobacco smoking pipes and large amounts of food refuse, supporting the accounts given by the special wardmasters in 1840.

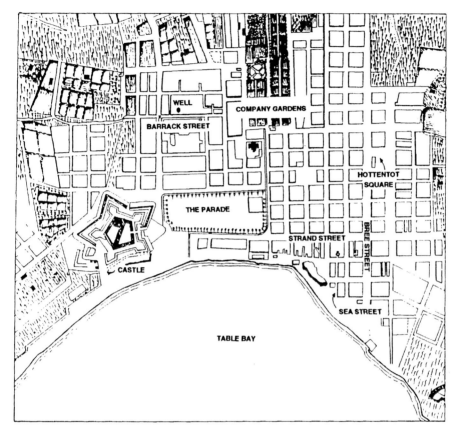

Figure 12.1   Cape Town in the early nineteenth century.

The four back yards in Sea Street tell a similar story for the waterfront area. These houses were built in the late 1830s by speculators taking advantage of the housing shortage in Cape Town.[2] Occupants listed in street directories for the time were fishermen, seamstresses, washerwomen and labourers, typical of Cape Town's underclass.[3] But the wardmasters' inspection revealed what the street directories were concealing. Rather than the individual householders whose names were published in the Almanac – giving the impression of a low-density population – the wardmasters revealed that many more people were living in each house. The text of the archaeological assemblages shows what this meant in everyday life. Food was prepared on open hearths, built in turn on the accumulated debris left behind by earlier occupants. Apart from broken ceramics and clay pipes, there were again large amounts of food waste (Hall 1991a).

The assemblages in the Barrack Street well built up under different circumstances – not so much the accumulation of everyday debris, but things accidentally lost or deliberately abandoned. Nevertheless, they tell a story similar to that of the Sea Street and Bree Street back yards. On the business premises and residences of bakers in the early nineteenth century, the well has preserved the imprint of the underclass. Apart from the tablewares of the householder, the well was also the repository of cheaper, commonplace domestic wares: the handpainted and annular wares turned out by the Staffordshire potteries for 'peasants' and the colonies. Food waste included bones from inferior cuts of meat and fish, principally snoek, described by the *Cape Argus* later in the century as a staple food of the underclass (Bradlow 1977). Personal items included leather shoes and military buttons and insignia, testimony to the presence of soldiers from the barracks across the street, who spent their leisure in nearby lanes and back yards to the consternation of their officers and the temperance movement.

Texts of domination and opposition

A semiotic approach to the study of material culture allows archaeology a role beyond the amplification of narrative: it allows us to discern how symbols were manipulated in everyday forms of domination and opposition (Scott 1985, 1990). All the underclass assemblages that we have excavated contain items of material culture that were archaic in the early nineteenth century. Seventeenth-century porcelain entered the archaeological record alongside cheap peasant wares. Dutch East India Company coins, long since valueless as currency, were kept for three or four decades before they were lost in the back yards where people lived. Cowrie shells – not part of the Cape's marine fauna – were clearly valued. Glass and ceramic sherds were fashioned into implements, using the long-established methods of Khoi herdsmen. There is little evidence for formal political organization amongst Cape Town's underclass this early in the century, although it has been argued that there was considerable social cohesion in the face of domination (Bank 1991). The evidence of material culture supports this suggestion.

This chapter, however, is more concerned with the role that material culture played in domination. The key actors here were Cape Town's bourgeoisie, who were concerned with social control and to present Cape Town as the ideal colonial city.

It is not surprising that Cape Town's bourgeoisie should be worried about the dark side of their world. In the earlier years of the nineteenth century, many of this class were themselves not far removed from humbler origins. Like Leonard Bast in E. M. Forster's (1941) *Howards End*, they must have felt themselves on the brink of an abyss, into which they could be tossed by misfortune. Illness for themselves, their families, their slaves and servants would directly threaten their livelihood.

Biographical outlines of members of the petty bourgeoisie suggest that many of them had achieved their position by taking advantage of the freer commercial opportunities which came with the end of Dutch East India

Company rule in 1795. In Barrack Street, Philip Anhuyzer, in his earlier life a soldier and a cook with the Company, had bought an elegant, but probably decaying, late eighteenth-century townhouse and established a retail business (Hall, Halkett, Klose & Ritchie 1990). When he died in 1827 he left the possessions of a respectable household: silver knives, forks and spoons, a large number of pictures, feather beds and three slaves. But his widow, Celia van der Kaap, had herself in all likelihood once been a slave, a relict of her husband's humbler origins. On the other side of town, close to Hottentot Square where farmers from the interior outspanned their ox-wagons on their periodic visits to town, Thomas Sinclair and his brother started their business as ships chandlers by renting a house that had earlier been the residence of an attorney of some substance. Sinclair was successful, eventually buying the property and the store next door (Hall, Halkett, Klose & Portuesi 1993). His neighbours in the same city block had similar life histories, starting off with small concerns – a wheelwright, gunsmith, wagon builder, snuff manufacturer and the like – and, if they could amass the resources, buying a few local properties (Hall 1989).

Of course, not all members of the bourgeoisie were so vulnerable, and many had considerable fortunes that allowed them to compete for the social status of the merchant princes. However, Anhuyzer, Sinclair and many of their neighbours must have been acutely aware of their vulnerability to indebtedness, economic collapse and life in the slums. This tension was exacerbated by the increasing involvement of the petty bourgeoisie in rented property (Warren 1986). With slave emancipation people flocked to the city and property owners took advantage of the consequent housing crisis to expand their incomes as landlords. Some had many properties – one man owning some 400 houses with about 4000 tenants – and many had a few. Apart from houses in backstreets such as Coffee Lane off Barrack Street, and Sea Street in the waterfront area, many had 'private yards' – a euphemism for the squalid corners tucked away behind respectable street fronts, and the places revealed briefly by the special wardmasters in 1840. For landlords extracting rent for poor housing from impoverished tenants, class conflict must have been a daily reality.

But apart from looking inward – at the need to control Cape Town's underclass – the bourgeoisie were looking outwards, to the expanding cosmopolitan world of the British Empire. For almost all of them prosperity depended, directly or indirectly, on trade, and trade depended on investment in the colony. For such investment to be realized it was essential that Cape Town was seen as a model of prosperity and propriety. The colonial bourgeoisie worked fervently at realizing such an image.

One set of texts that contributed to this end was written material, such as travellers accounts and newspaper reports. The accounts of poverty that came with the smallpox epidemic were an exception: newspaper accounts were, more usually, eulogies. Here, for instance, is Cape Town according to John Fairbairn, editor of the *South African Commercial Advertizer*:

Notwithstanding this comparative scarcity, and the high price of the first necessaries of life, there does not appear to be any unusual distress among the poor. In outward appearance, the classes commonly called the labouring poor, have greatly improved. They are well clad, or rather dressed, both they and their children; and from their looks it is manifest that if they ever fast, it must be, like Falstaff, 'immediately after dinner'. Beggary, properly so called, is still entirely unknown in the Cape.

(*South African Commercial Advertizer* 1/1/1840)

In similar vein were many travellers accounts. Ferdinand Krauss, a German naturalist who accompanied the high-born Baron van Ludwig back to the Cape in 1838, saw a clean, neat city:

In neat quarters and straight roads it gently rises from the lively beach up to the foot of the said mountains. At the outskirts we find friendly country houses surrounded by the most splendid gardens and vineyards. . . . The houses are well-nigh all of them double-storied and flat-roofed, and generally white-washed and built of brick, which is, in view of the oppressive heat and the strong winds, very suitable. High spacious rooms offer the occupier a cool abode in summer, while during the cool wet winters a little open fire gives sufficient protection. . . . The streets are broad, crossing at right angles, and very clean, though paved only along the houses. Their cleanliness is mainly due to the suitable lay-out and the sandy material; the latter, however, becomes a nuisance during the summer months because of the dust with which the mightily blowing south-east winds fill the air.

(Krauss 1966, p. 3)

In ways such as these, verbal texts explicitly denied the squalor, poverty and exploitation that were characteristic of Cape Town.

If we were to accept a simple notion of ideology, we could stop the analysis at this point, assuming that Cape Town's nineteenth-century bourgeoisie were explicitly and knowingly misrepresenting the true conditions of their town. However, ideological mechanisms were more complicated. For example, John Fairbairn was the author of newspaper editorials that one week praised Cape Town as a clean, ideal, colonial city and the next condemned it as a pit of poverty and degradation. But Fairbairn cannot be dismissed as a self-serving cynic. He was an advocate of the anti-slavery position and certainly no lackey of the landlord class. It is probable that he believed both images that he presented. But how did Fairbairn accommodate these apparently contrary positions? I would suggest that other texts of domination, in concert with the more explicit verbal sources, combined in presenting a world in which domination and subservience seemed naturalized. Two additional categories of text illustrate the point: architecture and graphic art.

Architecture and art

The earliest colonial buildings at the Cape were simple one- or two-roomed, mass-built rectangles with thatched roofs, an adaptation of basic European vernacular forms to allow for the great shortage of timber at the Cape that prevented the use of frame construction techniques (Walton 1965, 1989). But as the eighteenth century progressed this early form of Cape vernacular was relegated to the frontier or for the use of subservient groups in society. Today such buildings survive in limited areas, such as the Verloren Vlei on the Cape west coast (Gribble 1989). The aspirant gentry of the Cape of Good Hope built for themselves substantial mansions strictly symmetrical in facade and in plan, and decorated with ornate baroque-style front gables (Fransen & Cook 1980, Obholzer, Baraitser & Malherbe 1985). The need ever to be aspiring higher caused subsequent changes to this basic form of the Cape house. Particularly in the last quarter of the eighteenth century, Cape houses came to be adorned with gables on their side wings and at the back of the building, buildings were raised on solid platforms in order to give them command over the outbuildings as well as a dominant position in the landscape and, in a particularly elaborate form of conspicuous display, fowl runs, pig sties and other details of the farmyard were adorned in the lavish styles of high baroque architecture (Walton 1985).

This built environment daily asserted the politics of competition between factions of the Dutch East India Company hierarchy, and the domination of master over slave, of colonizer over colonized. This was the world that the British found in 1795 and, although the new administration changed the rules of social intercourse and altered the settings in which people of importance encountered one another, the ideological role of the built environment remained of central importance. To live in Cape Town in the eighteenth or nineteenth centuries was to be encased in a text, the code of which overwhelmingly asserted status. Achievement and social standing were mapped out for all to see in bricks and mortar.

But although such a townscape asserted status, it could not in itself deny poverty or the challenge of the underclass. Although the *South African Commercial Advertizer* routinely denied the fact, poor, ragged people moved conspicuously about the streets of Cape Town. Pictures – mostly watercolours or lithographic prints – helped the bourgeoisie forget this disturbing, dark side of life.

The role of painting and prints as text is illustrated through the work of one early nineteenth-century artist, Thomas Bowler (Hall 1991b). Bowler arrived at the Cape from England in 1834, setting himself up as an artist and producing in his lifetime more than 500 watercolours and 63 published lithographic prints (Bradlow 1967). Bowler was popular amongst the bourgeoisie in the early nineteenth century, many of whom bought his work. At first sight, his depictions of Cape Town seem accurate: it is clear that the topography is close to the topography that we would see today. It is possible to stand where Bowler stood, see the same outline of mountain contours and, where they survive, the same buildings. But was this Cape Town 'as it really was'?

First, Bowler was clearly selective in his choice of which parts of Cape Town to paint or draw. His interest in the picturesque is evident in panoramic views, whether from above (as in the set of four lithographs showing Cape Town from Kloof Nek, published in 1854) or whether from the sea (as in the numerous seascapes of Cape Town from Table Bay, Blouberg or near the Amsterdam battery). But in these pictures, of course, there is no detail of streets, buildings or people, except for figures placed in foregrounds for compositional reasons. Only limited parts of Cape Town are represented in more detail: the main commercial and residential streets, such as Adderley Street and Wale Street, and details of particular buildings, such as the Lutheran Church (from the front and the back), the Dutch Reformed Church and the entrance to the Castle. The busy back lanes, which would have drawn Hogarth a century earlier and which are revealed in the texts of wardmasters' reports and archaeological deposits, are absent from Bowler's known works (Hall 1991b).

Bowler's street scenes are usually dominated by the buildings. This is particularly the case in the lithographs, in which the buildings have crisp, clear lines and no evidence of wear and tear. They tower above the wagons in the street and the people walking alongside. Even when foregrounds are busy, the buildings still seem somewhat larger than life. It is only in the epic scenes, with their crowds of hundreds or thousands, that the buildings are allowed to slip away into the background (Hall 1991b).

Similarly selective are Bowler's representations of people. The overall impression is usually of industriousness, and only occasionally are people clearly idle. In the view of the Roman Catholic Cathedral two people lounge by a lamppost, the building in the left foreground is uncharacteristically tatty, and the horse looks decidedly weary as it pulls its load. Perhaps for Bowler, a nonconformist, this was the effect of proximity to Roman Catholicism. In the lithograph titled *Boor's Wagon*, part of the set of ten *South African Sketches* published in 1854, the farmers lounge against their wagon. But by this time, 'Boors' were considered the epitome of idleness by the British at the Cape (Coetzee 1988).

Apart from 'Malays' (invariably typed by their headgear) in the street scenes, the only other place where the underclass is regularly encountered in Bowler's art is at sea or on the seashore. In Bowler's first set of lithographs, *Four Views of Cape Town, Cape of Good Hope*, published in 1844, three out of the four prints have fishermen in the foreground, either at sea or working with their boat on the beach. Fishermen appear in many other watercolours, drawings and lithographs. For an artist fascinated by seascapes, fishermen, whether at sea or on the shore, would of course be a natural choice for the figures in the foreground that compositional rules demanded. At the same time, fishermen had an ambiguity in the class structure of Cape Town. While many were clearly seasonal workers and members of the underclass, others owned their boats and property in the town (Bickford-Smith 1988). By working hard, a fisherman could rise above his humble origins, much as Bowler himself had done. In Bowler's pictures, fishermen are invariably working hard (Hall 1991b).

Thus Thomas Bowler presented a particular image of Cape Town – the image that he expected prospective purchasers of his watercolours and lithographs to want to see. First, squalor and the life of the slums were completely excised. The underclass was busy, well dressed and not too numerous. There was the prospect that their labour could bring them social advancement. Streets were clean and wide, and buildings were tall and impressive, and showed no sign of decay. As a text, such a way of seeing neatly complemented the actual streetscapes of the colonial city, further naturalizing domination and subordination, and contributing powerfully to the ideological masque of the bourgeoisie.

Historical texts in present settings

Understanding the semiotic interaction of texts such as these with forms of opposition is a challenging research enterprise. But here I have a narrower concern: with the manner in which the early nineteenth-century bourgeois view of the world is used as an artefact of modern domination. This is, of course, not unique to South Africa: in many different parts of the world, versions of the past are used to validate power in the present. But in South Africa the naturalization of dominance, and in particular racial dominance, is particularly important because it helps to explain how ideology has worked to sustain apartheid.

Again, the role of the past in validating the present in South Africa is a wide and complex field. For practical reasons, I will restrict myself to the same three textual areas that I have already used in illustration: verbal accounts, architecture and art.

C. Graham Botha (1883–1973) had a long career in the Cape. Appointed the first Archivist of the Union of South Africa in 1912, Botha was particularly interested in making knowledge of archival sources widely available and was influential in developing a consciousness, among South Africa's white elite, of a version of the past. His popular text, *Our South Africa Past and Present*, illustrates his approach (Botha 1938).

In describing Cape Town in the early years of the nineteenth century, Botha followed, uncritically, the enthusiastic accounts developed by the bourgeoisie a century earlier:

> Cape Town at this time had grown and many changes and improvements had taken place in the last few decades. . . . The water supply for domestic use was greatly improved . . . iron pipes had been laid along the principal streets with taps at convenient

distances. This greatly increased the comfort of the people. . . .
Travellers remarked, as they did in the previous century, on the
whitewashed houses with their green shutters and doors, stoeps,
either high or low, built of Batavian bricks and floored with large
red tiles or blue slate slabs, and large airy and spacious rooms with
red tiled floors.

(Botha 1938, pp. 60–2)

Botha only acknowledged the dark side of the city with a slight, flippant
reference to 'rogues and vagabonds' who 'flourished and reaped a golden
harvest by carrying on their nefarious calling' causing, as a matter of inconvenience, the necessity of carrying a torch at night. Poverty was denied, and
racial categorization and prejudice entrenched, with passages such as the
following:

Among the inhabitants every shade of colour could be seen from
the fairest to the blackest. The town was indeed cosmopolitan in
many ways. The Mozambiques, black as Erebus, were an ugly lot
with faces all knobs and corners. The Malay women were hand-
some in their brightly coloured dresses; the Malay hadjis or priests
in their flowing eastern robes of bright hues, the Malay hawkers
with their broad-brimmed and pointed hats carrying their wares in
baskets hanging from a stick or pole across their shoulders, added
to the picturesqueness of a Cape Town street scene. Many of the
freed slaves dressed in European fashion and were good imitators in
this respect, for they often tried to ape their superiors.

(Botha 1938, pp. 64–5)

Botha's image of the past was simultaneously popularized and given authority
by the device of including the illustrations for the volumes as cards with 'C to
C' cigarettes, manufactured by the Union Tobacco Company.[4] The back of
each card claimed as its authority the 'Chief Archivist for the Union
Government', and the set depicted architecture, street scenes and racial stereotypes, many of them taken from early nineteenth-century artists. In this way
the bourgeois image of 1838 was reintroduced as the bourgeois image of 1938.
Botha, as an archivist of many years' experience, probably knew of contradictory texts, such as the accounts of the smallpox epidemic of 1840 and of the
poverty and degradation that fostered the disease. But this dark side was not
for the smokers of 'C to C' cigarettes.

A second example of corporate sponsorship of popular history was published nearly fifty years later. *A Tale of Three Cities* was promoted by Murray
& Roberts Buildings Ltd and was 'dedicated to Cape Town and to all the men
and women who have and will continue to shape its future' with the additional
comment that 'we have had the privilege to work in and be part of what ranks
as one of the most beautiful cities in the world; let us together make the most
of the opportunities ahead and make it a better place' (De Villiers 1985, p. 6).

Susan de Villiers, author of *A Tale of Three Cities*, opens her text with an explicit acknowledgement that all is not right in the world:

> Like any other city, Cape Town has its own set of contradictions. It is first and third world; it has a stunning natural environment and man-made structures that are sometimes beautiful, sometimes ugly; it has a fascinating historical heritage and an uncertain political and economic future; it has its exploiters and its benefactors. Above all, Cape Town is the sum of all its parts and to understand it means looking at what is good and bad.
>
> (De Villiers 1985, p. 7)

Clearly, this is not the style of C. Graham Botha, who was not prepared to acknowledge anything as bad. However, the oppositions that De Villiers sets up in her introduction serve just as thoroughly to direct her reader into the imagined, bourgeois view of the past. The positives are Cape Town's place in the First World, its natural setting and its fascinating history; the negatives are its place in the Third World, ugly buildings and an uncertain future. Interpreted, these negatives become black migrant labourers, their shacks and shelters on Cape Town's periphery and the political threat that they carry. As the construction industry, of which Murray & Roberts is a part, is a major employer of black migrant labour in Cape Town, the connection can hardly be taken as coincidental.

This theme runs on in the pages that follow, lurking behind the fine illustrations and the liberality of the content. The caption to a panoramic watercolour by Captain Walter Stanhope Sherwill, a contemporary of Thomas Bowler's and painting in his tradition, gives a further clue:

> This tranquil scene reflects a Cape Town still relatively untouched by the changes that came about in the mid-nineteenth century. . . . Soon the opening of the railways and the discovery of diamonds and gold in the interior were to change the face of the city.
>
> (De Villiers 1985, p. 12)

The part of history with which we are invited to relate lies before industrialization, before urbanization and labour migrancy that have carried such a political penalty. In the tradition which is, by now, familiar to us, we are presented with an idealized world:

> This was the age of Thibault the architect, Schutte the builder and Anrieth the sculptor – men whose works have had such a lasting impact on the built environment of Cape Town. . . . Cape Town was changing from a village of domestic-styled architecture and limited commercial activity into a market centre in its own right and, with the prospect of fortunes to be made, new immigrants began arriving at the Cape.
>
> (De Villiers 1985, pp. 21–3)

References to the bad side, promised in the introduction, are very sparse. 'For the working classes, clustered around the fringes of the city, social conditions were quite different to those of their more fortunate employers' (De Villiers 1985, p. 25). But we are never told how conditions were different.

References to architecture abound in such popular images of the past, emphasizing harmony and genteel living. One further example, from a successful cookery book, illustrates the genre further:

> With a fine instinct for what was harmonious, the people both at the Cape and in the Boland adapted the architectural styles of their original homelands to local conditions and created their stately Cape-Dutch houses. As the climate was well-suited to the cultivation of grapes, fruit and grain, this produce, too, was to have an influence on the emergence of a distinctive building style. Houses and outbuildings were erected with thatched roofs and thick outside walls so that fruit and grain might be preserved within their cool interiors and the highly prized Boland wines might mature there to perfection. In time these estates became the homes of an established and prosperous community consisting of farmers whose backgrounds were Dutch and German as well as French.
>
> (Coetzee 1977, pp. 37–8)

Many of these buildings still stand today, restored as images of the eighteenth and nineteenth centuries and providing the modern visitor with a text that recalls the past into the present. For example Groot Constantia, a substantial working wine estate in the eighteenth and nineteenth centuries, is now a museum. Buildings are meticulously well maintained and whitewashed and the distinctive green paintwork of doors and window frames is unfaded and unchipped. Visitors approach along a long avenue of oaks and see the imposing, gabled facade in front of them. To their left, over a clean, whitewashed wall, is a panorama of vineyards and the ocean. The noise and bustle of modern living – of any living – are not in evidence. In the house itself, furniture and furnishings are set out in contemporary tableaux. Groot Constantia was a major slave estate and, after emancipation, employer of apprenticed labour in the vineyards. This dimension is nowhere in evidence. For visitors, Groot Constantia offers the opportunity of stepping out of time and into a tranquil, secure past. The sub-text is clear: if our pioneer ancestors, with all the threats to their security, could survive, so can we.

The genre of 'Cape Dutch' architecture has been massively expanded in modern reconstructions and motifs. Electrical sub-stations, farm stalls, petrol stations, shops and offices have been built in eighteenth-century style, or with eighteenth-century architectural references. Holiday homes – the escape from the city – routinely recall simple frontier architecture (appropriate for the simple life of the weekend away) or more elaborate pretensions. The architecture of past dominance becomes the architecture of dominance in the present.

My third example of the way in which the bourgeois image of the nineteenth century serves the bourgeois image of the present comes from the graphic arts. Both C. Graham Botha and Susan de Villiers make extensive use of early nineteenth-century watercolours and lithographic prints, invariably presenting such images without comment, thus passing them as true to life. Indeed, Frank Bradlow, Thomas Bowler's historian, has made his subject's representational veracity a major point:

> Bowler's chief merit lies in his role of pictorial historian. He has left us an accurate record of the Cape and its people, a hundred and more years ago. Under his pen and brush, scenes from another age spring into vivid life. He is the social historian who relates how and where people lived, what they wore and what they did.
>
> (Bradlow 1967, p. 70)

In his introduction to Bowler's collected work, Bradlow himself explicitly makes the connection that is so generally utilized:

> My delight in, and appreciation of, Bowler as an artist has increased over the years. My eyes and emotions have always been receptive to the beauties of the Cape scene, but looking at it through the eyes of Thomas Bowler, my appreciation has been heightened. Even a cormorant drying on a rock – a vignette Bowler loved depicting – has assumed a new significance and becomes evocative of a time that is past and present. Bowler is pre-eminently an artist of the Cape.
>
> (Bradlow 1967, p. 12)

But, as I have shown earlier in this paper, the claim for Bowler's realism simply cannot be sustained, as Bradlow himself allows elsewhere:

> His work is often full of clichés and even tends to be somewhat unoriginal. His paintings depict what both artist and public wanted to see.
>
> (Bradlow 1967, p. 69)

Just as the contradictions in early texts of the Cape reveal the conflicts of class in the past, so the contradictions in commentaries such as Bradlow's reveal the conflicts of class in the present.

Conclusion

The connections between past and present examined in this chapter are only a small part of the myriad ways in which modern ideologies of dominance use history and archaeology. There is, of course, nothing new in noting these connections. The point I have tried to stress, however, is that textual analysis provides a way of understanding how these connections work and why they are so effective. From this understanding, we can begin to see how to subvert such modern ideological forms.

A necessary part of the transformation of South Africa from racial hegemony to a democratic, non-racial society will be an acceptance by white South Africans, as past holders of power and privilege, that their position is not part of the natural order. This will not be achieved by simply suppressing their icons, or by substituting for them a new set of black nationalist icons. Indeed, this course is likely merely to promote nostalgia and resentment – bitter memories over a gin and tonic as the sun sets on a better time. By breaking the icons – showing that the past was not what it has been made to be – effective change can be achieved: museum displays that show poverty in the past, the celebration of a different architecture, farm walls that are dirty rather than clean, popular histories that explore the lives of the underclass, art appreciation that sees artists as they were, rather than as they wanted to be – in short, the use of the past to create alternative texts for the present.

Notes

1 This interpretation is based on unpublished documents, Cape Archives AG2614, pp. 109ff, *Memorandum of the Attorney General relative to the desecration of the Sabbath. March 25th 1836*; Cape Archives C0490 (item 159), *Report on conditions of the poor in Cape Town in 1840.*
2 The original purchaser of the land on which the houses in Sea Street stand was Jan Marthinus Horak. Horak held the land as an investment until the late 1830s, when he built houses and sold them off to take advantage of the building boom in Cape Town.
3 Householders listed for Sea Street in 1840 were Widow Johannes Zeeman, Nicolaas Zeeberg, Saartje Davidse (laundress), William Edwards (shipwright), Christoffel Gerhardus Riel (carpenter) and Johannes Daniel Rosa (tailor). The Cape Calendar and Annual Register for 1840, Cape Town, Van de Sandt.
4 The name 'C to C' was itself part of the myth of domination, referring to the nineteenth-century ambition of a continent, from the Cape to Cairo, under British imperial rule.

References

Anon. 1990. It's partition or black domination. An interview with Carel Boshoff. *Monitor* April, 22–5.
Bank, A. 1991. *The Decline of Urban Slavery at the Cape, 1806 to 1843*. Cape Town: Centre for African Studies.
Bickford-Smith, V. 1988. Commerce, class and ethnicity in Cape Town, 1875 to 1902. Unpublished Ph.D. thesis, University of Cambridge.
Botha, C. G. 1938. *Our South Africa Past and Present*. Cape Town: Cape Times.
Bradlow, E. 1977. Cape Town's labouring poor a century ago. *South African Historical Journal*, 9, 19–29.
Bradlow, F. 1967. *Thomas Bowler, his Life and Work*. Cape Town: A. A. Balkema.
Coetzee, J. M. 1988. *White Writing. On the culture of letters in South Africa*. Sandton: Radix.

Coetzee, R. 1977. *The South African Culinary Tradition, with 167 Authentic Recipes*. Cape Town: Struik.

Cornevin, M. 1980. *Apartheid: power and historical falsification*. Paris: Unesco.

Deacon, J. 1984. Later Stone Age people and their descendants in southern Africa. In *Southern African Prehistory and Paleoenvironments*, Klein, R. G. (ed.), 221–38. Rotterdam: A. A. Balkema.

De St Croix, G. E. M. 1981. *The Class Struggle in the Ancient Greek World from the Archaic Age to the Arab Conquests*. London: Duckworth.

De Villiers, S. 1985. *A Tale of Three Cities*. Cape Town: Murray & Roberts Buildings Ltd.

Forster, E. M. 1941. *Howards End*. London: Penguin.

Fransen, H. & M. A. Cook 1980. *The Old Buildings of the Cape*. Cape Town: A. A. Balkema.

Gribble, J. 1989. Verlorenvlei vernacular: a structuralist analysis of sandveld folk architecture. Unpublished MA thesis, University of Cape Town.

Hall, M. 1987. *The Changing Past: farmers, kings and traders in southern Africa, 200–1860*. Cape Town: David Philip.

Hall, M. 1988. Archaeology under apartheid. *Archaeology* 41, 62–4.

Hall, M. 1989. Block 11 Cape Town – an archaeological assessment. Unpublished report, Archaeology Contracts Office, University of Cape Town.

Hall, M. 1990. 'Hidden history': Iron Age archaeology in southern Africa. In *A History of African Archaeology*, Robertshaw, P. (ed.), 59–77. London: James Currey.

Hall, M. 1991a. Archaeological work at Sea Street Cape Town. Unpublished report, Archaeology Contracts Office, University of Cape Town.

Hall, M. 1991b. Fish and the fisherman: art, text and archaeology. *South African Journal of Art and Architectural History* 2, 78–88.

Hall, M. 1992. 'Small things' and 'the mobile, conflictual fusion of power, fear and desire'. In *The Art and Mystery of Archaeology: essays in honor of James Deetz*, Yentsch, A. & M. Beaudry (eds), 373–99. Boca Raton: CRC Press.

Hall, M., D. Halkett, J. Klose & J. Portuesi 1993. Haupt's Yard: a late eighteenth-century site in Cape Town. Unpublished report, Department of Archaeology, University of Cape Town.

Hall, M., D. Halkett, J. Klose & G. Ritchie 1990. The Barrack Street well: images of a Cape Town household in the nineteenth century. *South African Archaeological Bulletin* 45, 73–92.

Judges, S. 1977. Poverty, living conditions and social relations – aspects of life in Cape Town in the 1830s. Unpublished MA thesis, University of Cape Town.

Klopper, S. 1989. Mobilizing cultural symbols in twentieth-century Zululand. Africa Seminar paper, Centre for African Studies, University of Cape Town.

Krauss, F. 1966. A description of Cape Town and its way of life, 1838–40. *Quarterly Bulletin of the South African Library* 21, 2–12.

Lewis-Williams, D. 1981. *Believing and Seeing: symbolic meanings in southern San rock paintings*. London: Academic Press.

Mentzel, O. F. 1921. *A Geographical and Topographical Description of the Cape of Good Hope*. Part 1. Cape Town: Van Riebeeck Society.

Mentzel, O. F. 1925. *A Geographical and Topographical Description of the Cape of Good Hope*. Part 2. Cape Town: Van Riebeeck Society.

Mentzel, O. F. 1944. *A Geographical and Topographical Description of the Cape of Good Hope*. Part 3. Cape Town: Van Riebeeck Society.

Obholzer, A. M., M. Baraitser & W. D. Malherbe 1985. *The Cape House and its Interior*. Stellenbosch: Stellenbosch Museum.

Scott, J. C. 1985. *Weapons of the Weak. Everyday forms of resistance*. New Haven: Yale University Press.

Scott, J. C. 1990. *Domination and the Arts of Resistance. Hidden transcripts*. New Haven:

Yale University Press.

Shepherd, N. 1990. The politics of material culture: ox-wagons and rock-musicians. Unpublished seminar paper, Historical Archaeology Research Group, University of Cape Town.

Smith, A. B. 1983. The Hotnot syndrome: myth-making in South African school textbooks. *Social Dynamics* 9, 37–49.

Stadler, A. 1987. *The Political Economy of Modern South Africa*. Cape Town: David Philip.

Stewart, P. & A. Mazel. 1986. Perpetual poisoning of the mind: a consideration of the treatment of the San and the origins of South Africa's black population in South Africa's school history textbooks since 1972 for Standards 8, 9, 10 and 1974 for Standards 5, 6 and 7. Paper presented at the Precolonial History Workshop, University of Cape Town.

Walton, J. 1965. *Homesteads and Villages of South Africa*. Pretoria: Schaik.

Walton, J. 1985. *Cape Dovecots and Fowl-runs*. Stellenbosch: Stellenbosch Museum.

Walton, J. 1989. *Old Cape Farmsteads*. Cape Town: Human & Rousseau.

Warren, D. 1986. Merchants, commissioners and wardmasters: municipal politics in Cape Town, 1840–54. Unpublished MA thesis, University of Cape Town.

13 Struggling with tradition in South Africa: the multivocality of images of the past

ANDREW D. SPIEGEL

The past is especially fascinating in South Africa, with its short colonial history of growing social polarization. Legitimation for that polarization and the socially engineered stratification that grew with it has been sought by appeals to the past, many re-creations of which have been in terms of the notion of tradition. Such appeals created images of essentialist continuities, helping to carry imagined characteristics of different population categories into present struggles over social and legislated differentiation.

This chapter examines ways that socially constructed images of the supposedly separate pasts of various categories of South Africa's population have been used both to legitimate, and to contest, socio-legal categorization and the domination that it has produced. Some of these constructed images involve notions of traditionality, often contributed by anthropological endeavour, which continue to influence many arguments. This chapter's concern is thus with the present and how it constitutes, and is constituted by, 'the traditional' for different portions of the South African population, particularly the African 'population group'.[1] Examples are considered of the use of tradition, both for domination and for resistance.[2]

South Africa is infamous for its coercive racist policies and political structure and I do not mean to suggest that that coercion has been effected solely through ideological means. Indeed, that would hide the extremely violent nature of much of the country's colonial history and of the coercion that has marked and marred its administration. But it is intriguing that many of South Africa's legally created social boundaries have been imbued with a sense of legitimacy that derives from appeals to an image of separate traditions and a divided past in which different populations are seen to have had different monadic cultures and traditions. This is still the ideological standpoint of reactionary opponents of transformation in South Africa. Ironically, it also provides the basis for some anti-apartheid positions whose protagonists appeal to similarly static and monadic contemporary representations/inventions of past traditions and cultures to legitimate their particular types of visions for the future.

Representing Africans as traditional

Dualist models of various forms litter the South African literature and media
(cf. Sharp 1988a). Representing Africans as 'traditional' has been just one
weapon in a discursive armoury used to deny Africans full participation in
the country's political and economic processes. Africans, represented as still
'traditional', have thereby been excluded from the 'western' (namely white-
dominated) political structures. The evidence used to demonstrate their traditionality includes that Africans 'still' engage in 'tribal' feuding, 'still' pay
bridewealth, 'still' practise initiation rituals, 'still' believe in the ancestors and
'still' resort to diviners for therapy. In other words they are conservative and
backward-looking, unable to meet the demands of modern society.

The epithet 'traditional' has long been used as an alternative to such labels as
'uncivilized', 'primitive', 'pre-literate', 'tribal' or 'non-western' – namely to
identify the 'other'. Indeed, much social science has contrasted 'tradition' on
the one hand, with 'reason', 'rationality' and 'science' on the other (Shils 1981),
and it has implied that the lives of 'traditional' people are 'bound by the
cultural horizons set by [their] tradition' whereas 'modern' people are conceived as 'culturally dynamic, oriented to change and innovation' (Eisenstadt
1973, p. 1).

This contrast between 'tradition' on the one hand, and 'reason', 'rationality'
and 'science' on the other, has been clearly symbolized in the Afrikaans
taalmonument (language monument) outside the western Cape town of Paarl
where, parochial popular history has it, the decisions were taken in 1875 to
create a formal lexicon and grammar for Afrikaans, and in 1896 to campaign
for its recognition as an official language of the local (colonial) state. As an
architect-designed monument to a living language,[3] the *taalmonument* is probably unique. Acknowledging that the Afrikaans language draws upon various
European as well as Asian and African languages, the monument includes
representations of each of these linguistic contributions. The contrived symbolism of the structure reflects how white South Africans contrast their roots
with those of their African compatriots.

It is also explicitly spelled out in pamphlets and a poster display at the
monument. Their texts explain what each segment of the monument was
designed to represent and how they culminate in the main 57m high open
concrete-and-granite cylinder representing the (ever-growing) Afrikaans
language, and in its somewhat shorter companion signifying attainment of
independent Republic status in 1961.[4] Three shorter rectangular and neatly
angled columns, representing European influences, are said to reflect the
'rationality and enlightenment of Europe'. By contrast, the 'magic, mystery
and tradition of Africa' is symbolized by three rounded (breast-like) forms
behind a low wall on the opposite side of the main steps. And, placed between
the 'structure' of Europe and the 'warmth' of Africa is a low almost unnotice-
able wall depicting the contribution made to the language by slaves from the
Far East who were settled in the Cape during the early Dutch occupation.

The distinction between 'traditional' and 'modern' has also been particularly suited to other more explicitly discursive representations of South Africa as a society comprising distinctly separate parts. It provides images on which the anonymous authors of South Africa's official yearbooks have drawn to emphasize the perceived differences between legislated categories of the population. Thus the yearbook for 1985 argues that 'the White and Black segments of the South African population have different cultures' and that 'traditional economics among the Black peoples of South Africa is based on a subsistence rather than a profit philosophy. The concept of overproduction in specialized fields for distribution by free marketing is foreign to traditionalist thinking' (South Africa, Department of Foreign Affairs 1985, pp. 94–5).

Further perceived differences in white and African economic values are used to illustrate the necessity of keeping these segments of the population separate. And images are conveyed of 'traditional' African culture that is unchanging, homogeneous and communal – just as it always was in some mythical past – as compared with a 'modern' white culture that follows an historical trajectory of dynamism, diversity and individualism. Used in this way, 'traditional' culture and 'traditional' economics are not simply descriptive labels. They are part of an argument calling upon and reinforcing deep-seated images of an imagined past in order to account for the marked contemporary discrepancies in wealth between whites and Africans in terms of supposed obstacles that 'traditional' beliefs and practices put in the way of progress and development – themselves core symbols of modernity. This argument allows one to ignore the long process of dispossession experienced by South Africa's African population, particularly since the discovery of minerals in the last third of the nineteenth century (e.g. Bundy 1979, Keegan 1982, Letsoalo 1987).

Such pictures of Africans as 'traditional' help mystify the historical political-economic processes that have created and maintained the inequalities pervading contemporary South African society. For those concerned to perpetuate apartheid and the racial differentiation it has produced, the image conveyed by traditionality offers much. This is because the description allows an entire category of the population to be labelled so as to portray their behaviour and thought negatively: Africans are thus socially constructed as 'conservative', 'backward', 'pre-rational' and thus fundamentally different from 'modern', 'progressive' or 'developed' people – namely whites. Although the reference to traditionality is cultural and not racial, such usages are entirely compatible with racist ideologies.

It is thus disquieting, although not entirely surprising, to find appeals to static images of traditionality drawn from mythical pasts in the work of some liberation ideologues. Keesing (n.d., p. 22) has recently reminded us that 'in a situation of subjugation, confrontational politics are [frequently] inherently structured in the terms and categories of the dominant . . . because of a strategic realization that one must meet the enemy on his own turf'.

Traditionality has also been used to 'account for' African workers' increasingly vociferous rejection of capitalism, and their unions' socialist positions.

Rather than recognizing it as a response to the extremely exploitative nature of the local wage-labour relation, the government-controlled South African Broadcasting Corporation (SABC) explained, to its assumedly white listeners in 1986, that this proclivity could be ascribed to Africans having only recently 'emerged' from communalist 'traditionalism':

> in a country in which a large group is barely emerging from a traditional culture of collectivism, and moreover feels itself to be disadvantaged, the apparent panaceas of socialism are a powerful attraction . . . and it is not surprising that many Black[5] people tend to favour socialism above free enterprise.
>
> (SABC 'Comment' 10 June 1986)

In part the image of Africans as having only recently emerged from traditionalism is the product of a thirty-year exercise of reinventing tradition for the country's Bantustans. Indeed a 1930s survey of African administration expressed similar sentiments, commenting that Africans were 'a primitive people rapidly emerging from barbarism' (Rogers 1933 quoted in Letsoalo 1987, p. 37). By having contrived to create 'traditional homelands' for the different 'ethnic groups' among the country's Africans, and by making it difficult for them to be permanently domiciled elsewhere in the country, apartheid's architects led themselves and their acolytes into believing that Africans really did still live in 'traditional' milieus in the 1970s and 1980s. Let us now examine the process of inventing African traditionality for the Bantustans.

Traditionality and the land

Land dispossession in South Africa reached its zenith with the 1913 Natives Land Act prohibiting Africans from owning land, or being self-employed agricultural tenants, in all but 7 per cent of the country.[6] The 7 per cent became reserves administered directly through appointed headmen (Hammond-Tooke 1975, p. 81). By 1936, with mining-industry pressure to extend the reserves so that they could continue to subsidize mine wages (cf. Wolpe 1972, Lacey 1981), a further 6 per cent of the country was scheduled for 'release' to the reserves.[7] As this happened areas were planned and settled under administration through headmen, just as in the rest of the reserves.

The 1950s saw a major shift in government perceptions of the significance of these areas of African-occupied land. They had by then become extremely overcrowded and their agricultural output was falling rapidly. With the exception of odd fertile pockets, they were unable any longer to support their populations, let alone provide any subsidy to wages, as a government-appointed commission of enquiry – the Tomlinson Commission (UG61/1955) – indicated. By this point, however, these Bantustans ('tribal homelands') were seen as the geographical loci of the ethnic-national units into which apartheid divided the African population through the 1959 Promotion of Bantu Self-Government Act. One way government thought to control this growing population was to divide it into imposed ethnic categories and establish indirect rule through reinvented 'traditional' chiefs overseeing renovated 'traditional' administrative and land-tenure systems. While the Tomlinson Commission recommended individualization of reserve land to encourage increased production, the apartheid government insisted on reviving 'traditional/communal' tenure, effectively to make places for as many people as possible.

In the perception of the then Minister of Native Affairs and his staff, a common feature of all these African peoples was that they had been traditionally administered by chiefs who remained the 'true leaders' of the people and who now needed to have their power reinstated. As a result a new system of regional government was introduced. In terms of the Bantu Authorities Act, a reinvented traditionality was created with a hierarchy of chiefs and paramount chiefs created for each Bantustan. That hierarchy, it was envisaged, would eventually administer its respective territory so that it could become an 'independent' state.

Chiefs' precolonial claims to allegiance had rested largely on their ability to allocate areas of land to their subjects. Thus '[t]he [precolonial] chief was the ultimate source of all authority. He embodied the material and spiritual welfare of his people [and a]s custodian of the land, he controlled its distribution . . . [and] regulated the sowing and harvesting of crops' (Murray 1980, p. 96). Building on such images, the apartheid administration reconstituted the chieftainship, building in significant control over land allocation. The Bantustans' land-tenure systems were thus also of an invented traditional form, in parallel with administration through chiefs. The land remained notionally the property of the chiefs and through them a government agency that held it 'in trust' for the population at large. No individual freehold or leasehold was envisaged, but rather land was allocated by the chiefs and their subordinate headmen, advised by agricultural officers.

There had, simultaneously, been another major government intervention in land-use patterns, ostensibly to prevent soil erosion (Yawitch 1981, 1988). But the motivation underpinning these efforts was the apartheid vision of all Africans 'returning' to their 'homelands' and attending the 'white' cities, towns and farms only as servants of whites. By insisting that land-tenure retain a 'traditional' form, with every householder entitled to some arable land, a residential site and access to communal pasturage, the government attempted to ensure that as many people as possible would feel or develop a commitment to the Bantustan area where they held such entitlements. That way the African population could be kept out of the towns and 'white' areas, except as short-term wage-workers. Responsibility for their general social reproduction would rest on the Bantustan and its chiefs-dominated administration, which in addition would have to bear responsibility for control of that population.

The 1980s saw the predominance of the last of these functions. The over-crowding that resulted from massive forced population relocation (SPP 1983, Platzky & Walker 1985) brought the demise of attempts to effect a 'traditional' land-tenure system in many Bantustan areas. While chiefs continued to call upon images of traditionality in their internecine struggles over the right to administer land and thus to gain power within their respective Bantustans (Quinlan 1986), the land basis of their authority was significantly transformed: all they could now offer was small residential sites on densely overcrowded 'closer settlements'[8] and 'protection' from other chiefs in the area. In this instance the appeal to traditionality on the land had failed – political-economic processes had overtaken ideological manipulation.

Yet appeals to reinstate a 'traditional' land-tenure system are still to be heard in South Africa, this time emanating from the work of Africanist opponents of the apartheid system (cf. Letsoala 1987, 1990).[9] In terms of these appeals and the view that supports them, all the country's 'lands should be vested in the state, but administered by chiefs who will distribute them amongst followers according to traditional norms in which differentiation indicates reciprocity rather than exploitation. Chiefs are seen as traditional democrats and it is held that the new "traditional" men will be paragons of gender sensitivity' (Sharp 1990a, p. 9).

Underlying these appeals is an implication that all previous attempts to document 'traditional' land-tenure have been insufficiently sensitive to the perversions that colonial and state intervention brought about. The documents have thus themselves perverted the 'traditional' and not represented it authentically. Letsoalo has argued that the authentically traditional 'land-tenure system of the Blacks (before colonization) produced in abundance and did so without ravaging the environment or the society. Land was distributed to all members of a tribe' (Letsoalo 1987, p. 78; cf. 1990). As a result, the inherent characteristics of precolonial land-tenure systems – in which completely equit-able land allocation is said to have occurred, and where there was neither the practice of, nor scope for, any form of exploitation or unfair appropriations either of labour or product – have allegedly been lost from view.

Despite their claims to the contrary, such calls romanticize a past 'traditional' African land-tenure system without providing any substantive evidence that the supposed equitability was ever realized in practice. Indeed, the primary source for such images has been the oral evidence of dispossessed Africans in today's 'homelands'; the instrumentality of their imagery is as necessary a part of their own local struggles for rehabilitation as it is transparent.

Clearly, political struggle over land may come to work with images of a past that at once reject the apartheid image of African 'traditionality' and suggest a newly contrived authentic past. But these remain merely images, as does all historiography. And in being constructed in oppositional dialogue these voices, as Keesing (n.d.) has pointed out, tend to use the same sets of categories as those used by the ideology that is under attack and which they are intended to reject and displace in its entirety (cf. Sharp 1990b). Another place where this may occur, albeit as a result of commercial success, rather than as part of the struggle for South Africa, is in the tourist industry.

Traditionality in the tourist industry

South Africa today is transforming itself into a non-racial democracy that no longer gives political credence to images of cultural difference between categories of the population. A result of this process is a rapid growth in foreign tourism to the country. Paradoxically, many such tourists visit the country for a taste of the very magical mystery and traditionality of Africa – the 'otherness' – that the *taalmonument* suggests the continent and its people possess. Albeit unwittingly, the categories of domination are thus again reinforced through appeals to traditionality, in this instance closely associated with images of pristine nature. The voices calling up these images have no explicit political reason for doing so. Indeed, the tourists' tacit understanding of Africa and Africans as pristine and 'other' is itself a product of a long ideological history that has created and reinforced such perceptions. And the fact that the local tourist industry meets such demands is a reflection of commercial self-interestedness, coupled with a distinct lack of self-conscious evaluation of the political implications of the images conveyed.

Tourist demand for experience of the African 'other' reflects a continuity with the enormous grip that African animals held over the British imagination during the nineteenth century (cf. Beinart 1990), although it is now conflated with interest in quaint and curious human social habits. And the tourist industry meets the demand in like terms, as became clear when a student-researcher interviewed an employee of one of Cape Town's postcard manufac- turers and distributors during June 1990. Asking whether, in addition to postcards of landscapes, flowers and wildlife, they produced and distributed any of people, she was told 'Only natives [Africans]. No people as such' (Westerhout 1990). Africans, in this perception, are so close to nature that they are not really people at all.

This combination of a wild Africa and its 'traditional' people appears in various places: in the ways booklets about the various fauna and flora of the country are intermingled on the bookshelves of curio-cum-tourist shops with booklets about various African 'tribal' groupings; in the fact that materials on African populations are housed in natural history museums (cf. Durrans 1988);[10] and in the advertising of safari tours and game-parks where the magic of the African bush and its proliferation of wildlife are offered along with experience of the 'traditional' lifestyles of Africans.

Similarly, tour-bus advertising brochures appeal to this image of 'otherness' to attract clientele. One brochure thus advertises:

We leave Durban [the country's main commercial-port city] for a land of sugar cane, trees, bustling small towns and traditional Zulu homesteads . . . [to] arrive at Shakaland [a contrived 'traditional' Zulu settlement]. Our . . . visit to this unique cross-cultural programme includes lectures on Zulu history, etiquette and tradition and gives the visitor an opportunity to experience, at first hand, traditional dancing and folklore. An authentic Zulu meal is served in the traditional manner, at the main hut. After lunch [we] continue into the unspoilt thornveld of Zululand to Ubizane Game Reserve.

. . . Passengers electing the Sabi Sabi option will be . . . taken to Sabi Sabi Game Reserve . . . set in the heart of a vast expanse of *pristine* African bushveld . . . explored in open landrovers with highly trained game rangers and trackers . . . [followed by] dinner in the open air 'Boma' including a traditional barbecue with venison dishes, while *Shangaan tribal dancers entertain under the starlit African sky.*

(Touring South Africa 1990. Springbok Atlas 1990
Coach Tours of South Africa, p. 15)[11]

Another indication of the representation of Africans as 'traditional' and living in the pristine state of an idealized 'natural' past can be found in the wide array of postcards and tourist booklets that publish some of the only readily available semi-nude photographs in the country. A very powerful puritanical Calvinist philosophy controls the South African publishing industry under a government which has enforced strict censorship of both political and pornographic materials. Definition of the latter extends to include items such as advertising calendars of topless (white) women. Yet in departmental stores, on newsstands and in curio shops, one finds postcards depicting topless African women – ostensibly in their 'traditional' African garb including beadwork decorations manufactured from glass beads of European origin.[12] Virtually nowhere in the country can one find people actually dressed in this manner – whether in the supposedly 'traditional' Bantustans or in the industrial cities – except where there are explicit displays of African 'traditionality' for tourist purposes. Yet a curio-shop assistant responded to another student-researcher's questions in June 1990 that 'of course people dress like that in the homelands – boobs and all. If they didn't then why would people bother to make postcards of that sort of scene? People dress like that in the countryside. It is traditional to do so' (Ferguson 1990, p. 30).

It is true that for some more intimate rituals, young women – and young men too – may have to attire themselves thus. This is particularly so for initiation rituals held in secluded places out of general view. But such attire is not commonplace today, although thirty and more years ago it might have been in selected parts of the country. Its representation on postcards and in pictorial 'colour guides' for today's tourists represents an appeal to an imagination that would expect nature – and semi-nude men and women – in the 'darkness' of Africa where animals run wild. Explicit statements reflecting this attitude came from a clerk in a postcard factory who retailed the contents of a letter received from a California customer who had placed regular orders over the past two to three years. Suggesting that she assumed that the customer was interested in the postcards for exclusively pornographic reasons, she quoted his letter: 'Send as many postcards as you can of blacker black women, Zulu girls. Don't send postcards of men, or boys or animals or birds or even Cape Town . . . being a white man's son I do not worship blacks' (Westerhout 1990, p. 24). She also indicated that the company for which she worked was beginning to reconsider its marketing of such artefacts.

That topless African women somehow represent tradition is reflected in various places. As I have indicated elsewhere (Spiegel 1989), one such place is the glossies published during the 1970s and 1980s to mark the various Bantustans' achievement of apartheid-styled constitutional 'independence'. In those cases tradition was contrasted with modernity by the photographic counterposing of topless with dressed African women. Another such place is in postcard captions. Thus the bilingual caption to a photograph of an attractive, bare-breasted teenager with beads around her neck and a colourful skirt around her waist as she stands holding a hoe next to a banana tree in a lush setting, reads:

English:
African life – Natal – South Africa

In the communal life of a typical village, the maidens hoe the ground in preparation for planting, or clearing the area of weeds.

Afrikaans (my translation):
Traditional tribal life – Natal – South Africa

In the communal life of a typical African village maidens hoe the ground in preparation for the planting of maize or wheat, or to remove weeds from the area.[13]

The divergence in the English and Afrikaans captions suggests that the makers either saw an equivalence between African and 'traditional tribal' or that they felt safer using the latter terms in a language not likely to be understood by foreign tourists (Dutch and German excluded).

Using tradition as a resource in gender struggles

Domination, and resistance to it, is no more restricted to the public political domain in South Africa than elsewhere, and as in the former sphere, tradition is used as a resource in both local and domestic contexts. Recent work has begun to indicate the extent to which images of traditionality have been used in gender struggles in various parts of the country; many appeals to images of the past as 'tradition' are not directly related to apartheid. Yet they too are used either to reinforce or challenge domination. And they too may reinforce perceptions of a fundamental opposition between 'tradition' (which is African) and 'modernity' (white).

The particular forms which gender relations take are largely determined by people's material circumstances and their recent experiences of historical processes. Such factors produce significant regional and temporal differences in the nature of gender relations among Africans in Bantustans: where there has been a long continuous occupation of the same area, with agricultural resources and steady access to the labour market for migrant wage-workers, gender relations are more stable and less intensely patriarchal than where people have recently been subjected to forced removal from white-owned farms into densely settled Bantustan relocation areas offering nothing more than a minuscule residential site and erratic access to the wage-labour market. In each case, the ideology of gender relations is underpinned by people's expectations built upon their memories of past experience (Sharp & Spiegel 1990). Those memories and expectations are often reinforced by appeals to images of the past couched in terms of an African traditionality that is then set up in opposition to (white) modernity. This process reflects the hegemonic ideological division of the South African population and the manner in which it is often taken up by the oppressed themselves. Thus in the small Eastern Cape town of Grahamstown, 'Traditional Xhosa culture' was constantly mentioned as a reference point. It referred to a time preceding the coming of the whites, or persisting until some unspecified time in the recent past, or sometimes still continuing in the rural areas. Indeed, informants often slipped from one time frame to another in discussion. The image of 'modern' marriage was likewise manipulated for strategic ends (van der Vliet 1991, p. 220).

Looking at marriage patterns and expectations, van der Vliet goes on to show that the discourse of disputes and tensions between spouses was often phrased around these two opposing images. For the most part men appealed to the 'traditional' in order to claim their 'right' to dominate and indeed some-times abuse their wives. This was particularly notable as regards men's justifi-cations of their frequent philandering by appeals to the Xhosa tradition of polygyny. An informant of van der Vliet (1991, p. 231) argued that 'You have a string of girlfriends in the place of the many wives your grandfather used to have.'

Women, on the other hand, appealed to an image of the jointness, closure and fidelity of idealized 'modern' marriage to reject these assertions and to claim that companionship and mutual help were the requirements of a mar-riage. Yet there were other cases where the tables were turned, where wives appealed to 'tradition' to bring their husbands to book if that 'cultural script' was more likely to provide a satisfactory strategic outcome.

Similar gender-distinctive appeals to tradition occur among people in the Thongaland area of northern Natal near Kosi Bay (Webster 1991).[14] There, however, the competing 'scripts' were not African traditionality and modernity but local people's perceptions of Zulu and Thonga traditions regarding gender relations, particularly between spouses, and regarding the expected behaviour of wives in their affines' presence.

The area in which Webster worked has been variously occupied over some centuries by both the Thonga state under Mabudu in what is now Mozambique, and, in recent times, by Shaka's Zulu state, and its various successors. The people living there had therefore often had to change their political allegiances: 'the people in the area between Lake St Lucia in the south and Delagoa Bay in the north have experienced a bewildering series of changes in political control over their lives' (Webster 1991, p. 248). They have thus experienced 'successive waves of political authority washing over them, lending weight, authority and enlightened self-interest to the espousal of one set of cultural practices and identities or another, with the ebb and flow of Thonga and Zulu influence' (Webster 1991, p. 249).

By the 1980s, the area was part of the KwaZulu Bantustan. Its men were predominantly labour migrants in and around Johannesburg, while the women remained in the area, engaging in householding in its broader sense. Having to search for work in the hostile environment of Johannesburg, the men presented themselves as Zulu to suit 'white stereotypes of the suitability of Zulus for jobs such as nightwatchman' – a niche occupied by many of them in one of Johannesburg's high-rise apartment areas (Webster 1991, p. 254). Their self-presentation as Zulu was also because they felt that 'in the hazardous circumstances of hostel-dwelling in the city, it is better to be thought a member of a powerful dominant group than a small and vulnerable one' (Webster 1991, p. 254). Women too presented themselves as Zulu when it came to public occasions to do with the KwaZulu Bantustan authorities – such as on pension-payday – and its 'national cultural movement' Inkatha.

In the domestic domain, however, women preferred to regard themselves as Thonga while men continued to consider themselves as Zulu. Why was this? As Webster pointed out, it is ethnographically puzzling that men have spurned the Thonga heritage while their own sisters and wives embrace it. His answer to the conundrum, which is the issue of significance here, was that it was in women's interests to appeal to Thonga traditions of domesticity and expectations of wives, while men preferred the Zulu ways – or the local rendering of these – because they legitimated patriarchy and male dominance.

Thonga tradition was understood to give wives much greater independence than did Zulu tradition. It allows women to keep their own patronymics; to rise to positions of great status as father's-sister (*hahane*) and mother-in-law in their affinal groups; to maintain an independent dignity with regard to their fathers-in-law that, in their eyes, the Zulu tradition of *hlonipha* (elaborate rules of respect/avoidance) undermines; and especially to obtain a divorce (Webster 1991, pp. 256–9). Furthermore, 'Thonga women had various rights not commonly recognized among their Nguni [Zulu] neighbours. First, husbands could not maltreat wives; second, wives had the right to sexual gratification; third, they had the right to luxury items, beyond subsistence, if available; and fourth, they could dissolve a marriage' if both parties agreed . . . [so that] if a man becomes a migrant and is absent for a continuous period of four years, or fails to support his wife by sending remittances, she may end the marriage (Webster 1991, p. 259).

But it was not only in the ideological sphere that women's appeals to Thonga tradition were in their interests. 'While the ideological weaponry . . . provides a shield of legitimacy for male dominance and women's resistance, it is in the hard arena of economic relations that relative strengths are tested against each other' (Webster 1991, p. 261). The fact that male labour migration is as entrenched as it is in Bantustan areas such as Kosi Bay means that women are extremely dependent on men for the means of subsistence (cf. Sharp & Spiegel 1990). While men develop their macho-Zulu image as labour migrants, they spurn domestic and local agricultural work as 'women's work' – an attitude supported by Zulu tradition, at least in the locally shared perception of it. In terms of a similarly shared understanding of Thonga tradition, however, men are expected to assist their wives in the fields and gardens, and women therefore rehearse their own and their men's 'Thonganess' in efforts to claim their menfolk's assistance, to claim equality of status with their men, and to 'negotiat[e]' the quality of their relationship with their husbands: the men's interests lie in patriarchy framed in a "Zulu" model, while the women attempt to retain some areas of equality by retaining the "Thonga" model' (Webster 1991, p. 263).

Conclusion: South Africa, anthropologists and tradition

Anthropological research has long documented the variety of traditions that occur world-wide. Indeed, that has been one of its prime *raisons d'être*, and – as Boyer (1987) has indicated – anthropologists have shared a set of assumptions about what constitutes traditionality without ever addressing these explicitly. Moreover, for the most part they have been oblivious of how tradition has been used as a resource for purposes of domination and resistance.

Recent years have seen an important shift in this regard (Keesing & Tonkinson 1982, Hobsbawm & Ranger 1983). That people invent and reinvent tradition in order to reconstruct the past as images for the present is there in virtually every fieldwork encounter and experience. The past has a salience that makes such invention particularly worthwhile, not only for those in the seats of power, but also for those trying to confront power-holders. It is also an important resource for people concerned to use images of the past in their everyday struggles over personal rights and freedoms.

It is for this reason that anthropologists have begun to study the processes whereby tradition is used and invented. Tradition is, and has the potential to be, multivocal, as this chapter has tried to show for the South African case. Everyone in society at some time looks to images created in the name of tradition to further their socio-political ends. Anthropologists are particularly well suited to find ways of understanding that kind of multivocality. This is particularly important in contemporary South Africa as the old order crumbles. As we enter the post-apartheid era, members of South African society need to come to terms with the ways in which domination has loaded the intellectual categories used for that domination into the consciousness of the oppressed. We need to recognize that different interest-groups use their own inventions of secular and parochial traditions to resist their domination, and that the intensity of struggle in which these inventions are forged makes them particularly resilient. To be able to recognize such processes at work, to be able to deconstruct the images created, and yet not to fly in the face of popular opinion requires immense sensitivity.

South African anthropologists have another reason, however, for having to do what is outlined above. For many years some of the (broader) discipline's members have been active participants in the process of constructing parochial traditions in order to give legitimacy to apartheid. I refer here to the branch of South African anthropology that we describe in our country as *volkekunde* (ethnology in the fashion of Mühlmann 1938 and Shirokogoroff 1935; cf. Sharp 1981, Gordon 1988).

Particularly from the 1950s through to the late 1970s, many *volkekundiges* (practitioners of *volkekunde*) were centrally involved in the work of inventing an ideology of difference in order to give credibility to apartheid.[15] Despite the clearly racist political control function intended for the Bantustans created during the 1950s, attempts were made to hide this behind a facade of cultural relativism that insisted on the uniqueness of each ethnos or *volk* and its respective traditionality.

Working *inter alia* through the then government-sponsored South African Bureau of Racial Affairs,[16] *volkekundiges* insisted that the traditions and customs of each South African ethnos were so distinctive that they each deserved their own separate ethnic-national territory and administration – a Bantustan or 'homeland' in which members of the Zulu, Xhosa, Southern Sotho, etc. ethnoses could each continue to practise their respective primordial customs without hindrance from outsiders. As each ethnos was seen to be imbued with its own virtually immutable culture and traditions, the self-perceived work of the *volkekundige* was to find means to collect and systematize items of those pristine cultures and record and codify them. Their job, then, was to find the essential elements of each *volk*'s culture so that its *Volksgeist* could be captured, codified, systematized and revived for the benefit of each *volk* respectively.

Social anthropologists did not, for the most part, participate in these political endeavours or subscribe to the *volkekundiges*' essentialist epistemology. Some were, indeed, employed as government ethnologists, but as apartheid began to unfold they attempted to divorce themselves from its implementation. One of these was David Hammond-Tooke who subsequently published critical analyses of the implementation of the apartheid policy of tribal authorities in the Transkei (Hammond-Tooke 1964, 1975).

Despite their efforts to distance themselves from the crude representations of the past, however, some social anthropologists still found themselves increasingly drawn to trying to 'salvage', in textual form, what was understood to be the precolonial past, and thus to reinvent tradition (cf. Wilson & Thompson 1969, 1971, Hunter 1979). In part this was understood to be for scientific posterity. In part it was seen as necessary to correct the false image of the past that then prevailed regarding especially the nature of precolonial society in South Africa. On the one hand, these scholars were trapped in working with an image of stasis as they constructed precolonial base-lines (cf. Spiegel 1989). On the other, their intention was to provide an historiographical corrective that revealed change and fluidity rather than stasis, a process of incorporation of indigenous populations into a single political-economy where they had become oppressed, rather than an image of continuing god-given separateness that required nurturing.

Today, with a lively awareness of the instrumentality of the *volkekundiges'* project and a clear recognition that traditions are social constructions of the past, a younger generation of South African social anthropologists has begun the task of deconstructing tradition and the various images of the past that its multivocality has generated (e.g. Sharp 1991, Spiegel & McAllister 1991, White 1991). Although it is now easy to do this as regards the inventions of apartheid's ideologues (cf. Boonzaier & Sharp 1988), it remains an important task to demonstrate the extent to which they have been internalized and used to structure ideologies of resistance to apartheid. The challenge lies then in being able sensitively to deconstruct those images of traditionality that have been used for purposes of resistance. As pointed out, these are likely to be extremely resilient and their purveyors particularly jealous of their authenticity.

The rewards for such deconstructive efforts are more likely to be slaps in the face than motions of gratitude. This is because South African society has for so long been built around images of historical difference that to draw upon them is still a fundamental part of the political process. Because our exercise aims to understand inventions of tradition and uses of images of the past in terms of contemporary socio-political circumstances, we cannot ever write a 'correct' history. We will therefore be unable to legitimate particularist claims.

Yet we can and must engage with the transformation of South Africa. The contemporary wider world gives clear indication of the power of primordialism through the violence that it brings in its wake. As South African social anthropologists, our task must be to point to the dangers of primordialism and to draw attention to the circumstances in which traditions are invented and histories constructed. And we must do this to help bring about an open dialogic discourse amongst the creators and purveyors of tradition, rather than merely to act as self-satisfied critics. As they reconstruct histories and draw upon images of the past to bolster their struggles, South Africans of all persuasions need to recognize the instrumentality behind, and the dangers of, their actions. Engaged social anthropologists must accept the challenge of acting as guides.

Notes

1 Official usage in South Africa distinguishes four broad 'population groups': black, 'coloured', Asiatic/Indian and white (cf. West 1988). Each of these comprises a legislatively imposed racial category, although the necessarily vague criteria used to determine boundaries depend on a variety of factors, including primordialist culture groupings overlaid on crude conceptions of race. As the term black is more popularly used to include all of the first three categories, I use the term African here to refer to the first of them. My usage does not imply approval of such legal classification. It is, however, important to recognize that the classification and its legitimation is part of the concern of this chapter and it is thus necessary to use it in discussion. People in each legally defined category are treated differently, and this has had profound repercussions for their lives.

2 The chapter adds some new examples to others used previously (Spiegel & Boonzaier 1988, Spiegel 1989). I am grateful to Emile Boonzaier for his comments and suggestions. Any errors, omissions or misinterpretations are, of course, my own.

3 Various architects participated in a competition to find an appropriate design during the late 1960s and early 1970s.

4 With recognition of Afrikaans as an official language, independence as a Republic divorced from British imperial influence was an important symbol of Afrikaner nationhood since the end of the Anglo–Boer war (1898–1902).

5 As stated above (see note 1), 'Black' here refers to Africans.

6 In fact Africans were still allowed to purchase land in the Cape Province, although very few had the resources to do so, and fewer still actually did. I include share-contracting peasant farmers in the designation self-employed agricultural tenants.

7 This did not mean that all of these 'released' areas were immediately turned over as reserves. Indeed, this process took many years, still occurring in the 1970s.

8 'Closer settlement' refers to areas of nominally rural land, often in remote corners of the country, for which there is so great a demand that households are allocated just a small residential site and there is minimal infrastructure. 'Closer settlements' are administered by chiefs and headmen in terms of the Bantu Authorities Act.

9 Applied researchers working in the semi-arid north-west of the country have recently been concerned to defend 'traditional' use of range-land in the face of government-orchestrated attempts in those areas – 'Coloured Rural Areas' – to impose a system of individual tenure on 'economic units' of grazing land that would destroy most local people's access to common pasturage (cf. Sharp 1990a). They have, however, called for careful studies of the logic and ecological rationality of 'communal grazing' in those areas rather than accepting the 'traditional' merely on blind faith (Boonzaier, Hoffman, Archer & Smith 1990).

10 Cape Town's natural history museum is the South African Museum which includes displays of various African 'tribal'/ethnic scenes and artefacts (Davison 1990). Its Bushman diorama – with life-casts made early this century to depict a supposed eighteenth-century scene at a foragers' camp – is a favourite with many tourists and local (mainly white) children, the latter spending their rainy Sunday afternoons going on to see stuffed birds, fish and wildlife, or listening to the sounds of whales at sea while examining a whale skeleton.

11 The same image is reflected in the title of another operator's tour of the same area: 'The East – The Beast – The Zulu – Durban', 1990/1, Welcome Tours and Safaris Welcome to South Africa (Pty) Ltd.

12 Westerhout (1990) has suggested that the postcards of semi-clad African men portrayed as warriors in their animal skins and bearing spears and shields, which are to be found on the shelves alongside those of the bare-breasted women, represent an imagery of the wild savagery of Africa, while the women represent the unspoilt and passive.
13 The postcard referred to here is marked Ref. No. 833 produced by Art Publishers (Pty) Ltd, Durban, Johannesburg, Cape Town. It was purchased at Johannesburg's Jan Smuts Airport 17 May 1989.
14 This is the last paper David Webster wrote before his assassination on 1 May 1989. For many reasons, he should have been the first South African social anthropologist to have attended a meeting of the World Archaeological Congress.
15 As Sharp (1988b) has pointed out, their commitment to an essentialist theory appears to derive from the struggle of Afrikanerdom for its own invention during the 1920s and 1930s when a new South African white petty-bourgeoisie forged an alliance with a large newly dispossessed white fraction of the regional working class, using symbols of race and common cultural features and history to mobilize what was initially a quite disparate assemblage of people.
16 Since 1983, when SABRA rejected the government's 'tricameral' parliamentary constitution (one chamber each for whites, 'coloureds' and Asians, none for Africans – their Bantustans were to suffice), the bureau has been a haven for right-wing white reactionaries (Zille 1988, p. 58).

References

Beinart, W. 1990. Empire, hunting and ecological change in southern and central Africa. *Past and Present* 128, 162–86.
Boonzaier, E. A., M. T. Hoffman, F. M. Archer & A. B. Smith 1990. Communal land use and the 'tragedy of the commons': some problems and perspectives with specific reference to semi-arid regions of southern Africa. *Journal of the Grassland Society of South Africa* 7, 77–80.
Boonzaier, E. & J. Sharp (eds) 1988. *South African Keywords: the uses and abuses of political concepts.* Cape Town: David Philip.
Boyer, P. 1987. The stuff 'traditions' are made of: on the implicit ontology of an ethnographic category. *Philosophy of the Social Sciences* 17, 49–65.
Bundy, C. 1979. *The Rise and Fall of the South African Peasantry.* London: Heinemann.
Davison, P. 1990. Rethinking the practice of ethnography and cultural history in South African museums. *African Studies* 49, 149–67.
Durrans, B. 1988. The future and the other: changing cultures on displays in ethnographic museums. In *The Museum Time-Machine*, Lumley, R. (ed.), 144–69. London: Routledge.
Eisenstadt, S. N. 1973. Post-traditional societies and the continuity and reconstruction of tradition. In *Post-Traditional Societies*, Winter number of *Daedalus* 102(1), 1–28.
Ferguson, J. 1990. Tourists and traders: the demand for and production of traditionality in a segment of Cape Town's tourist industry. Unpublished BA dissertation, University of Cape Town, Department of Social Anthropology.
Gordon, R. 1988. Apartheid's anthropologists: notes on the genealogy of Afrikaner *volkekundiges*. *American Ethnologist* 15, 535–54.
Hammond-Tooke, D. 1964. Chieftainship in Transkeian political development. *Journal of Modern African Studies* 2, 513–29.
Hammond-Tooke, D. 1975. *Command or Consensus: the development of Transkeian local government.* Cape Town: David Philip.
Hobsbawm, E. & T. Ranger 1983. *The Invention of Tradition.* Cambridge: Cambridge University Press.

Hunter, M. 1979. *Reaction to Conquest.* Cape Town: David Philip.
Keegan, T. 1982. The share-cropping economy, African class formation and the 1913 Natives Land Act in the Highveld Maize Belt. In *Industrialisation and Social Change in South Africa,* Marks, S. & R. Rathbone (eds), 195–211. London: Longman.
Keesing, R. M. n.d. Colonial and counter-colonial discourse in Melanesia. Mimeo – revised version of a paper presented to a seminar at Macquarie University, 19 April 1988.
Keesing, R. & R. Tonkinson (eds) 1982. *Reinventing Traditional Culture: the politics of Kastom in Island Melanesia.* Special issue of *Mankind* 13, 295–400.
Lacey, M. 1981. *Working for Boroko.* Johannesburg: Ravan Press.
Letsoalo, E. M. 1987. *Land Reform in South Africa: a black perspective.* Johannesburg: Skotaville.
Letsoalo, E. M. 1990. Land reforms – state initiatives. Unpublished paper presented to an IDASA workshop on the rural land question.
Mühlmann, W. 1938. *Methodik der Völkerkunde.* Stuttgart: Ferdinand Enker.
Murray, C. G. 1980. The political community: from tribe to nation. In *Transformations on the Highveld,* Lye, W. & C. G. Murray (eds), 88–105. Cape Town: David Philip.
Platzky, L. & C. Walker 1985. *The Surplus People: forced removals in South Africa.* Johannesburg: Ravan Press.
Quinlan, T. 1986. The tribal paradigm and ethnic nationalism: a case study of political structures in Qwaqwa. *Transformation* 2, 31–49.
Rogers, H. 1933. *Native Administration in the Union of South Africa.* Johannesburg, Witwatersrand University Press.
SABC 1986. '"Comment" on South African Broadcasting Corporation', English Service 10 June 1986.
Sharp, J. 1981. The roots and development of *volkekunde* in South Africa. *Journal of Southern African Studies* 8, 16–36.
Sharp, J. 1988a. Two worlds in one country: 'First World' and 'Third World' in South Africa. In *South African Keywords,* Boonzaier, E. & J. Sharp (eds), 111–21. Cape Town: David Philip.
Sharp, J. 1988b. Ethnic group and nation: the apartheid vision in South Africa. In *South African Keywords,* Boonzaier, E. & J. Sharp (eds), 79–99. Cape Town: David Philip.
Sharp, J. 1990a. Contested terrain: agriculture and development in the 'rural coloured areas'. Unpublished paper presented to an IDASA workshop on the rural land question.
Sharp, J. 1990b. Comment on Michèle Dominy's 'New Zealand's Waitangi tribunal: cultural politics of an anthropology of the high country'. *Anthropology Today* 6, 8–9.
Sharp, J. 1991. Controlled ethnogenesis: a comparative perspective on ethnic mobilization in South Africa. Unpublished paper presented at the University of Toronto.
Sharp, J. & A. Spiegel 1990. Women and wages: gender and the control of income in farm and bantustan households. *Journal of Southern African Studies* 16, 527–49.
Shils, E. 1981. *Tradition.* London: Faber & Faber.
Shirokogoroff, S. M. 1935. *Psychomental complex of the Tungas.* London: Kegan Paul, Trench & Tubner.
South Africa (Republic of) 1985. *Official Yearbook of the Republic of South Africa.* Pretoria: Department of Foreign Affairs.
Spiegel, A. D. 1989. Towards an understanding of tradition: uses of tradition(al) in apartheid South Africa. *Critique of Anthropology* 9, 49–74.
Spiegel, A. & E. Boonzaier 1988. Promoting tradition: images of the South African past. In *South African Keywords,* Boonzaier, E. & J. Sharp (eds), 40–57. Cape Town: David Philip.
Spiegel, A. D. & P. A. McAllister (eds) 1991. *Tradition and Transition in Southern Africa.* Johannesburg: Witwatersrand University Press.

SPP 1983. *Forced Removals in South Africa.* 5 vols. Cape Town, Surplus People Project.

van der Vliet, V. 1991. Traditional husbands, modern wives?: constructing marriages in a South African township. In *Tradition and Transition in Southern Africa*, Spiegel, A. D. & P. A. McAllister (eds), 219–42. Johannesburg: Witwatersrand University Press.

Webster, D. 1991. *Abafazi bathonga bafihlakala*: ethnicity and gender in a Kwazulu border community. In *Tradition and Transition in Southern Africa*, Spiegel, A. D. & P. A. McAllister (eds), 243–71. Johannesburg: Witwatersrand University Press.

West, M. 1988. Confusing categories: population groups, national states and citizenship. In *South African Keywords*, Boonzaier, E. & J. Sharp (eds), 100–10. Cape Town: David Philip.

Westerhout, L. 1990. A world in one country, a country in two minds: dualism in media representation within the South African tourist industry. Unpublished BA dissertation, University of Cape Town, Department of Social Anthropology.

White, H. 1991. Images of a late modern tribe: mass media representations of the Kruiper family at Kagga Kamma. Unpublished BA dissertation, University of Cape Town, Department of Social Anthropology.

Wilson, M. & L. Thompson (eds) 1969. *The Oxford History of South Africa.* Vol. I. London: Oxford University Press.

Wilson, M. & L. Thompson (eds) 1971. *The Oxford History of South Africa.* Vol. II. London: Oxford University Press.

Wolpe, H. 1972. Capitalism and cheap labour power: from segregation to apartheid. *Economy and Society* 1, 425–56.

Yawitch, J. 1981. *Betterment: the myth of homeland agriculture.* Johannesburg: South African Institute of Race Relations.

Yawitch, J. 1988. Betterment as state policy in South Africa. In *Towards Freehold*, Cross, C. & R. Haines (eds). 101–11. Cape Town: Juta.

Zille, H. 1985. The right-wing in South African politics. In *A Future South Africa: visions, strategies and realities*, Berger, P. L. & R. Godsell (eds), 55–94. Cape Town: Human & Rouseau & Tafelberg Publishers.

14 Intellectuals in South Africa and the reconstructive agenda

MALA SINGH

> The honeymoon of intellectuals and policy-makers is often nasty, brutish and short.
>
> (Merton 1968, p. 276)

> In as much as an intellectual puts himself at the service of a popular movement, he must observe its discipline, and refrain from weakening the organization of the masses. But in as much as he must clarify the practical relationship between means and ends, he can never renounce his critical faculties if he is to preserve the fundamental meaning of the ends pursued by the movement.
>
> (Sartre 1985, p. 263)

Intellectuals as the articulators, interpreters and disseminators of ideas, concepts, theories and symbols have, through their work, served a variety of ideological interests, not excluding their own. Depending on the differing demands made upon them and their work, they occupy variously contested social territories, within which they intervene in complex and contradictory ways. The perceptions of intellectuals of their own social value and how that is to be measured, especially in socio-political struggles, have not necessarily coincided with the estimations of other social agents. Consequently, their role and social positioning generate tensions among intellectuals themselves and between intellectuals and other groups, depending on the social, political and economic goals that are at stake.

In this chapter I focus on some of the ambiguities surrounding the work of intellectuals in South Africa within the transition – a phase where conceptualizing an alternative future has become a growth industry. I explore the nature and role of critically engaged intellectual work in the present conjuncture, especially in relation to the tremendous demand for and the urgency of policy research which can be used for reconstructive purposes as well as for more short-term electioneering gains. A great deal of progressive intellectual work is underpinned by the discourses of transformation and reconstruction, which are both contested notions for different ideological groupings even within the liberation movement. The problems and challenges which this poses for that work and the implications of linking intellectual work with broader struggles for a democratic transformatory process will form the core of my analysis.

The notion of intellectuals

The literature on intellectuals[1] and their roles, both in general and in specific historical contexts, is enormous. One of the lessons to be learned from a survey of this mass of materials is the difficulty (and danger) of elucidating a homogeneous and unified general definition of intellectuals and their roles, which could then serve as a decisive reference point for more historically specific reflections on the issue. And yet, despite its contested nature, one needs some general parameters to demarcate the nature of the agency at work. Debates about intellectuals have centred on their individual characteristics, their role and function, their structural and institutional location, their aspirations and interests, their interrelationships with other social forces and the social effects of their practices. The plethora of analyses reflects the attempt to understand the historical emergence and increasing social prominence of the phenomenon of intellectuals operating within specific structural contexts and social relations. Different and even antinomic definitions which abound in the literature encompass the tensions, ambivalences and polarities of intellectual work itself. More often than not, questions concerning the validity and acceptability of definitions hinge as much on their ideological usefulness as on their analytical intent.

Mazrui (1978, p. 368) views the intellectual as a person 'who has the capacity to be fascinated by ideas and has acquired the skill to handle some of these ideas effectively'. Shils (1972) chooses to depict intellectuals in terms of the special inner qualities which distinguish them from other human beings.

> In every society, there are some persons with an unusual sensitivity to the sacred, an uncommon reflectiveness about the nature of their universe and the rules which govern their society. There is in every society a minority of persons who, more than the ordinary run of their fellow men, are inquiring, and desirous of being in frequent communion with symbols which are more general than the immediate concrete situations of everyday life.
>
> (Shils 1972, p. 3)

The elitist and essentialist inclinations of this approach are shown up, by contrast, in Gramsci (1971, p. 9), who maintains that all human activity involves the use of the intellect to some degree and that only social function counts as a demarcator. For Gramsci, 'All men are intellectuals, one could therefore say: but not all men have in society the function of intellectuals'. Merton (1968, p. 263), Mannheim (1968, p. 9) and Wright (1979, p. 192) allow us to home in on the actual activities of intellectuals within specific ideological contexts. For Wright, given the division between mental and manual labour within capitalist social relations, intellectuals constitute that social category of 'people whose primary activity is the elaboration and dissemination of ideas'. Merton sees them as people devoted to 'cultivating and formulating knowledge'. And, for Mannheim, the 'intelligentsia' is a social group 'whose special task it is to provide an interpretation of the world for that society'.

It is, however, the perception of intellectuals as a *societal* resource that is as threatening to some as it is valuable to others, which has led to the most passionate contestation about the political dimensions of intellectual activity. Claims have been made locating the essence of intellectual work beyond social and political engagement as well as within it. For example, the intellectual as inhabitant of the world of ideas, removed from the world of political passions, is upheld by Julien Benda (in de Huszar 1960, p. 217) as those 'whose activity is essentially *not* the pursuit of practical aims, all those who seek their joy in the practice of an art or a science or metaphysical speculation, in short in the possession of non-material advantages, and hence in a certain manner say: "My kingdom is not of this world" '. [2] Lenin, on the other hand, directs the 'intelligentsia' to revolutionary political tasks within actual socio-economic relations:

> their theoretical work must be directed towards the concrete study of all forms of economic antagonism in Russia, the study of their connections and successive development; they must reveal this antagonism wherever it has been concealed by political history, by the peculiarities of legal systems or by established theoretical preju-dice. They must present an integral picture of our realities as a definite system of production relations, show that exploitation and expropriation of the working people are essential under this system, and show the way out of this system that is indicated by economic development.
>
> (Lenin 1983, pp. 21–2)

Lenin also argued that the principles of socialism had to be brought to the working class by revolutionary intellectuals but insisted on the necessity for them to be subordinated to centralized organizational discipline.

In addressing the politics of intellectual work, the class origins, class location and class loyalties of intellectuals have come under close scrutiny, with a range of positions distinguishable between Marxist and non-Marxist theorists as well as among Marxist theorists themselves.[3] This provides us with a typology of sorts, at least as far as structural location and class relations are concerned. Mannheim (1968, p. 155) sees modern intellectuals as displaying heterogeneity when it comes to class origins and constituting a 'relatively classless stratum . . . "the socially unattached intelligentsia (*freischwebende Intelligenz*)" '. He went on to argue that education is the 'sociological bond' uniting intellectuals across differences of 'birth, status, profession and wealth', although this fact still does not knit them into a class. Gramsci (1971, p. 5), on the other hand, does not see intellectuals as an autonomous social group, maintaining rather that every social group produces its own intellectuals who 'give it homogeneity and an awareness of its own function not only in the economic but also in the social and political fields'. This enables them to focus not on intellectual activities as such but on their function in furthering the struggle of class interests within the 'ensemble' of social relations within which they are located. His development of Marxist theory as a theory of the struggle for hegemony draws intellectuals into centre stage as the organizers of that hegemony. In fact, Gramsci defines intellectuals primarily in terms of their organizational function, in the field of production as much as in cultural and political matters. In contrast to the above two conceptions of intellectuals as representing either a class-independent or a class-connected stratum are the views of the New Class theorists (Djilas, Gouldner, Konrad and Szelenyi and others) who see intellectuals as acting not on behalf of other classes but as constituting a separate class with a distinct set of interests and with aspirations to power based on control over and monopoly of the production of knowledge. With the increase in contemporary society of the numbers of the 'highly educated' as well as the centrality of specialized forms of knowledge to the process of social production and reproduction, the theory of the new class has been employed, in various formulations,[4] to explain the role of intellectuals in late capitalist as well as in state-socialist societies.

The above depictions point to some of the core issues which are so keenly contested about intellectuals and their work. Across the changing historical and institutional landscape of their activity, intellectuals have been evaluated by others and by themselves in a way represented frequently by the notion of ambivalence[5]. They have been celebrated as the creators of 'high culture' and as sages and guardians of wisdom. They have also been reviled as being extremely dangerous and threatening, especially to the proletarian masses on the very grounds of their access to knowledge.[6] They have been viewed as legitimators and supporters of existing social relations as well as delegitimators and opponents, if not as outright enemies, of the *status quo*. They have been depicted as being drawn to powerful elites as well as to 'the wretched of the earth' in constant pursuit of 'social legitimacy' (Kolakowski 1986, p. 165). They are claimed to be as desirous of political influence as of independence from the political. Their interventions in the socio-political arena have been urged as well as condemned. Heated disputes, often among themselves, have also occurred about the most appropriate forms of those interventions. The widening composition and membership of the constituency of intellectuals as well as the increasing sophistication of its self-understanding as a social force has not spared it from critiques of race and gender exclusions in the production and dissemination of ideas.[7] Intellectual work has been depicted as lying beyond the capacity of women and black people, and has been dominated for most of human history by white men.

Despite or perhaps because of their ambiguous social function, the role of intellectuals in revolutionary transformation has been crucial. Martin points out that from the time of

> the Reformation, ideology and intellectuals have been central elements in all the major social revolutions . . . that have produced the modern world-system. The leadership of the Reformation, the American and French revolutions, the Russian and Chinese revolutions (as well as most revolutions in the Third World) have combined intellectual production with political action.
>
> (Martin 1987, p. 73)

Mazrui (1978) underscores the dominant role of African intellectuals in the leadership of anti-colonial struggles as well as in several early postcolonial governments. Wright (1979, p. 191) brings a vital perspective to the above by reminding us that the ideas of intellectuals were 'nurtured through their contact with the masses' but affirms, nevertheless, that intellectuals rather than peasants or proletarians have been the key contributors to revolutionary theory.

Sartre (1985) describes contradiction as the 'natural element of the combatant intellectual'. In the debates about intellectuals, many of the tensions and polarities which have emerged could be viewed as being almost constitutive of the social identity and existence of intellectuals. These are often posed as choices and dichotomies, for example, between traditional and organic intellectuals, between universal and specific intellectuals, between the 'transcendent' and the 'historical' role of the intellectual, between intellectuals as critics or opponents of ruling relations and the advisers, allies or servants of those in power, between intellectuals as teleocrats and technocrats, between autonomy and social constraint for intellectuals, between promoting the interests of other classes and promoting their own, and between the individual and organizational or institutional nature of their work practices. Many of these contradictions serve to highlight the problem of the ambivalent relations between intellectuals and those in power but they also inform us about the equally ambivalent connection between intellectuals as a social grouping and those who are impoverished and powerless.

Intellectuals and the political struggle

The range of contradictions which beset intellectual work applies as much in the South African case and is likely to be accentuated within the transition. The events of 2 February 1990, signalling the beginning of the negotiations phase, have unleashed a range of possibilities which could be both advantageous and threatening to the progressive transformation of South African society. The 'normalization' of the political terrain through the entry of formerly banned organizations into the political process could lead in the direction of a more legitimate economic and political dispensation. And yet these events may also shape a dispensation which is new but requires too many compromises with existing constellations of power and is unable to dislodge existing arrangements of privilege. For those who spent long years in the liberation struggle and for those who pinned their political and material hopes on that struggle, there is no certainty that the transitional process will deliver on the key aspirations that underpinned the struggle. This uncertainty is compounded by the fact that negotiations have become somewhat abstracted from the public political process. The essential features of the new order and the new power relations emerging from the reconfiguration of social forces in the country are still confused and murky.

What the state and its challengers have in common, despite their differing political agendas, is the urgent search for new conceptualizations of a future South Africa and the attendant policy implications in the areas of education, housing, health and welfare, the economy, urban and rural development, etc. On the one hand, the apartheid framework and its policies have lost their legitimacy almost completely. On the other, the ideals and programmatic visions of the forces of resistance have to be translated into reality in the form of implementable policies. Within such a conjuncture, those who 'wield the power of the spoken and written word' (Schumpeter in de Huszar 1960, p. 70) are clearly in a privileged position to become central to the generation of new discourses concerning the shape and direction of a restructured society. But in considering the ways in which intellectuals in South Africa can take their place in the new conjuncture, we need to confront the ways in which their existence, function and location as a social category have been marked by enormous ideological heterogeneity.

Intellectuals in South Africa, not unexpectedly, manifest an array of contradictions and ambiguities relating to their self-understandings, their social and ideological location, their modes of work and the resulting effects. The usual fissures of race, class, gender and ideology have marked the category of intellectuals as a functionally identifiable agency and have articulated potently with the peculiar inclusions and exclusions of South African society. Whether they have been academics and researchers, teachers, journalists and film-makers, politicians, policy-makers and technocrats, novelists, playwrights and poets, unionists, clerics or student – historically – they have all been located along these various lines of fissure. They may have had in common an engagement with elaborating and disseminating ideas which propelled or challenged specific ideological interests but their operations have not proceeded from a single coherent social, intellectual or cultural framework. Critical differences in material and ideological interests have served to divide them and direct them into contending camps.

The lines of fissure along which intellectuals have been located have not been straightforward or clear-cut. The ideological location of intellectuals in the process of legitimating or resisting the hegemony of state and capital in the various phases of South African history is accompanied by its own complexities and tensions. Afrikaner intellectuals, for example, have furnished both the ideological articulations that helped to sustain Afrikaner nationalism as well as contributed to its delegitimation through their critiques of it (see Du Troit 1981). Liberal white intellectuals, for example, who took a stand against the racially discriminatory policies of the state, did not link this stand with a critique of capital. They may even have viewed capitalism minus the dysfunctional effects of apartheid as holding the key to a more just and equitable South Africa. Further, those intellectuals roughly on the same side of the demarcator did not necessarily see themselves as allies in a common struggle. The intellectuals of the Black Consciousness movement, with their concern for the development of authentic black autonomy and agency at all levels, were extremely critical of white leadership of anti-apartheid initiatives and dismissive of the claims of the white liberal establishment concerning 'nonracialism'. Even the role of radical white intellectuals in the struggle has not gone uncontested. The debates in the union movement at the end of the 1970s around the issue of registration threw up a host of thorny problems, including the position of the white left in workers' struggles. The ambiguities surrounding their intervention are couched in the form of a tension between the value of the 'crucial resources and expertise' (*South African Labour Bulletin* 7, 1981, p. 2) furnished by them and the danger of their dominance to the possibilities of more inclusive and democratic decision-making. In the present phase, similar concerns are being expressed about the continuing underrepresentation of black and women participants in the policy research arena, despite some conscious attempts to address this imbalance.

In general terms, intellectuals in South Africa have been both legitimators and delegitimators of state power. There have been those who have participated in the formulation and dissemination of the 'philosophy' and strategies of the apartheid state, both in its nationalist and technocratic-reformist phases. Others have engaged in producing the 'philosophy' and strategies which have come to constitute the history of resistance – in analysing the race/class foundations of the state, in exposing state moves and plans especially in their reformist guises and in articulating the ideas which have directed mobilization and organization. In the last few years, oppositional intellectuals have also been exploring alternative conceptualizations of policy issues in preparation for the restructuring of almost all areas of public life.

Progressive intellectuals, despite the common bond of opposition, have been at odds with each other through holding differing paradigms of repression and resistance, organization and transformation. Differing assessments of the centrality of race, nation and class and of the intersection of class struggle and the national liberation struggle in the South African formation have vied with each other for explanatory and organizational hegemony. Differing accounts have not only emanated from contending political organizations but have also sometimes formed the history of the same organization as well. Lodge (1990, pp. 161–88) points to the presence of Africanist, Christian-Liberal and Marxist-Leninist interpretations, articulated by different generations of ANC intellectuals in the various phases of the struggle. In some cases, the ideological differences marked the transitions made by those intellectuals who moved beyond their original political affiliations to other affiliations, for example, the Black Consciousness adherents who went on to embrace Charterism (see Halisi 1990).

As is evident from a survey of the bulk of the debates, gender as a distinct and specific social category has not been sufficiently integrated into the analytical and mobilizing mechanisms employed within progressive work. Despite the role of gender in the complex forging of relations of superordination and subordination within South African society and despite the substantive participation of women in many areas of struggle, the gender issue has generally been viewed as a 'secondary contradiction', to be subsumed to the organizational needs of national liberation struggle and/or class struggle. Within the limits of this significant gap, a tremendous ideological heterogeneity has characterized progressive intellectual work, even within the radical tradition as it developed in the 1970s. This has provided for an increasingly sophisticated understanding of the mechanisms of domination and resistance, of the complex relationships among the various stratifications of the population and of the intermeshing of different modes of struggle.

A further issue dividing intellectuals in South Africa has been contending conceptions of the nature and function of intellectual work. Some, mostly university-based academics, have argued for autonomy and distance from the concerns of power in the pursuit of their academic disciplines and their theoretical concerns. Those others, who view their work and its effects as being inextricably meshed with economic and socio-political interests, have themselves manifested varying modes and levels of solidarity and organic connection with mass struggles of the resistance movement. Their positions have encompassed vanguardist conceptions of their role as well as attempts (sometimes made by intellectuals themselves) to render intellectual work as a lesser form of activism, to be subordinated to or postponed in favour of other tasks. Intellectuals have also ranged from being 'organic' to various ideological tendencies to those who, in situating themselves in close proximity to the resistance movement, attempted to juggle the often conflicting demands of solidarity with some measure of critical distance. Those who have located themselves under the discipline of specific political organizations have displayed varying measures of critical engagement with party lines. This issue must be seen in conjunction with the degree of critical space which was available within political organizations operating under conditions of great repression for the articulation of internal critique.[8]

The production of knowledge

As can be expected in a society subjected to decades of racial domination, a striking feature of the internal stratification of the constituency of intellectuals is the racial division of intellectual labour. At a formal level, whether located at the universities or at research institutes or in the think-tanks of state, capital and labour, white intellectuals, mostly males, have dominated the production of knowledge in South Africa. One obvious and often cited set of reasons for this skewed pattern is the critical degree of intellectual impoverishment in vast masses of the population as a result of 'Bantu education', the denial of opportunity and access to information through repression and censorship and, in general, because of the continuing distribution of racial power and privilege that the system still manifests. Evans (1990, p. 23) cites white control of the academic process as central to the 'exclusion of blacks from shaping the intellectual life of South Africa'. Muller & Cloete (1991, p. 29) point to other factors connected more integrally to the pressing activist demands of the liberation movement on black intellectuals as well as the disastrous consequences for educational struggle of the phase of 'liberation before education'. Although the above factors have, no doubt, severely constrained the development of a black intelligentsia proportionate to the country's demographic realities, one should be wary of approaching the issue of intellectual under-representation only through looking at formal sites of knowledge production. This is an issue which Evans, for instance, passes over too quickly. Revisionist history has documented the interventions of many black intellectuals outside the academy. The Unity Movement intellectuals represent perhaps the most striking instance of intellectuals who pursued their work sometimes in conscious distance from the halls of academia.[9] It is interesting to note that many women and black members of the intelligentsia have found more prominent expression in areas like literature, art and journalism where their visions and representations have served to illuminate the key issues of South African politics in rich and powerful ways, while also laying some of the roots of new South African cultural traditions.

That this issue was not confined to the question of black intellectuals at the universities as formal sites of knowledge production is demonstrated, for example, in the account of Bozzoli & Delius (1990, pp. 14–15). In their overview of twenty years of radical historiography in South Africa, they point to the fact that three of the four patterns of radical thought preceding the radicalism of the 1970s were integrally linked to social and political movements rather than to the universities. This raises the question of the history and significance of the South African university as an institutional site conducive to the production of radical discourses, an issue that encompasses but also goes beyond the production of a black intelligentsia. In the 1970s, the 'liberal' white universities provided the institutional space, if not the unambiguous institutional blessing, for radical scholarship to take root, while the historically black universities provided the political context for the rise of the Black Consciousness intellectuals. However, the institutional distance of the universities from the material interests and experiences of the majority of the population may have rendered them, in popular perception, as mostly marginal to the articulation of mass concerns and sentiments. Hence, those who

have been intellectually productive outside of the universities may, as a matter
of political choice, have preferred an academically or institutionally un-
mediated form of intellectual work. In producing an account of a South
African intellectual tradition, those within the academy have to guard against
producing self-serving or myopic narratives that marginalize or render invisible those outside and which do not address the interlocking complex of causes
and consequences that have located intellectuals in formal as well as informal
sites of intellectual engagement. In the present period, when various policy
research investigations are being located at the universities, it is an interesting
issue as to whether such community orientated initiatives will be enveloped by
the enclosed professional culture of the university or whether they will serve to
open up the universities to the urgent demands of a society in need of massive
restructuring.

Intellectuals and the 'powers'

The acute ideological contestation within South African society about the
legitimate guiding principles of the body politic, which effectively constitutes
the history of that society, has posited a variety of social groupings (including
intellectuals) against the claims and authority of those in power. The relationship between intellectuals and 'the powers' frames the question of the political
engagement of intellectuals in an instructive way, encompassing their links
with the 'powerless' as much as with the powerful. This relationship has
exercised the attention of social theorists largely with respect to two key issues
– the role of intellectuals in the revolutionary transformation of crisis-ridden
societies on the one hand and, on the other, their role in the reproduction of
complex industrial states to which process the production and implementation
of scientific and technical knowledge is central. These are, in effect, two
distinguishable domains of intellectual activity. There is also a third which is
linked to and yet differentiated from those mentioned above. This domain,
which has not received the same degree of analytic attention as the other two is
one that, according to Martin (1987, p. 75) is concerned with 'intellectual
status and function in the newly established and institutionalized revolutionary
order'. Martin goes on to identify the central issues in such a context as 'the
role of the philosopher-king, the intellectual in power, the intellectual as
bureaucrat, the intellectual as propagandist and servant of power, and the role
of the dissident in the revolutionary order'.

   Given these different possibilities, how is the relationship between intellectuals and the 'powers' to be understood in South Africa? In the face of acute
repression and exploitation, resistance became the prism through which the
interventions of all opposing social forces came to be judged. In the long and
bitter history of resistance to state repression, many intellectuals have been
among those who have endured severe state sanction in the form of assassination, banning, house arrest, prosecution, imprisonment, censorship, etc. Even

in exile to which many were driven, the state cast its panoptic shadow through various forms of surveillance, threats and violence. Offering their skills to the liberation movement as part of the resistance meant engagement for intellectuals in a variety of ways. Some essentially put aside the path of intellectual production to choose a more directly activist role. Others made their contribution through various combinations of scholarship and activism, inserting themselves into different terrains of struggle in accordance with prevailing needs. In the present conjuncture, the transition in power relations has complicated the framework within which the relationship between intellectuals and the 'powers' can be defined. Who the 'powers' are or will be is not completely clear. On the one hand, existing power blocs are making their bid to control the nature and pace of restructuring. On the other, new power blocs are emerging out of the processes of negotiation. A variety of interest groups are jostling with one another to establish their hegemonic claims. Many intellectuals are being drawn into this process of producing a new social order in South Africa through engaging in policy work on behalf of various stakeholders, some of whom have aspirations to state power.

Given the urgency of the need for new policy options and the acute shortage of intellectual resources to address this need, it is to be expected that intellectuals and aspirant policy makers will move purposively closer to each other and that intellectuals will play an important role in this phase. However, within the context of the uncertainties and pressures of negotiation, the preparation of future reconstructive policies in a process conducted mainly by such aspirant policy makers and their intellectual advisers carries the danger of a distanciation from the needs and hopes of the majority of the population. Already, within the liberation movement, there are concerns that key decisions of policy and strategy, especially as they concern the transitional process, are being taken at the top. Many of the intellectuals who are currently engaged in policy work, no doubt, are energized and driven by the intellectual challenge of producing knowledge that may actually be put to work in a new democratic dispensation. There are also clearly those who are using the policy phase to position themselves to climb into the bureaucracy of the new state or up other ladders of opportunity. The change in emphasis from resistance-related intellectual work to reconstructive policy research and advocacy means that long-standing debates about intellectual autonomy, accountability and responsibility have to be revisited within the emergent ensemble of power relations, not laid to rest or glossed over in an unreflective preoccupation with the technical details of restructuring or in uncritical relationships and alliances with political and other patrons.

Despite their internal stratifications, intellectuals in South Africa are in a privileged position, on account of various forms of social advantage, to be central to the continuing generation of the discourses of transformation and reconstruction. With the energies of other social groupings occupied by organizational, ideological and material struggles on different fronts, many intellectuals, through their very marginality to the direct political process, are

well placed to concentrate their energies on future-orientated reconstructive
tasks involving the conceptualization of policy options and the appropriate
routes to their implementation. However, closer proximity to new sets of
power relations will pose a host of problems for critical intellectual work.
Intellectuals themselves in their role as 'experts' and 'authorities' may, through
their monopoly of certain forms of knowledge, pose dangers to the building of
a democratic reconstructive process in South Africa.[10] The present conjuncture
is generating new pacts and alliances which will come to form the horizon of
intellectual work and extract compromises and accommodations from intellectuals in order for them to be relevant and useful to the task of reconstruction.
Intellectuals preparing for reconstruction may also be preparing to operate
within the direct orbit of the state and its agencies – as bureaucrats and servants
of power. The newly emerging social relations hold dangers both for intellectuals and from them. The nature of the transition process will determine the
more specific character of the dominant power relations that will eventually
shape the reconstructive environment. However, whatever the specific political scenario, the extent and quality of popular democratic involvement in the
reconstructive process and a reconstructive agenda that addresses itself to
majority needs cannot be displaced as the central issues of South African
politics. Unless reflections on the role of intellectuals in the new conjuncture
are grounded in these issues, they run the risk of being narcissistic and self-
serving estimations of intellectual endeavour. Such a perspective also places
intellectuals within a framework that requires appropriately nuanced relationships with both state and civil society formations.

Intellectuals and social transformation

A brief glance at some of the debates in South Africa about the relationship of
intellectuals to the transformative project raises some crucial issues. The
debates by intellectuals themselves and others about the nature and effects of
the role of intellectuals in various struggles are not extensive but they do cover
many of the key concerns. They range through reflections on the relationship
between social science and social planning, the harnessing of intellectual work
to state projects, the social responsibility of intellectuals in the face of a strong
and repressive state, types of appropriate research and action, the dominance
of white intellectuals and the invisibility or virtual absence of black intellectuals, questions of academic autonomy and accountability, and increasingly
self-reflective accounts of the politics of knowledge production and their
implications for mass empowerment.

Some core issues concerning intellectuals in the new conjuncture are
addressed in the work of Muller & Cloete (1991) who focus on the present
function and location of intellectuals in a phase characterized as much by the
need for reconstruction as by the opening up of civil society. Already in 1987,
the same authors had begun to reflect on a model of engagement for intellec-

tuals that tried to go beyond the 'handmaiden' or 'midwife' conceptualizations. Building on the methodology of 'participatory action research' and Touraine's intervention sociology, they attempted to locate engagement within a model involving community participation that would suspend 'the academic's monopoly over authorization, while it re-authorizes a previously de-authorized voice or knowledge' (Muller & Cloete 1987, p. 151). They concluded from this that, through engaging with the community in the construction of a 'progressive political voice', intellectuals give up their vanguardist pretensions to lead the struggle and 'become part of the struggle in terms of their usefulness for the struggle and partially subordinated to it'. This observation was obviously important at a time when more intellectuals were being drawn into progressive research initiatives and it became necessary to reflect on their 'power base'. With the dramatic catapulting of the struggle on to a negotiations terrain, the above position demanded further elaboration. In their 1991 article, Muller & Cloete took up the question of intellectual engagement on just this new terrain.

The events of 2 February opened up the possibility for the liberation movement to operate in the form of political parties, in this way signalling a more complex relationship between the spheres of political and civil society. The tensions and differences between the two had been blurred in the phase of massive resistance to the state. The question to which Muller & Cloete address themselves is, in the opening up of the gap between political and civil society, where will the intellectuals position themselves? The second issue which engages them, which is a continuation of a theme from their 1987 paper, concerns the democratic generation and implementation of knowledge, given the dynamics of the new terrain. For the two authors, ensuring the second is crucial to understanding the first. They argue that intellectuals, whether critics or reconstructors, must be

> brought into public sites where their conclusions can be mediated in relation to other worldly discourses before they are brought to bear on policy formulation. . . . It is only by means of such encounters that citizens can participate in the compromises which necessarily have to be made in arriving at social and public policy.
> (Muller & Cloete 1991, p. 35)

Despite their acknowledgement of the extremely fragile and tenuous nature of these public fora, they propose them, nevertheless, as the decisive mechanism within which 'the civic, intellectual and political functions can engage with each other' in order to ensure a fully participatory social existence.

Muller & Cloete illuminate problems which have become even more urgent in the present context – the interaction between the discourses of intellectuals and those of others in a critical phase when new social foundations are being prepared, and the establishment and role of public fora to address national reconstruction issues. There are, however, questions which they do not raise or pass over too hastily which have a central bearing on any reconstructive process which seeks to be more than just formally democratic. They do not sufficiently challenge or problematize the Habermasian echoes in the 'public spaces or fora' which they espouse. To what extent can the fora be understood on the paradigm of the ideal speech situation where the force of the better argument will prevail over all other (ideologically determined) considerations? A number of national fora have already come into existence or are imminent and whose purposes have to do both with crisis resolution and a restructuring process that is inclusive of all concerned interests. The key question requiring deeper analytical attention concerns the balance of power among these different interests, the nature of their power bases and their varying abilities to force different kinds of compromises within the fora – all of which will determine how policy choices will be driven forward and by whom. Further, the discourses of intellectuals, especially about policy issues, are not self-contained, 'free-floating' products to be assessed alongside those of others. They may be explicitly or implicitly tied to the conceptualizations and agendas of political elites who are moving closer to state power. This makes the task of a disciplinary mediation of intellectual discourses by other discourses into a more complicated task. Muller & Cloete also draw a distinction between intellectuals as critics and as reconstructors that is too stark, ignoring the present continuum within which critique and reconstruction must interact with each other in order to be socially and politically useful. Ultimately, it is their overoptimistic reading of the rationality of the 'reconstructive moment' and its possibilities which obscures their view of the ambivalent alliances that intellectuals could be making within the domain of power.

The commitment to end apartheid as a system predicated on racial categorization is now a commonplace one, articulated even by those who have been central to its maintenance. The substance of transformation is another matter altogether. The question of how to restructure a society that is a web of competing and intersecting inequities and imbalances is one that has confronted the proponents of radical transformation in many crisis-ridden societies. The issue of restructuring involves, among other things, the complex accommodation of ideals and hopes that have driven the struggle forward with pragmatic imperatives emerging from prevailing material conditions. Policy deliberation is one such form of accommodation while intellectuals engaging in such work are an agency of accommodation. What can progressive intellectuals do to make more transparent the nature and extent of proposed accommodations in policy-related work in such a way that it invites and necessitates greater public access and participatory debate? A greater measure of self-reflectivity about the nature of such intellectual work is urgently needed. Opening up the policy project to critical reflections on the nature and objectives of policy research, the ideological horizons circumscribing such work and its place within the transformative project would be as valuable for intellectuals as it would be for other citizens. Such reflections will not be able to avoid some of the following concerns. Is it appropriate to conceptualize one grand version of reconstruction in the light of the fact that different political tendencies interpret the 'struggle' and its resolution differently? What compromises are decision-making elites inserting into reconstructive scenarios based on their reading of the 'new world order' and of local conditions? Are the policy scenarios that are being produced more likely to be of value for statist purposes or can they also be usefully accessed by civil society formations? How can expertise enhance rather than undermine democracy? Can policy options be investigated, collated and delivered up in an ideologically neutral way?[11] What is the appropriate intersection of mass aspirations and needs with the policy conceptualizations of intellectuals and party planners? How can the values of autonomy, accountability and non-sectarianism be consciously upheld within the context of policy investigation? Has there been a significant shift in the race and gender composition of the intellectuals who are preparing the policy paths of the future? If reconstructive policy work is viewed as a set of technical or instrumental tasks within a given or uncontested moral and political vision, intellectuals may be on their way to becoming technicians and apparatchiks of specific ideological tendencies. Hegemonizing parties are sure to represent their own visions and programmes as setting the parameters of reconstruction. It is crucial, therefore, to posit the discourses of reconstruction against the background of the transformative project as a whole and to conceptualize both notions as normative tasks as well as terrains of ideological contestation. Such a problematization of policy research could be one way of confronting the ideological closures of party planners and aspirant policy makers. It could also enable intellectuals who have become 'advisors' to the organizations of the resistance movement to find a way of straddling the challenge of remaining critical in their advisory roles.

The commitment of intellectuals was and is, no doubt, valued and needed by the liberation movement. In a period of extreme polarization, their political loyalties and allegiances may even have been a precondition for their intellectual participation. In this phase, however, it is their professional 'know-how' and specialist 'expertise' which is likely to be the key to their political value. In this capacity, what will be their political brief? Kissinger (in Gella 1976, p. 118) points out that the intellectual as expert is 'asked to solve problems, not to contribute to the definition of goals'. In the phase dominated by the needs of resistance, intellectuals, together with others, were a part of the process of defining and articulating goals. As such, their intellectual products in the form of theories and interpretations helped the process of mobilization. Conceptualizing their present intervention as means-oriented problem-solving within an agreed set of goals would be a grave distortion of intellectual responsibility. It also opens up the possibility for the ensuing intellectual products, carrying all the authority of 'scientific expertise', to be used to pacify an expectant and then discontented populace. Muller & Cloete (1991, p. 30) distinguish between a discourse of needs and a discourse of means and the increased focus in a policy-hungry conjuncture on a discourse of means. The ability of intellectuals to do justice to a discourse of means without reducing them to technocratic programmes depends on an ongoing engagement not only with discourses of needs but also with discourses of ends. The pressures generated by the need to be 'pragmatic' and 'realistic' in the new conjuncture have to be counterbalanced by a clear-eyed view of the ways in which ends may be compromised by the means resorted to in order to achieve specific benefits.

Merton (1968) distinguishes between two types of intellectuals: those who function in an advisory capacity within a bureaucracy and those not attached to a bureaucracy. His observation about the difference in the nature of the 'client' of the two types of intellectual is instructive for the South African context. 'For the bureaucratic intellectual, it is those policy-makers in the organization for whom he is, directly or remotely, performing a staff function; for the unattached intellectual, the clientele is a public.' How do intellectuals engaged in policy research view the distinction as well as the relationship between the organization as client and the public as client? In this phase of the emptying out of the liberation movement into political parties, such parties are still likely to postulate 'the people' as the client on whose behalf reconstructive policy work is being undertaken. Intellectuals who are engaged in such work and who are seeking to straddle the tensions between critical and advisory work may find Merton's distinction useful in order to understand the complex identity of the 'client' on whose behalf they are working. This may enable them to insert the aspirations and needs of the population at large into the centre of reconstructive scenarios against moves to reduce those scenarios to party-specific programmes.

Intellectual work which seeks to be useful for the purposes of transition must be able to locate itself within the parameters of urgent social concerns but not become trapped within party- or movement-specific briefs. One way of conceptualizing the attempt to be both relevant and critical would be not to posit intellectuals as being able to stand above the fray somewhat, distancing themselves from their own ideological inclinations and interests, but as having the 'independence to criticize radically within some common framework' (Fisk 1989, p. 161). Gouldner (1976a, pp. 11–12) talks about intellectuals taking 'the standpoint of the totality', something that is possible for them on account of their training and social positioning. He rightly draws attention to the ambiguity of this attempt, especially in so far as it concerns the representation of the interests of other classes through the 'selective mediation' of the interests of intellectuals as a distinct stratum. He also points to the tendency to perceive the standpoint of the totality from a 'top down' perspective. However, his argument that, though the consciousness may be 'false', the consequences of the stand are real, is a useful basis for exploring what taking the standpoint of the totality and its consequences might mean for intellectuals in South Africa.

The scarcity of resources to sustain an intellectual system and the absence of a significant intellectual public that could relate to intellectuals (and ruling elites) in a critical way has been pointed out as a common feature of many developing countries. In South Africa this problem, exacerbated by decades of structurally generated intellectual impoverishment and combined with the urgency of the reconstructive task, poses the dangerous temptation to those with skills to be drawn into a model of transformation that seeks to set people free from above. Intellectuals, as we are often reminded by many theorists, are central to the modernizing project. In the light of the violence and irrationality of apartheid as well as the more recent irruptions of violence among an increasingly fractured people, the temptation to step into the gap, to see South Africa as a canvas on which to impose a vision of rationality, planning and the efficient utilization of resources is great indeed for intellectuals and policy makers alike. Taking the standpoint of the totality could very well be the 'top down' claim of intellectuals operating within the notion of a benevolent modernity, buttressed possibly by a recurrent notion about traditional intellectuals as the guardians of universal values. A recent version of this position articulated by Bourdieu (1989) leads him to conclude that intellectuals are entitled to defend their own interests in their capacity as defenders of 'major universal causes'. This interpretation will fit well into the strong possibility that modernity as it is shaping up in South Africa is likely to benefit intellectual and other elites more than it is likely to facilitate encompassing systemic transformation.

The notion of the standpoint of the totality has to be historicized within the new conjuncture in order for it to be at all useful. It is not a static or self-evident universal. It is as ideologically contestable as that other favourite universal 'the people' which is now being disaggregated into the various formations of political and civil society. Intellectuals can only hope to approach the notion through consistently upholding and addressing the multiple discourses of needs which will continue to be generated in various organizational and other contexts as the touchstone of all means-orientated discourses. In their struggle to be critical advisors, intellectuals will have to work with others to prevent a fatal cleavage developing, at a discursive and operational level, between the discourses of needs of the citizenry and the discourses of means of policy makers. Despite the problem of false consciousness mentioned by Gouldner, despite the murky mixture of personal and political motives underlying intellectual engagement in this conjuncture, taking the standpoint of the totality in the sense mentioned above could have the consequence of not solidifying any single reconstructive vision, thus allowing for the possibility of democratic debate about a variety of such visions and the means to accomplish them. In asserting the need to be critical advisors, intellectuals will clearly be attempting to forge a political space that caters for their special interests as those committed in form at least to the culture of critical discourse.[12] And yet, the culture of dissent, valuable as it may be for them, is not cherished by intellectuals alone. In their search for an intellectually and politically balanced role within the newly forming social relations in South Africa, intellectuals will, therefore, be participating in the more encompassing task of opening up a space for critical engagement in the reconstructive project for the citizenry as a whole.

Conclusion

The present conjuncture in South Africa is forcing all constituencies and social agents to accommodate to the demands of a rapidly changing situation. Cherished visions have to be overhauled or defended in new ways. Long-preferred strategies have to be rethought and reformulated. The discourses of transformation and reconstruction are so seductive that they often obscure the pitfalls, obstacles and compromises that lie in wait. The key question, now as before, is the measure of democratic participation in the social, political and economic life of the country. In the process of building democracy, many social forces, employing a range of strategies and mechanisms, will have to play a role. Intellectuals seeking a place in the struggle in this conjuncture need be neither 'free-floating', nor 'handmaidens' nor 'midwives' of the struggle. For the present, at least, it is necessary and possible to become engaged as critical participants in the search for reconstructive scenarios.

Since 'the struggle' is now a complex of struggles and 'the people' a complex of social forces, the notion of 'progressive intellectual' can also cease to be a homogeneous category in terms of role, function and location within the new conjuncture. The unfolding of political and civil society will make it possible for intellectuals to find their place not only within the policy-making forums of political society but also in the organizations and activities of civil society as well. Their role in this sphere will be no less linked to the purposes of transformation and will be crucial to the building and strengthening of the realm of civil society. In fact, the insertion of intellectuals along different points of this complex of struggles will be a useful safeguard against the large-scale absorption of intellectuals into legitimating functions on behalf of the emergent order. The ability of critical intellectuals to operate in the domain of power without co-option or threat will become one of the indicators of the health of the body politic in a way not reminiscent of many African polities.

Although moving into new sites and conditions of work, progressive intellectuals in South Africa will continue to inhabit the difficult place between 'the powers' and the rest of the citizenry. The demands of the reconstructive agenda are beginning to shape the relations between intellectuals and other social agencies (specifically with political leadership, organizational bureaucracy and the 'masses'). As presently constituted, they will continue to be vulnerable to the charges of race, class and gender determinants as the basis of their privileged position. With the opening up of educational and political opportunity in the country, their composition and, therefore, their outlook and role is likely to change in the future. They are not on the way to becoming a new class whatever their individual aspirations or opportunisms. This phase of policy research assistance within a negotiated transition may well be the high point of their prominence and power. They are an ambiguously formed stratum with ambivalent motives and contradictory social effects, encompassing activities of subversion as well as legitimation. The issue for them is not a choice between political engagement and non-engagement, between modernist interventionism and 'postmodernist' non-interventionism (Fisk 1989, p. 157). It is essentially about the modalities of engagement. On the shifting ground of the present, the struggle for them as a constituency is to control the drive for hegemonic control over knowledge production processes, to avoid the snares of ideological closure and to facilitate, through their specific skills and interests, the democratic transformation of South African society.

Notes

1 The origin of the word 'intellectual' is usually ascribed to a manifesto which appeared in a French newspaper in 1898, signed by several French 'men of letters' in support of a new trial for Alfred Dreyfus, a member of the French military who was accused and convicted of spying for Germany. Emile Zola, André Gide and Marcel Proust were among those who became involved in what the Dreyfusard intellectuals saw as the struggle for truth and justice in the Third Republic. The word is sometimes used interchangeably with and sometimes distinguished from 'intelligentsia'. Komorowski (1976, p. 201–3) maintains that 'intelligentsia' first appeared in Polish literature around the middle of the nineteenth century to refer to a stratum that originally belonged to the nobility but had been disinherited after the partition of Poland, whose members 'felt responsible for and entitled to the spiritual leadership of the nation' and who were 'inclined to social radicalism'. The designation was later used in Russia to refer to a grouping of people from 'different ranks' in the latter half of the nineteenth century, who on account of their poverty were also inclined towards the same kind of radicalism. More recent discussions about the notion, especially within the context of so-called Third World countries, emphasize the possession of education, specialized knowledge and professionalization as key characteristics of the stratum. Some theorists, in maintaining a distinction between 'intellectuals' and 'intelligentsia', argue that the latter term refers to the sector of generally educated people who may be given over to technical tasks whereas the former refers to a smaller grouping within that sector who are the creators and innovators and the actual producers of knowledge. In this chapter, the word 'intelligentsia' is used as a collective expression to refer to the stratum of intellectuals.
2 Popiel & Mohan (1987, p. 49) interpret this not as the exhortation to stand apart from worldly concerns but rather as a warning against the 'surrender of the intellect to partisan passions that move those immersed in material and immediate interests'.
3 See Wright (1979) for a useful outline of some of the different interpretations within Marxist theory about intellectuals and their class position.
4 See Szelenyi & Martin (1988) for a discussion of the different phases of New Class theories.
5 Mannheim (1968) speaks of the 'sociological ambivalence' of the intellectuals as a social trait not characteristic of other strata in society.
6 Bakunin and Machajski are often cited as the arch sceptics and critics of the role of intellectuals in the struggle for socialism. Bakunin (in Chomsky 1978, p. 4) argues that intellectuals will attempt to create 'the reign of scientific intelligence, the most aristocratic, despotic, arrogant and elitist of all regimes . . . the world will be divided into a minority ruling in the name of knowledge, and an immense ignorant majority'.
7 The use of gender as an analytical to demystify the universalizing claims made by and about intellectuals has not been anywhere nearly as insistent as the resort to the concept of class. Robbins (1990, p. xvii) points to the title of Lewis Coser's book

Men of Ideas (1970) as indicative of the archetypal attitude towards the gender issue in discourses by and about intellectuals.

8 The institutionalization of critical space within political organizations and the acknowledgement that these spaces have to be publicly utilized in the interest of generating a critically arrived at consensus is vital. The unpacking of the liberation movement into political parties which must now compete for the allegiance of 'the people' on the basis of party-specific programmes and agendas, and the articulation of different discourses within a liberation movement moving from homogeneity to increasing heterogeneity opens up the possibility of a more public evaluation and critique of the conceptions and strategies of different elements of the liberation movement. A fruitful engagement between political and civil society is predicated on the possibility of just such a critical encounter.

9 See Nasson (1990) for an account of the Unity Movement and the social location, activities and influence of its intelligentsia.

10 Highly industrialized societies with long traditions of formal democracy and a more evenly educated citizenry are not immune to the dangers posed by intellectuals usurping democratic decision-making (see Smith 1991 for a study of think-tanks and intellectual experts in American public life).

11 In seeking to understand the nature of their present work, intellectuals doing policy research have sought to draw distinctions between articulating policy options and goals, the choice of policy options by political groupings and the actual policies that will emerge from political contestation.

12 See Gouldner (1976b) for an elaboration of the notion that intellectuals are the bearers of a 'special grammar of rationality' which enables them to judge 'the actions of any social class and all power elites'.

References

Bourdieu, P. 1989. The corporatism of the universal: the role of intellectuals in the modern world. *Telos* 81, 103.

Bozzoli, B. & P. Delius (eds) 1990. *Radical History Review*. New York: City University of New York.

Chomsky, N. 1978. *Intellectuals and the State*. London: Frits Stoepman.

de Huszar, G. B. (ed.) 1960. *The Intellectuals*. Glencoe, Ill.: The Free Press.

Du Toit, A. 1981. Facing up to the future: some personal reflections on the predicament of Afrikaner intellectuals in the legitimation crisis of Afrikaner nationalism and the apartheid state. *Social Dynamics* 7, 1–27.

Evans, I. 1990. The racial question and intellectual production in South Africa. *Perspectives in Education* 11, 21–36.

Fisk, M. 1989. Intellectuals, values and society. *Philosophy and Social Criticism* 15, 151–65.

Gella, A. 1976. *The Intelligentsia and the Intellectuals*. California: Sage Publications.

Gouldner, A. W. 1976a. Prologue to a theory of revolutionary intellectuals. *Telos* 26, 3–36.

Gouldner, A. W. 1976b. *The Future of Intellectuals and the Rise of the New Class*. New York: The Seabury Press.

Gramsci, A. 1971. *Selections from the Prison Notebooks*. New York: International Publishers.

Halisi, C. R. D. 1990. Intellectuals and black political thought in South Africa. Paper presented at SARP, Yale University.

Kolakowski, L. 1986. A discussion on the responsibilities of intellectuals. *Salmagundi* 70–1, 164–95.

Komorowski, Z. 1976. The class of the intelligentsia in Africa. In *The Intelligentsia and the Intellectuals*, Gella, A. (ed.), 201–9. California: Sage Publications.

Lenin, V. I. 1983. *On the Intelligentsia*. Moscow: Progress Publishers.

Lodge, T. 1990. Charters from the past: the African National Congress and its historiographical traditions. *Radical History Review* 46/7, 161–88.

Mannheim, K. 1968. *Ideology and Utopia*. New York: Harcourt, Brace & World.

Martin, W. C. 1987. The role of the intellectual in revolutionary institutions. In *The Mythmakers*, Mohan R. P. (ed.), 61–77. New York: Greenwood Press.

Mazrui, A. A. 1978. *Political Values and the Educated Class in Africa*. London: Heinemann.

Merton, R. K. 1968. *Social Theory and Social Structure*. New York: The Free Press.

Muller, J. & N. Cloete 1987. The white hands: academic social scientists, engagement and struggle in South Africa. *Social Epistemology* 1, 141–54.

Muller, J. & N. Cloete 1991. To outwit modernity: intellectuals and politics in transition. *Transformation* 14, 24–41.

Nasson, B. 1990. The unity movement: its legacy in historical consciousness. *Radical History Review* 46/7, 189–211.

Popiel, G. & R. P. Mohan 1987. Intellectuals and powers: S. M. Lipset, Julien Benda and Karl Mannheim. In *The Mythmakers*, Mohan, R. P. (ed.), 35–59. New York: Greenwood Press.

Robbins, B. (ed.) 1990. *Intellectuals*. Minneapolis: University of Minnesota Press.

Sartre, J.-P. 1985. *Between Existentialism and Marxism*. London: Verso Press.

Shils, E. 1972. *The Intellectuals and the Powers*. Chicago: University of Chicago Press.

Smith, J. A. 1991. *The Idea Brokers: think tanks and the rise of the new policy elite*. New York: The Free Press.

Szelenyi, I. & B. Martin 1988. The three waves of new class theories. *Theory and Society* 17, 645–67.

Wright, E. O. 1979. Intellectuals and the class structure of capitalist society. In *Between Labor and Capital*, Walker, P. (ed.), 191–211. Boston: South End Press.

Index

academic neglect of blacks in Colombia 69–70; academic canons 5, 10; academic discourse 20
acculturation 60; in Brazil 82
Africa 16; 'inventing of' 16: *see also* South Africa
African National Congress 168, 209–10
Africanism 16
Afrikaaner Volkswag 168, 169
Alencar, J. de, and influence on Brazilian thought 78; as a representative of indianism 77–8
Almeida, M. de, demystification of *Caramuru* 76: *see also Caramuru*, legend of
American Society of Equity 35–8: *see also* Black Patch War, Kentucky
American Tobacco Company 35–7: *see also* Black Patch War, Kentucky
Ancient Egypt and its role in the development of Ancient Greece: *see* Ancient Model of Greek origins
Ancient Greece: Ancient Model of Greek origins 119, 125, 127: its cultural debt to Ancient Egypt, *see* Ancient Model of Greek origins; its social construction 119–27; Aryan Model of Greek origins 119–20, 123–7; historiography of 119–25; reasons for the overthrow of the Ancient Model 120–4; as the root of western civilization 9
Ancient Model of Greek origins 9, 119, 120, 125, 127; reasons for its overthrow 120–4
Andes: *caciques*, role of in Spanish

colonial administration 92–4; documents and bestowal of authority in Peru 94–6; effects of literacy on native thought 90, 92; effects of literacy on native culture 89–109; forms of native representation 103; importance of wills in colonial Peru 94, 96–7; legal documents and enfranchizement 93–4; literacy and the replacement of native forms of representation 102–3; native readings of documents 98–101; oral nature of colonial Spanish writing 91; perception of documents as objects 99–101; political importance of Inca symbols of authority 94; political uses of colonial documents in post-colonial Peru 93; political uses of writing and documents in colonial Peru 92–3; pre-colonial conceptions of communication and the preservation of knowledge 100–1; *quipu* 100, 102; replacement of oral tradition by written documents 91; social context of the production of Spanish legal documents 93; Spanish documentary writing and the recording of Inca history 92–3; Spanish legal system and its sociopolitical effects 90; Spanish recording of Inca ritual 91–3; use of documents to support land claims 97–8; writing and enfranchizement 102: *see also* legal documents and enfranchizement; writing and the legitimation of political authority 96

anthropological 'other', and the academic neglect of blacks in Colombia 69–70
anthropological conceptions of tradition, discussion of 196
anthropological discourse 85–6; and construction of the past 116–17
anthropological writing and power 116
anthropologists 13, 16; and future role in South Africa 198–9; and legitimation of apartheid 197; South African 5
anthropology 1, 2, 4, 14, 19; epistemology of 1, 2; in Brazil and Edenic discourse and nativism 85–6; methodology of 2; praxis of 2; theory of 2
anti-Semitism 123–5
apartheid 4, 5, 15, 167, 177, 187, 188, 189, 190, 197, 198, 208, 209, 216, 219; ideology of 197
appropriation: European appropriation of the concept of civilization 126; of western civilization by the extreme right 127
archaeological knowledge: and bias 130; and objectivism 144–6; role of gender in the construction of 115, 144–51; social construction of, discussion of 141
archaeological naivety, discussion of 129, 130, 136
archaeologists and the production of knowledge 136
archaeology 6; and acquisition of authority 137; of colonialism, project of 138–9; and the construction of identity 132–3; and the construction of national identity 138, 168; and cultural identity 130; and the empowerment of local groups 132–3; and gender/women 6, 147–51; gender division of labour 147–51; gender politics in 150–1; and generalization, discussion of 138; men and the construction of archaeological knowledge 149; and nationalism 11, 132–4, 141–2; and the political manipulation of identity 132; and politics 130, 134, 168; and poststructuralism 168–9; relationship between archaeology and anthropology in Africa 137–8; role of

gender in construction of archaeological knowledge 144–51; role of men in lithic analysis 147–9; role of women in faunal analysis 150; role of women in lithic analysis 147–9; role of women in palaeoethnobotany 149; role of women in palaeozoology 150; and self-reflexivity 134; and social identity 130; and the state, supplier of history to 133;
Aryan Model of Greek origins 4, 8–9, 114, 115, 119–20, 123, 125, 127; 'Broad' version of 123–5; denial of the role of African and Asian people in shaping Ancient Greek civilization 114; and justification of European colonialism 126, 127; and justification of European cultural superiority 127; and racism 120, 126
authenticity: discussion of cultural authenticity 85; construction of cultural authenticity in South Africa 191–3
Ayodhya (northern India) 14–15, 156, 158, 159; its place in Hindu thought 156, 158, 159, 160

Babar, Mughal emperor 15, 156–7
Bantustans (tribal homelands) 188–90, 197; gender relations in 194–6; invention of traditions 188–90
Black Consciousness Movement (South Africa) 209, 210, 211
black intellectuals: relationship with South African academia 211–12
Black Patch War (Kentucky) 31, 35–8
black social mobility in Colombia 64, 70–1
blacks: academic neglect of in Colombia 69–70; denial of educational opportunity in South Africa 211
blanqueamiento (whitening): ideology of 18, 26, 27, 61–5, 66, 67, 68–71; and Colombian national identity 63–5, 67; as a system of knowledge 67
Bogey Man 18, 113–14, 117
Bourdieu, P. 140–1; on intellectuals 219
Brazil 6, 8, 9, 26, 27, 74–86; anthropology and Edenic discourse and nativism 85–6; the army and protection of indians 82–3; effects of

colonialism on indigenous population 75–6; effects of the Enlightenment 76; ecological movement 79; genocide 75–6, 80; indianism and nationhood 77–8; indians and forced acculturation 82; indians and white protest 86; modernist movement and racial representations 79; National Indian Foundation 82–3; nativist movement 76, 77–8; racial representation of blacks 26, 63; racial representations and the construction of identity 78; representation of indians as inferior 80–1, 83–4; representation of indigenous peoples 74–86; role of racial representations in reproducing white dominance 83–4; romantic movement 77–8: *see also* civilizing discourse, Edenic discourse, indianism and nativism
Broad Aryan Model 123–5; and Jewish scholars 124–5

caciques, role of in the Spanish colonial administration in the Andes 92–4: *see also* Andes
cannibalism, and its use to justify civilizing discourse in South America 80–1: *see also* civilizing discourse
canons, academic 5, 10
Cape Town (South Africa) 168, 169–80; architecture of 175; artistic representation of 175–7; artistic representations of its people 176–7; class relations 172–4; ideology 174; during the nineteenth century 169–74; textual representations of 177–80
Caramuru, legend of 76–7; as an example of nativistic discourse 76–7: *see also* Brazil
civilization 18; European appropriation of the concept 126
civilizing discourse 26, 74, 75, 80–6: *see also* Edenic discourse
class 6; Marxist theory of 169
class analysis in Kentucky 30–1, 37–8, 40
class conflict: in Kentucky 31, 39–40; use of racial representations to avoid development of class consciousness in Kentucky 29–31, 34–8

class relations in Cape Town (South Africa) 172–4
Code Noir 53–4
Colombia 6, 8, 9, 26; academic neglect of blacks 69–70; black social mobility 64, 70–1; eugenics 62–3; hegemony 70–1; ideology of race mixture 59–60, 63, 65: *see also lo mestizo;* ideology of racial representations and their political use 59–71; importance of racial lineage 61–2; intermarriage 60; *lo mestizo* 65–71; national identity and *blanqueamiento* (whitening) 63–5, 67; political use of the past 69–70; racial discrimination 60, 61, 63, 69–71; racial representations 26; racial segregation 59; racism 70–1; reclaiming history 70; representations of the past 70; slavery 60
colonial discourse 16
colonialism 3, 27
competing interpretations 11; of the past 116
concept of progress, and the decline of the Ancient Model of Greek origins 121–2
construction: of African society via encounter with colonial rule 137; of British national identity 133; of difference in South Africa 185, 187, 197; of ethnicity 25; of gender 27, 46; of gender roles in Haiti 48; of history 10, 17; of history in the USA 26; of identity 13; of identity and archaeology 132–3; of knowledge 144–6: *see also* constructivist approach to knowledge; of nationalism in South Africa 168; of the past 17; of the past and its political uses 38–40, 115–16; of sexuality 27; social 3, 20; of social categories 46; of white identity in South Africa 186
constructivist approach to knowledge 144–6
contestatory histories 12, 16, 17, 134; in India 156–7; their political effects 134
cultural authenticity: construction of in South Africa 191–3; discussion of 85
cultural domination 3, 27
cultural evolution 8–9
cultural heritage and the development of the concept of identity 131

cultural representations, political use of in South Africa 187, 191
culture: of dissent in South Africa 219; of resistance 7
Cunliffe, B.C., and debate with P.J.Ucko over first World Archaeological Congress 134

debt peonage in Kentucky 32, 33, 37
difference, construction of in South Africa 185, 187, 197
discourse: academic 20; alternative 6; anthropological 85–6; civilizing 26, 74, 75, 80–6; colonial 16; ecological 79; Edenic discourse 8, 26, 74, 75–7, 79, 80, 84–6, indianism 74, 77–8; nativism 76, 77–8; of reconstruction in South Africa 203, 213, 216, 220; of transformation in South Africa 203, 213, 220; racial in South Africa 211–12
documents: and bestowal of authority in Peru 94–6; native readings of in the Andes 98–101; use of to support land claims in the Andes 97–8; as objects 99–101: see also Andes
dominant culture, alternative views of 27
domination 20; forms of 25; intellectual 7
Dutch East India Company 168, 172, 173, 175

ecological movement: denial of indian agency and paternalism towards indians 79–80; discourse, account of 79, similarities with nativistic and romantic discourses 79
Edenic discourse 8, 26, 74, 75–7, 79, 80, 84–6: see also Brazil
empowerment: discussion of the role of history in 29–31, 38–40; female 44–5, 55; and female sexuality in Haiti 51, 52; of local groups via archaeology 132–3
epistemology 1, 2
essentialism 13, 16, 19, 25, 185
ethnic representation: its role in nation-states 25–6
eugenics in Colombia 62–3

false consciousness, discussion of 60–1, 64–5

Farmer's Alliance (Kentucky) 31–5, 39, 40: see also Black Patch War
female sexuality: and empowerment in Haiti 51, 52; as a resource in Haiti 48–51
feminism: critique of science 146–7, 151; perspectives on power 44–5
folk history 6, 11–12, 17
folk racial categorizations in Latin America 67–8
Foucault, M. 8, 9–10; on systems of knowledge 60–1
fusion of Inca and Spanish traditions: see Andes

gender 2; and archaeology 6; construction of 27, 46; and construction of archaeological knowledge 115; division of labour in archaeology 147–51; division of labour in Haiti 51–2; inequality, discussion of reasons for 55; and intellectuals in South Africa 206, 210, 220; and tradition in South Africa 193–5; politics in archaeology 150–1; relations, Thonga 195–6; relations, Zulu 195–6; relations in Bantustans 194–6; roles, construction of in Haiti 48
genocide in Brazil 74–6, 80
Gramsci, A.: distinction between organic and traditional intellectuals 15–16; discussion of function of intellectuals 204, 205–6
Greece (Ancient) 15–16, 119–28; and Indo-European languages 119–20

Haiti 4, 27; conjugal relations 46; construction of gender roles 48; female participation in formal politics 47–8; female sexuality 46, 48, 51; female sexuality as a resource 48, 51; forms of conjugal union 46; forms of social domination 45; gender division of labour 51–2; ideology of gender 48; ideology of marriage 48; ideology of sexuality 48; male control of female labour 45–6; male dominance over women 45; marriage customs 46–7; men's dependence on women 50; paternalism 50; resistance to slavery 52–3; sex/gender system 44–5; sexual behaviour 48; sexual politics 44–55; sexuality and female empowerment 51, 52; slavery 52–4; slavery and its legacy 49, 50–1, 52; social organization 46–7, 49–50; women and the economy 50–2

hegemony 7; in Colombia 70–1; European hegemony in Brazil 79; and intellectuals 206, 208, 209; in Kentucky 29–30, 39; in South Africa and its subversion 181–2

Hindus: construction of history 154–67; their history in India 158–9

historiography of Ancient Greece 119–25

history 2; contested 12, 16, 17; construction of 10, 16; and the construction of nationalism 168; dominant versions of 1; and empowerment 29–31, 38–40; folk 6, 11–12, 17; and nationalism 133–4; public 17; reclamation of in Colombia 70; state 6, 11; subjugated 8

Homelands: see Bantustans, and South Africa

Iberian colonialism in Latin America 59–61

identity: archaeology and the construction of identity 132–3; construction of white identity in South Africa 186; discussion of models and theory of 131–2; primordialist conception of 132, 136; roots of 131–2

ideological contestation in South Africa 211–12

ideological identification between oppressed and dominators 30

ideology: of apartheid 197; of assimilation 27; of blackness 18; of blanqueamiento (whitening) 18, 26, 27, 61–5, 66, 67, 68–71; in Cape Town (South Africa) 174; of colour 18; definition of 61; as false consciousness, discussion of 60–1, 64–5; of gender in Haiti 48; of gender relations in South Africa 194, 196; of lo mestizo 65–71; of marriage in Haiti 48; of race in Colombia 67: see also blanqueamiento and lo mestizo; of race mixture in Colombia 59–60, 63, 65: see also lo mestizo; racist in South

Africa 187; of sexuality in Haiti 48; of whiteness: see blanqueamiento

imagined communities 17; definition of 133

India 4, 14–16; conflict between Muslims and Hindus and their use of archaeology and history 115–16; contested histories 156–7; creation of Hindu identity 155–6, 160; Hindu construction of history 154–67; history of Hinduism 158–9; Muslim construction of history 154–67; negation of colonial past 154–5; negation of Muslim identity 155–6; political use of the past 154–61; religion and legitimation of state power 157–8; symbolism of the past in India 157–9, 160–1

indianism: and Brazilian nationhood 77–8; discourse of 74, 77–8: see also Edenic discourse, civilizing discourse, discourse of nativism

indigenism, discourse of 8, 26

indigenismo, glorification of the Indian in Mexico 65–6

Indo-European languages and Ancient Greece 119–20

inequality 4, 20; representation of 25

Inkatha 168, 169, 195

intellectual domination 7, 8

intellectuals 5, African 16; and the African National Congress 209–10; black 16, 211–12; bureaucratic 218; definitions of and discussion of 204–7, 214–16, 217; and gender in South Africa 206, 210, 220; and hegemony 206, 208, 209; indigenous 6; and the invention of culture 15–16; Marxist theories of 205–6; and nationalism in South Africa 209; organic 15–16; and political struggle in South Africa 205, 206, 209, 210–17; and production of knowledge 217–18; and race in South Africa 206, 220; relationship with the South African state 212–13; repression of in South Africa 212–13; and resistance in South Africa 212–13, 217; role of in South African society 203–21; role of in South African trade unions 209; South African 5, 203–21; Third World 7, 20; traditional 15–16; and

transformation of South African society 214–21
interpretations: competing 11; multiplicity of 2
inventing traditions 13, 14, 15–16, 133, 137, 196

Kentucky 7, 18, 29–40; Black Patch War 31, 35–8; black–white relations 29–31; class conflict 31, 39–40; Farmers' Alliance 31–5, 39, 40; Jim Crow legislation 32–4; political use of racial representations 29–40; and racism 31; system of debt-bondage 32, 33, 37; use of racism to support status quo 34–5, 37
knowledge: archaeological 6; archaeology and the production of knowledge 136; 'buried' 8; construction of archaeological knowledge 115; construction of knowledge 144–6: see also constructivist approach to knowledge; construction of the past 2; construction of the present 2; constructivist approach to knowledge 144–6; hierarchies of 12; intellectuals and the production of knowledge 217–18; and politics 1; politics of 20; knowledge and power 2, 60–1; production of in South Africa 210; subjugated 8, 9–10; use of 1
Kultur 127

legal documents and enfranchizement in the Andes 93–4
Lenin, V.I. on intellectuals 205, 206
literacy 10; effects of on native culture and thought in the Andes 89–109; and power 10; and the replacement of native Andean forms of representation 102–3; and its social effects, discussion of 90
lo mestizo: ideology of race mixedness (Colombia) 65–71; as a system of knowledge 67

Marxism: theories of class 169; of intellectuals 205–6
master narratives 3, 11
Merton, R.K. on intellectuals 204–5, 218

mestizo (s) 9, 60, 62, 63–4, 65: see also ideology of lo mestizo
Mexico: and the cult of the mestizo 65; indigenismo (glorification of the Indian) 65–6; pre-Columbian forms of pictographic writing 102; sexual politics 54
modern culture, representation of in South Africa 186–7
modernity 18, 135–136, definition of 134; and identity 131
multi-racial societies 17, 18
multiple pasts 140–1, 185
multiplicity of interpretations 2, 11

nationalism and history 133–4
nation-states, role of ethnic representation in 25–6
National Indian Foundation (Brazil) 82–3
nationalism 11; and archaeology 11, 132–4, 141–2; history 133–4; and intellectuals in South Africa 209; and traditionalism 133
native readings of documents in the Andes 98–101: see also Andes
native representation, forms of in the Andes 103: see also Andes
nativism, discourse of 76, 77–8: see also Edenic discourse
nativistic movement 76, 77–8
negation of colonial past in India 154–5
noble savage 9, 74, 78: see also Edenic discourse

objectivist view of science, discussion of 144–6
objectivity 1, 2, 20
Occidentalism 16, 19
oral tradition and its replacement by written documents: see Andes
organic intellectuals 15–16
Orientalism 16, 19
other, anthropological 13, 16
ownership of the past 136

partisan scholarship 20
past: analogy with text 168–9; and empowerment 29–30; and individual identity 3; and legitimation of the present 28; and legitimation of the present in South Africa 177, 181–2, 185; its malleability 134, 154, 160–1;

multiple pasts 140–1; and national identity 3; ownership of 136; political use of 14–15, 28; political use of in Colombia 69–70; political use of in India 154–61; political use of in South Africa 185, 167–82; representation of in Colombia 70; representation of in South Africa 167–8, 177, 185, 190, 198: *see also* representation of tradition and Bantustans, invention of tradition; representations of 1, 5, 14–15; rhizome 140; role of in the construction of national identity 133–4, 138; social construction of and its political uses 5, 14–15, 38–40; symbolism of in India 157–9, 160–1; and its use to justify cultural superiority of the West 114–15: *see also* Ancient Greece, its social construction; versions of 1, 5, 14–15 and political

People's Party (Kentucky): *see* Farmers' Alliance

poetic power 1

poetics of meaning 16

political: struggle and intellectuals in South Africa 205, 206, 209, 210–17; use of racial representations in Kentucky 29–40; use of the past in Colombia 69–70; uses of colonial documents in post-colonial Peru 93; uses of tradition, discussion of 196; uses of writing and documents in colonial Peru 92–3;

politics: of archaeology 130; of knowledge 20; of racial representations 26, 29–40; of scholarship 7; sexual 27

postmodernism 14; account of 139–40; and identity 140; implications for archaeology 139

poststructuralism 14, 25; and the decentring of science and knowledge 25; definition of a poststructuralist approach to archaeology 168–9; implications for archaeology 140–1

power 1, 13, 17; definition of 44–5, 116; feminist perspectives 44–5; and knowledge 60–1; and literacy 10; and scholarship 116; and text 13; white 17

primitivism 139

primordialism: conception of identity 132, 136; and history 133

production of knowledge and intellectuals 217–18

progress and development, concepts of 4, 8, 18

quipu, Andes 100, 102

race 2, 6, 13; race mixture in Colombia 60: *see also* ideology of *lo mestizo*; relations 7, 18, 25

racial categorization in Latin America 67–8; in New Spain and Peru 61–2

racial discourses in South Africa 211–12

racial discrimination in Colombia 60, 61, 63, 69–71

racial division of intellectual labour in South Africa 211, 220

racial representations: in Brazil 63, 77–8, 80; and construction of identity (Brazil) 78; and the modernist movement in Brazil 79; and their political use in Colombia 59–71; and their political use in South Africa 186; role in reproducing white dominance in Brazil 83–4; in South Africa 186, 191–3

racial segregation: in Colombia 59; in South Africa 188–9

racism 19; in Colombia 70–1; and the decline of the Ancient Model of Greek origins 121–2, 123, 124; in Kentucky 31; use of to support status quo in Kentucky 34–5, 37

Ram Janmabhoomi/Babri Marsjid controversy: *see* India, political use of the past

raza cosmica (cosmic race) 65, 66–7: *see also lo mestizo*

reconstruction, discourse of (South Africa) 203, 213, 216, 220

relativism and its challenge to European cultural superiority 126

representation: of black–white cultural differences in South Africa 186–7, 194; of inequality 1, 25; of indians as inferior in Brazil 80–1, 83–4: *see also* civilizing discourse; of modern culture in South Africa 186–7; of the past 1; of the past in Colombia 70; of the past in South Africa 167–8, 177, 185, 198; of race 25, 26, 29–40; of race, political uses of 29–40; of race and the justification of hegemony 29;

of South Africa 187; of tradition in
South Africa 186–9, 192–3
representations: of Africans in South
Africa 186, 191–3; cultural, political
use of in South Africa 187, 191; of
the past and the state 137, 138
repression of intellectuals in South
Africa 212–13
resistance 7, 19; culture of 7; and
intellectuals in South Africa 212–13,
217; to slavery in Haiti 52–3
rhizome pasts 140
romantic movement and glorification
of the Indian (Brazil) 77–8

scholarly canons 5, 10
scholars, subalterns 3, 11, 14
scholarship and power 116
science, discussion of objectivist view
of 144–6
sexual politics: in Ecuador 54; in Haiti
44–55; in Mexico 54; in Uruguay 54
sexuality: construction of 27; female
and empowerment in Haiti 51, 52;
ideology of in Haiti 48
slavery 4, 10, 25, 27; in Colombia 60;
in Haiti 52–4; and its legacy in Haiti
49, 50–1, 52; in South Africa 168,
169
social construction 3, 20; of Ancient
Greece 121–7; of archaeological
knowledge, discussion of 141; of
ethnicity 25; of gender 27; of the past
5, 119–27; of the past and its political
uses 38–40; of sexuality 27
society, multi-racial 17, 18
South Africa 4, 5–6, 11, 15, 17; African
National Congress intellectuals
209–10; Afrikaaner Volkswag 168,
169; anthropologists 5;
anthropologists and the legitimation
of apartheid 197; attitude of blacks to
whites 115; Bantustans (tribal
homelands) 188–90, 197; Black
Consciousness movement 209, 210,
211; black intellectuals 211–12; black
intellectuals and relationship with
academia 211–12; coercion 212–13;
conceptualizations of future South
African society 208; construction of
cultural authenticity 191–3;
construction of difference 185, 187,
197; construction of white identity

186; culture of dissent 219; denial of
educational opportunity to blacks
211; discourse of reconstruction 203,
213, 216, 220; discourse of
transformation 203, 213, 220;
divisions among intellectuals 208–10;
future role of anthropologists 198–9;
gender relations in Bantustans 194–6;
hegemony and its subversion 181–2;
ideological contestation 211–12;
ideology of apartheid 197; ideology
of gender relations 194, 196, Inkatha
168, 169, 195; intellectuals,
perceptions of the nature and
function of their work 210;
intellectuals and Afrikaaner
nationalism 209; intellectuals and
gender 206, 210, 220; intellectuals
and political struggle; 205, 206, 209,
210–17; intellectuals and race 206,
220; intellectuals and relationship
with the state 212–13; intellectuals
and resistance; 212–13, 217;
intellectuals and the transformation
of society 214–21; invention of
traditions for Bantustans 188–90: see
also tourist industry and construction
of native tradition; land dispossession
188; Native Lands Act 188; the past
and the construction of nationalism
168; political use of cultural
representations 187, 191; political use
of racial representations 186; political
use of the past 185, 167–82;
production of knowledge 210; racial
discourses 211–12; racial division of
intellectual labour 211, 220; racial
segregation 188–89; racist ideology
187; representation of black–white
cultural differences 186–7, 194;
representation of modern culture
186–7; representation of the past
167–8, 177, 185, 198; representation
of tradition 186–9, 192–3;
representations of Africans 186,
191–3; repression of intellectuals
212–13; role of intellectuals in society
203–221; role of intellectuals in trade
unions 209; slavery 168, 169; Soweto
115; taalmonument, symbolism of 186,
191; Thonga gender relations 195–6;
tourist industry 191–3; tourist
industry and the construction of

native tradition 191–2; tradition and gender struggles 193–5; Unity Movement 211; use of the past to legitimate the present 185; *volkekundiges* and apartheid 197, 198; Zulu gender relations 195–6: *see also* Cape Town (South Africa)

Spanish documentary writing and the recording of Inca history 92–3: *see also* Andes

Spanish recording of Andean ritual 91–3: *see also* Andes

state histories 6, 11

state and: intellectuals (South Africa) 212–13; representations of the past 137, 138

Subaltern Studies Project 13

subaltern: populations 3; scholars 3, 11, 14

subalterns 12, 13

subjugated history 8

subjugated knowledge 8, 9–10

subjugation 3, 20

submission to domination 4

taalmonument (South Africa), symbolism of 186, 191

text and power 13

Third World: and the creation of an authentic precolonial past 135; intellectuals 7, 20; scholars 14, 25

Thonga gender relations 195–6

tourist industry: and construction of native tradition in South Africa 191–2; in South Africa 191–3

tradition: anthropological conceptions of 196; and gender struggles in South Africa 193–5; invention of 13, 14,

15–16, 133, 137, 196; invention of in South Africa 188–90: *see also* tourist industry; and legitimation 14; political uses of, discussion of 196; representation of in South Africa 186–9, 192–3

traditional intellectuals 15–16

traditionalism 5; and nationalism 133

transformation, discourse of (South Africa) 203, 213, 220

Ucko, P. J., and debate with B. C. Cunliffe over first World Archaeological Congress 134

USA and black inequality 26: *see also* Kentucky

volkundiges and apartheid 197, 198

western civilization: concept of superiority of 8; deconstruction of 127

western civilization courses, development of 126–7

whitening, *see blanqueamiento*

women and archaeology 6, 147–51

World Archaeological Congress I 130, 134

writing: and legitimation of political authority in the Andes 96; effects of on 'traditional' cultures 10: and enfranchizement in the Andes 102: *see also* legal documents and enfranchizement, and Andes

Zulu gender relations 195–6

Printed in the United Kingdom
by Lightning Source UK Ltd.
128UKS00001B/133-135

9 780415 152242